SPEECHES, LETTERS,

AND SAYINGS

OF

CHARLES DICKENS.

TO WHICH IS ADDED A SKETCH OF THE AUTHOR

BY GEORGE AUGUSTUS SALA,

AND

DEAN STANLEY'S SERMON.

University Press of the Pacific
Honolulu, Hawaii

Speeches, Letters, and Sayings of Charles Dickens

by
Charles Dickens
To Which is Added a Sketch of the Author by
George Augustus Sala, and Dean Stanley's Sermon

ISBN: 0-89875-633-2

Reprinted from the 1870 edition

University Press of the Pacific
Honolulu, Hawaii
http://www.universitypressofthepacific.com

In order to make original editions of historical works
available to scholars at an economical price, this
facsimile of the original edition of 1870 is
reproduced from the best available copy and has
been digitally enhanced to improve legibility, but the
text remains unaltered to retain historical
authenticity.

CHARLES DICKENS,

At the age of 29

From a Drawing by Count D'Orsay, taken on the completion of
"The Old Curiosity Shop."

CONTENTS.

INTRODUCTION.

CHARLES DICKENS was born at Landport, Portsmouth, on February 7, 1812. At that time his father, Mr. John Dickens, held an office in the Navy Pay Department, the duties of which obliged him to reside alternately at the principal naval stations of England. But on the conclusion of peace in 1815 a considerable reduction was made by Government in this branch of the public service. Mr. John Dickens, among others, was pensioned off, and he removed to London with his wife and children, when his son Charles was hardly four years of age.

No doubt the varied bustling scenes of life witnessed by Charles Dickens in his early years, had an influence on his mind that gave him a taste for observing the manners and mental peculiarities of different classes of people engaged in the active pursuits of life, and quickened a naturally lively perception of the ridiculous, for which he was distinguished even in boyhood.

It is curious to observe how similar opportunities of becoming acquainted practically with life, and the busy actors on its varied scenes, in very early life, appear to influence the minds of thinking and imaginative men in after-years. Goldsmith's pedestrian excursions on the Continent, Bulwer's youthful rambles on foot in England and equestrian expeditions in France, and Maclise's extensive walks in boyhood over his native county, and the mountains and valleys of Wicklow a little later, were fraught with similar results.

Charles Dickens was intended by his father to be an attorney. Nature and Mr. John Dickens happily differed on that point. London law may have sustained little injury in losing Dickens for "a limb." English literature would have met with an irreparable loss, had she been deprived of him whom she delights to own as a favorite son.

Dickens, having decided against the law, began his career in "the gallery," as a reporter on "The True Sun;" and from the first made himself distinguished and distinguishable among "the corps," for his ability, promptness, and punctuality.

Remaining for a short term on the staff of this periodical, he seceded to "The Mirror of Parliament," which was started with the express object of furnishing *verbatim* reports of the debates. It only lived, however, for two sessions.

The influence of his father, who, on settling in the metropolis, had become connected with the London press, procured for Charles Dickens an appointment as short-hand reporter on the "Morning Chronicle." To this period of his life he has made some graceful and interesting allusions in a speech delivered at the Second Anniversary of the Newspaper Press Fund, about five years ago.

It was in "The Monthly Magazine" of January, 1834, before he had quite attained his twenty-second year, that Charles Dickens made his first appearance in print as a story-teller.* Neither the editor of the magazine, nor the readers, nor even the ardent and gratified young author himself (who has described in the preface to the "Pickwick Papers" his sensations on finding his little contribution accepted), then dreamt that he would become in five short years from that time one of the most popular and widely-read of English authors; that his name would shortly become familiar as a household word, and that his praise would be on every tongue on both sides of the Atlantic.

Encouraged by his success, Charles Dickens continued to send sketches in the same vein, and for the next twelve months was a tolerably constant contributor to the magazine. All, or nearly all, of these little papers were reprinted in the collection of "Sketches by Boz;" but as it will perhaps be interesting to some of our readers to trace their original appearance in the magazine, we give a list of them here:

February, 1834, Horatio Sparkins.
      Marriage à-la-Mode.
April, " The Bloomsbury Christening.
May,   " The Boarding-House.
August, " *Ibid.* (No II.)†
September, " The Goings-on at Bramsby Hall.
October, " The Steam Excursion.
January, 1835, Passage in the Life of Mr. Watkins
      Tottle.
February, " *Ib.* Chapter Second.

A similar series was afterwards contributed to the evening edition of "The Morning Chronicle,‡" then edited by Mr. John Black, and on

---

* This first sketch was entitled, "Mrs. Joseph Porter, 'over the way,'" which is still one of the favorite and most effective readings of Mr. Bellew. The "Monthly Magazine," in which this appeared, was published by Cochrane and M'Crone, and must not be confounded with "The New Monthly Magazine," published by Colburn.

† This was the first paper in which Dickens assumed the pseudonym of "Boz." The previous sketches appeared anonymously.

‡ Of these Sketches two volumes were collected and published by M'Crone (with illustrations by George Cruikshank), in February, 1836, and a third in the December following.

which Dickens was engaged as parliamentary reporter.

While writing the " Sketches," a strong inclination towards the stage induced Mr. Charles Dickens to test his powers as a dramatist; and his first piece, a farce called " The Strange Gentleman," was produced at the St. James's Theatre on the opening night of the season, September 29, 1836. The late Mr. Harley was the hero of the farce, which was received with great favor. This was followed by an opera, called "The Village Coquettes," for which Mr. Hullah composed the music, and which was brought out at the same establishment, on Tuesday, December 6, 1836. The quaint humor, unaffected pathos, and graceful lyrics of this production found prompt recognition, and the piece enjoyed a prosperous run. "The Village Coquettes" took its title from two village girls, Lucy and Rose, led away by vanity, coquetting with men above them in station, and discarding their humble though worthy lovers. Before, however, it is too late they see their error, and the piece terminates happily. Miss Rainforth and Miss Julia Smith were the heroines, and Mr. Bennet and Mr. Gardner were their betrothed lovers. Braham was the Lord of the Manor, who would have led astray the fair Lucy. There was a capital scene, where he was detected by Lucy's father, played by Strickland, urging an elopement. Harley had a trifling part in the piece, rendered highly amusing by his admirable acting.

On March 6, 1837, was brought out at the St. James's Theatre a farce called " Is she his Wife; or, Something Singular," in which Harley played the principal character, Felix Tapkins, a flirting bachelor, and sang a song in the character of Pickwick, "written expressly for him by Boz."

Under the pseudonym of Timothy Sparks Charles Dickens published about this time a wholesome, wise, and cleverly written little pamphlet against Sabbatarianism, in which he cogently and forcibly advocated more liberal views respecting the observance of Sunday than generally obtain in this country.*

In March, 1836, appeared the first number of "Pickwick," with illustrations by Seymour. It was continued in monthly shilling numbers until its completion, and this has been Mr. Dickens's favorite and usual form of publications ever since. The success and popularity of the work—which, in freshness and vigor, he has never surpassed in his later and maturer writings — were unmistakable. Several playwrights dramatized it, with more or less success; and a swarm of obscure scribblers flooded the town with imitations and sequels, which, like Avanelleda's second part of " Don Quixote," came mostly to grief, and were quickly forgotten.

Before the work had reached its third number, the talented artist who had undertaken the illustrations, and who has immortalized the features of Mr. Pickwick, was unfortunately removed by death, and Mr. Hablot Browne (the well-known *Phiz*) was chosen to replace him, and continued to illustrate most of Mr. Dickens's novels for many years after. During the years 1837–1838, Mr. Dickens carried on the editorship of "Bentley's Miscellany," where his novel of "Oliver Twist" (illustrated by George Cruikshank) first appeared. To this magazine, during the time that he conducted it, he also contributed some humorous papers, entitled "Full Report of the Meetings of the Mudfog Association for the Advancement of Every Thing." But, finding his editorial office irksome, he soon abandoned it.

During his engagement with Mr. Bentley, he edited and partly wrote the "Memoirs of Joseph Grimaldi,"* a book now almost forgotten, though not without passages of pathos and humor. Dickens, in the introductory chapter (dated February, 1838), gives the following account of his share in the work:

"For about a year before his death, Grimaldi was employed in writing a full account of his life and adventures, and as people who write their own lives often find time to extend them to a most inordinate length, it is no wonder that his account of himself was exceedingly voluminous.

"This manuscript was confided to Mr. Thomas Egerton Wilks, to alter and revise, with a view to its publication. While he was thus engaged, Grimaldi died; and Mr. Wilks having, by the commencement of September (1837), concluded his labors, offered the manuscript to Mr. Bentley, by whom it was shortly afterwards purchased.

"The present editor of these volumes has felt it necessary to say thus much in explanation of their origin. His own share in them is stated in a few words. Being much struck by several incidents in the manuscript—such as the description of Grimaldi's infancy, the burglary, the brother's return from sea, and many other passages—and thinking that they might be related in a more attractive manner, he accepted a proposal from the publisher to edit the book, and *has* edited it to the best of his ability, altering its form throughout, and making such other alterations as he conceived would improve the narration of the facts, without any departure from the facts themselves."

His next work was "Nicholas Nickleby," published in monthly numbers. The following passage from the original preface, which is only to be found in the old editions, alludes to the great success that attended this story:

"It only now remains for the writer of these pages, with that feeling of regret with which we leave almost any pursuit that has for a long

---

* The pamphlet was entitled " Sunday under Three Heads: As it is, as Sabbath Bills would make it; as it might be made." By Timothy Sparks. London, Chapman and Hall, 1836, pp. 49 (with illustrations by Hablot K. Browne).

* "Memoirs of Joseph Grimaldi," edited by *Boz*. With illustrations by George Cruikshank. In two volumes. London, R. Bentley, 1838.

time occupied us and engaged our thoughts, and which is naturally augmented in such a case as this, when that pursuit has been surrounded by all that could animate and cheer him on—it only now remains for him, before abandoning his task, to bid his readers farewell."

This was followed by "Master Humphrey's Clock," the publication of which, in weekly numbers, with illustrations by Cattermole and Hablot Browne, was commenced in April, 1840. "Master Humphrey's Clock" comprised the two novels of "The Old Curiosity Shop" and "Barnaby Rudge," which are now published in a separate form, stripped of the introductory portion relating to Master Humphrey, and of the intercalary chapters in which Mr. Pickwick and the two Wellers appear again on the scene. It was pleasant to meet once more these familiar humorous creations, and it may be a matter for regret that this portion of the book has been consigned to oblivion. But the author considered that these passages served only to interrupt the continuity of the main story, and they were consequently eliminated.

These three characters (the Wellers and Mr. Pickwick) have all the same raciness and inexhaustible humor in this sequel as in the work in which we were first introduced to them. As the original edition of the work we are alluding to is now somewhat rare, the reader may not be displeased to have a few specimens laid before him. Here is Mr. Weller senior's opinion of railways:

"I con-sider," said Mr. Weller, "that the rail is unconstitootional and an inwaser o' priwileges, and I should wery much like to know what that 'ere old Carter as once stood up for our liberties and wun 'em too—I should like to know wot he vould say if he wos alive now, to Englishmen being locked up with widders, or with any body, again their wills. Wot a old Carter would have said, a old Coachman may say, and I as-sert that in that pint o' view alone the rail is an inwaser. As to the comfort, vere's the comfort o' sittin' in a harm cheer lookin' at brick walls or heaps o' mud, never comin' to a public house, never seein' a glass o' ale, never goin' through a pike, never meetin' a change o' no kind (horses or otherwise), but alvays comin' to a place, ven you come to one at all, the wery picter o' the last, vith the same p'leesemen standing about, the same blessed old bell a ringin', the same unfort'nate people standing behind the bars, a waitin' to be let in; and every thin' the same except the name, vich is wrote up in the same sized letters as the last name and vith the same colors. As to the *honor* and dignity o' travellin', vere can that be vithout a coachman; and wot's the rail to sich coachmen and guards as is sometimes forced to go by it, but a outrage and a insult? As to the pace, wot sort o' pace do you think I, Tony Veller, could have kept a coach goin' at, for five hundred thousand pound a mile, paid in adwance afore the coach was on the road? And as to the ingein—a nasty wheezin', creaking, gasping, puffin, bustin' monster, alvays out o'

breath, vith a shiny green and gold back, like a unpleasant beetle in that 'ere gas magnifier—as to the ingein as is alvays a pourin' out red-hot coals at night, and black smoke in the day, the sensiblest thing it does, in my opinion, is, ven there's somethin' in the vay and it sets up that 'ere frightful scream vich seems to say, 'Now here's two hundred and forty passengers in the wery greatest extremity o' danger, and here's their two hundred and forty screams in vun!'"*

While Mr. Pickwick is listening to Master Humphrey's story above, the Wellers are entertained by the housekeeper in the kitchen, where they find Mr. Slithers, the barber, to whom Sam Weller, drawing extensively, we may suppose, upon his lively imagination, relates the following anecdote:

"I never knew," said Sam, fixing his eyes in a ruminative manner upon the blushing barber, "I never knew but von o' your trade, but *he* wos worth a dozen, and wos indeed dewoted to his callin'!"

"Was he in the easy shaving way, sir," inquired Mr. Slithers; "or in the cutting and curling line?"

"Both," replied Sam, "easy shavin' was his natur, and cuttin' and curlin' was his pride and glory. His whole delight wos in his trade. He spent all his money in bears and run in debt for 'em besides, and there they wos a growling avay down in the front-cellar all day long, and ineffectooally gnashing their teeth, vile the grease o' their relations and friends wos being re-tailed in gallipots in the shop above, and the first-floor winder wos ornamented vith their heads; not to speak o' the dreadful aggrawation it must have been to 'em to see a man alvays a walkin' up and down the pavement outside, vith the portrait of a bear in his last agonies, and underneath in large letters, 'Another fine animal wos slaughtered yesterday at Jinkinson's!' Hows'ever, there they wos, and there Jinkinson wos, till he wos took wery ill with some inn'ard disorder, lost the use of his legs, and wos confined to his bed, vere he laid a wery long time, but sich wos his pride in his profession even then, that wenever he wos worse than usual, the doctor used to go down stairs and say, 'Jinkinson's wery low this mornin'; we must give the bears a stir;' and as sure as ever they stirred 'em up a bit, and made 'em roar, Jinkinson opens his eyes if he wos ever so bad, calls out, 'There's the bears!' and re-wives agin. Vun day the doctor happenin' to say, 'I shall look in as usual to-morrow mornin',' Jinkinson catches hold of his hand and says, 'Doctor,' he says, 'vill you grant me one favor?' 'I will, Jinkinson,' says the doctor. 'Then, doctor,' says Jinkinson, 'vill you come unshaved, and let me shave you?' 'I will,' says the doctor. 'God bless you,' says Jinkinson. Next day the doctor came, and arter he'd been shaved all skillful and reg'lar, he says, 'Jinkinson,' he says, 'it's wery plain this does you good. Now,' he says, 'I've got a coachman as has got a beard

* "Master Humphrey's Clock," vol. i. p 72.

that it 'd warm your heart to work on, and though the footman,' he says, ' hasn't got much of a beard, still he's a trying it on vith a pair o' viskers to that extent, that razors is Christian charity. If they take it in turns to mind the carriage wen it's a waitin' below,' he says, ' wot's to hinder you from operatin' on both of 'em ev'ry day as well as upon me? You've got six children,' he says, ' wot's to hinder you from shavin' all their heads, and keepin' 'em shaved? You've got two assistants in the shop down stairs, wot's to hinder you from cuttin' and curlin' them as often as you like? Do this,' he says, ' and you're a man agin.' Jinkinson squeedged the doctor's hand, and begun that wery day; he kept his tools upon the bed, and wenever he felt his-self gettin' worse, he turned to at vun o' the children, who wos a runnin' about the house vith heads like clean Dutch cheeses, and shaved him agin. Vun day the lawyer come to make his vill; all the time he wos a takin' it down. Jinkinson was secretly a clippin' avay at his hair vith a large pair of scissors. ' Wot's that 'ere snippin' noise?' says the lawyer every now and then, ' it's like a man havin' his hair cut.' ' It *is* wery like a man havin' his hair cut,' says poor Jinkinson, hidin' the scissors and lookin' quite innocent. By the time the lawyer found it out, he was wery nearly bald. Jinkinson was kept alive in this vay for a long time, but at last vun day he has in all the children, vun arter another, shaves each on 'em wery clean, and gives him vun kiss on the crown of his head; then he has in the two assistants, and arter cuttin' and curlin' of 'em in the first style of elegance, says he should like to hear the woice o' the greasiest bear, vich rekvest is immedetly complied with; then he says that he feels wery happy in his mind, and vishes to be left alone; and then he dies, previously cuttin' his own hair, and makin' one flat curl in the wery middle of his forehead."*

There is a great deal more in the same vein, not unworthy of the "Pickwick Papers." We must leave the curious reader to find it out, however, for himself.

During the progress of this publication, it seems that certain officious persons, mistaking it for a kind of *omnium gatherum*, by "several hands," tendered contributions to its pages, and the author was compelled to issue the following advertisement:

"MASTER HUMPHREY'S CLOCK."

Mr. Dickens begs to inform all those Ladies and Gentlemen who have tendered him contributions for this work, and all those who may now or at any future time have it in contemplation to do so, that he can not avail himself of their obliging offers, as it is written solely by himself, and can not possibly include any productions from other hands.

This announcement will serve for a final answer to all correspondents, and will render any private communications unnecessary.

After " winding up his clock," as he termed it, Dickens resolved to make a tour in the United States. Before he went away, however, some of the most distinguished citizens of Edinburgh gave him a farewell banquet.* He was then only twenty-nine years of age, and this was the first great public recognition of his genius, and the first occasion that was afforded him of displaying his powers as a public speaker. Professor Wilson (Christopher North) presided, and spoke of the young author in the following terms:

"Our friend has dealt with the common feelings and passions of ordinary men in the common and ordinary paths of life. He has not sought—at least he has not yet sought—to deal with those thoughts and passions that are made conspicuous from afar by the elevated stations of those who experience them. He has mingled in the common walks of life; he has made himself familiar with the lower orders of society. He has not been deterred by the aspect of vice and wickedness, and misery and guilt, from seeking a spirit of good in things evil, but has endeavored by the might of genius to transmute what was base into what is precious as the beaten gold. * * * But I shall be betrayed if I go on much longer—which it would be improper for me to do—into something like a critical delineation of the genius of our illustrious guest. I shall not attempt that; but I can not but express in a few ineffectual words the delight which every human bosom feels in the benign spirit which pervades all his creations. How kind and good a man he is, I need not say; nor what strength of genius he has acquired by that profound sympathy with his fellow-creatures, whether in prosperity and happiness, or overwhelmed with unfortunate circumstances, but who do not yet sink under their miseries, but trust to their own strength of endurance, to that principle of truth and honor and integrity which is no stranger to the uncultivated bosom, which is found in the lowest abodes in as great strength as in the halls of nobles and the palaces of kings.

" Mr. Dickens is also a satirist. He satirizes human life, but he does not satirize it to degrade it. He does not wish to pull down what is high into the neighborhood of what is low. He does not seek to represent all virtue as a hollow thing, in which no confidence can be placed. He satirizes only the selfish, and the hard-hearted, and the cruel; he exposes in a hideous light that principle which, when acted upon, gives a power to men in the lowest grades to carry on a more terrific tyranny than if placed upon thrones. I shall not say—for I do not feel—that our distinguished guest has done full and entire justice to one subject—that he has entirely succeeded where I have no doubt he would be most anxious to succeed—in a full and complete delineation of the female character. But this he has done: he has not endeavored to represent women as charming merely by the aid of acomplishments, however elegant and graceful. He has not depicted those accomplishments as the essentials of their character, but has spoken of them rather as always inspired by a love of do-

---

* "Master Humphrey's Clock," vol. 1 pp 98, 99.

* June 25, 1841.

mesticity, by fidelity, by purity, by innocence, by charity, and by hope, which makes them discharge, under the most difficult circumstances, their duties; and which brings over their path in this world some glimpses of the light of heaven. Mr. Dickens may be assured that there is felt for him all over Scotland a sentiment of kindness, affection, admiration, and love; and I know for certain that the knowledge of these sentiments must make him happy."

Dickens left Liverpool, on his voyage across the Atlantic, in the "Britannia" steam-packet, Captain Hewett, on the 3d of January, 1842. At Boston, Hartford, and New York, he was received with ovations (Washington Irving on one occasion presiding at a banquet held in his honor), until he was obliged to decline any further appearance in public. During this first visit to America, he made three long and eloquent speeches, which are all given in this volume *in extenso*. In each of these he referred in an earnest way to the great question of International Copyright, urging upon his transatlantic friends the necessity of doing right and justice in this matter. He returned to England in the month of June, and a few weeks afterwards addressed the following circular letter to all the principal English authors:

"1 Devonshire Terrace, York Gate, Regent's Park,
"7th July, 1842

"You may perhaps be aware that, during my stay in America, I lost no opportunity of endeavoring to awaken the public mind to a sense of the unjust and iniquitous state of the law in that country in reference to the wholesale piracy of British works. Having been successful in making the subject one of general discussion in the United States, I carried to Washington, for presentation to Congress by Mr. Clay, a petition from the whole body of American authors, earnestly praying for the enactment of an International Copyright Law. It was signed by Mr. Washington Irving, Mr. Prescott, Mr. Cooper, and every man who has distinguished himself in the literature of America; and has since been referred to a Select Committee of the House of Representatives. To counteract any effect which might be produced by that petition, a meeting was held in Boston—which you will remember, is the seat and stronghold of Learning and Letters in the United States—at which a memorial against any change in the existing state of things in this respect was agreed to, with but one dissentient voice. This document, which, incredible as it may appear to you, was actually forwarded to Congress and received, deliberately stated that if English authors were invested with any control over the republication of their own books, it would be no longer possible for American editors to alter and adapt them (as they do now) to the American taste! This memorial was, without loss of time, replied to by Mr. Prescott, who commented, with the natural indignation of a gentleman and a man of letters, upon its extraordinary dishonesty. I am satisfied that this brief mention of its tone, and spirit is sufficient to impress you with the conviction that it becomes all those who are in any way connected with the literature of England to take that high stand to which the nature of their pursuits and the extent of their sphere of usefulness justly entitle them, to discourage the upholders of such doctrines by every means in their power, and to hold themselves aloof from the remotest participation in a system from which the moral sense and honorable feeling of all just men must instinctively recoil.

"For myself, I have resolved that I will never from this time enter into any negotiation with any person for the transmission across the Atlantic of early proofs of any thing I may write, and that I will forego all profit derivable from such a source. I do not venture to urge this line of proceeding upon you, but I would beg to suggest, and to lay great stress upon the necessity of observing one other course of action, to which

I can not too emphatically call your attention. The persons who exert themselves to mislead the American public on this question, to put down its discussion, and to suppress and distort the truth in reference to it in every possible way, are (as you may easily suppose) those who have a strong interest in the existing system of piracy and plunder, inasmuch as, so long as it continues, they can gain a very comfortable living out of the brains of other men, while they would find it very difficult to earn bread by the exercise of their own. These are the editors and proprietors of newspapers almost exclusively devoted to the republication of popular English works. They are, for the most part, men of very low attainments, and of more than indifferent reputation; and I have frequently seen them, in the same sheet in which they boast of the rapid sale of many thousand copies of an English reprint, coarsely and insolently attacking the author of that very book, and heaping scurrility and slander upon his head. I would therefore entreat you, in the name of the honorable pursuit with which you are so intimately connected, never to hold correspondence with any of these men, and never to negotiate with them for the sale of early proofs of any work over which you have control, but to treat on all occasions with some respectable American publishing house, and with such an establishment only. Our common interest in this subject, and my advocacy of it, single-handed, on every occasion that has presented itself during my absence from Europe, form my excuse for addressing you.

"I am, etc., CHARLES DICKENS."

By his "American Notes," and by some of the scenes in "Martin Chuzzlewit," Dickens gave for a time great offense to the Americans, though he only satirized some of their foibles (with just a spice of piquant exaggeration), as he had ours at home. Let the reader hear what two candid Americans have recently written on this subject:

"The 'American Notes' are weak, and unworthy of their author; but the American sketches in 'Martin Chuzzlewit' are among the cleverest and truest things he has ever written. The satire was richly deserved, well applied, and has done a great deal of good. To claim that it was mere burlesque and exaggeration, is sheer nonsense, and it is highly disingenuous to deny the existence of the absurdities upon which it was founded. Moreover, the popular implication that there is really nothing now in the country justly to provoke a smile—to urge with so much complacency that we have changed all that—argues the continued existence of not a little of the same thin-skinned tetchiness, the same inability 'to see ourselves as others see us,' which made us so legitimate a target before."

"As for certain American portraits painted in Martin Chuzzlewit," says an American lady,[*] "I should as soon think of objecting to them as I should think of objecting to any other discovery in natural history. To deny the existence of Elijah Pogram, Jefferson Brick, Colonel Diver, Mrs. Hominy, and Miss Codger, is to deny facts, somewhat exaggerated, that are patent to any keen observer who has ever travelled through the United States. The character of Elijah Pogram is so well known as to constantly figure in the world of illustration; and we can well afford to laugh at foibles of native growth when Mr. Dickens devotes the greater part of this same novel to the exposition of English vice and selfishness."

The following letter, referring to Martin Chuz-

* Kate Field.

zlewit, which was then in course of publication, was addressed by Mr. Dickens to a friend in January, 1844:

"Devonshire Terrace, January 2d, 1844

"MY DEAR SIR,—That is a very horrible case you tell me of. I would to God I could get at the parental heart of ——, in which event I would so scarify it, that he should writhe again. But if I were to put such a father as he into a book, all the fathers going (and especially the bad ones) would hold up their hands and protest against the unnatural caricature. I find that a great many people (particularly those who might have sat for the character) consider even Mr. Pecksniff a grotesque impossibility, and Mrs. Nickleby herself, sitting bodily before me in a solid chair, once asked me whether I really believed there ever was such a woman.

"So ——, reviewing his own case, would not believe in Jonas Chuzzlewit. 'I like Oliver Twist,' says ——, 'for I am fond of children. But the book is unnatural, for who would think of being cruel to poor little Oliver Twist!'

"Nevertheless I will bear the dog in my mind, and if I can hit him between the eyes so that he shall stagger more than you or I have done this Christmas under the combined effects of punch and turkey, I will.

"Thank you cordially for your note. Excuse this scrap of paper. I thought it was a whole sheet until I turned it over. My dear sir, faithfully yours,

"CHARLES DICKENS."

To a collection of Sketches and Tales by a Working-man, published in 1844,[*] Charles Dickens was induced to contribute a preface, from which we select the following passages:

"I do not recommend it as a book of surpassing originality or transcendent merit. * * * I do not claim to have discovered in humble life an extraordinary and brilliant genius. I can not charge mankind in general with having entered into a conspiracy to neglect the author of this volume, or to leave him pining in obscurity. I have not the smallest intention of comparing him with Burns, the exciseman; or with Bloomfield, the shoemaker; or with Ebenezer Elliott, the worker in iron; or with James Hogg, the shepherd. I see no reason to be hot, or bitter, or lowering, or sarcastic, or indignant, or fierce, or sour, or sharp, in his behalf. I have nothing to rail at; nothing to exalt; nothing to flourish in the face of a stony-hearted world; and have but a very short and simple story to tell.

"John Overs is, as is set forth in the title-page, a working-man. A man who earns his weekly wages (or who did when he was strong enough) by plying of the hammer, plane, and chisel. He became known to me nearly six years ago, when he sent me some songs, appropriate to the different months of the year, with a letter, stating under what circumstances they had been composed, and in what manner he was occupied from morning until night. I was just then relinquishing the conduct of a monthly periodical,[†] or I would gladly have published them. As it was, I returned them to him, with a private expression of the interest I felt in such productions. They were afterwards accepted, with much readiness and consideration, by Mr.

Tait, of Edinburgh, and were printed in his Magazine.

"Finding, after some further correspondence with my new friend, that his authorship had not ceased with his verses, but that he still occupied his leisure moments in writing, I took occasion to remonstrate with him seriously against his pursuing that course. I told him his persistence in his new calling made me uneasy; and I advised him to abandon it as strongly as I could.

"In answer to this dissuasion of mine, he wrote me as manly and straightforward, but withal, as modest a letter, as ever I read in my life. He explained to me how limited his ambition was: soaring no higher than the establishment of his wife in some light business, and the better education of his children. He set before me the difference between his evening and holiday studies, such as they were; and the having no better resource than an ale-house or a skittle-ground. He told me how every small addition to his stock of knowledge made his Sunday walks the pleasanter, the hedge-flowers sweeter, every thing more full of interest and meaning to him.

* * * * *

"He is very ill; the faintest shadow of the man who came into my little study for the first time, half-a-dozen years ago, after the correspondence I have mentioned. He has been very ill for a long period; his disease is a severe and wasting affection of the lungs, which has incapacitated him these many months for every kind of occupation. 'If I could only do a hard day's work,' he said to me the other day, 'how happy I should be!'

"Having these papers by him, amongst others, he bethought himself that, if he could get a bookseller to purchase them for publication in a volume, they would enable him to make some temporary provision for his sick wife and very young family. We talked the matter over together, and that it might be easier of accomplishment I promised him that I would write an introduction to his book.

"I would to Heaven that I could do him better service! I would to Heaven it were an introduction to a long, and vigorous, and useful life! But Hope will not trim his lamp the less brightly for him and his because of this impulse to their struggling fortunes, and trust me, reader, they deserve her light, and need it sorely.

"He has inscribed this book to one[*] whose skill will help him, under Providence, in all that human skill can do.[†] To one who never could have recognized in any potentate on earth a higher claim to constant kindness and attention than he has recognized in him." * * *

The beautiful series of Christmas stories with

---

* "Evenings of a Working-man." by John Overs, with a Preface relative to the Author, by Charles Dickens. London, Newby, 1844.
† "Bentley's Miscellany," edited by Mr. Dickens during the years 1837-'38.

* Dr. Elliotson.
† We are told that Overs did not live long after the publication of his little book: "the malady under which he was laboring terminated fatally the following October."—Communicated.

which during the last fifteen years the public have become so familiar, was commenced by Mr. Dickens in December, 1843, with "A Christmas Carol in Prose," illustrated by John Leech. What Jeffrey, what Sydney Smith, what Jerrold, what Thackeray thought and wrote about this little story is well known. "Blessings on your kind heart, my dear Dickens," wrote Jeffrey, "and may it always be as full and as light as it is kind, and a fountain of goodness to all within reach of its beatings! We are all charmed with your Carol; chiefly, I think, for the genuine goodness which breathes all through it, and is the true inspiring angel by which its genius has been awakened. The whole scene of the Cratchits is like the dream of a beneficent angel, in spite of its broad reality, and little Tiny Tim in life and in death almost as sweet and touching as Nelly. You may be sure you have done more good, and not only fastened more kindly feelings, but prompted more positive acts of benevolence by this little publication, than can be traced to all the pulpits and confessionals since Christmas, 1842."

"It is the work," writes Thackeray,[*] "of the master of all the English humorists now alive; the young man who came and took his place calmly at the head of the whole tribe, and who has kept it. Think of all we owe Mr. Dickens since those half-dozen years—the store of happy hours that he has made us pass, the kindly and pleasant companions whom he has introduced to us; the harmless laughter, the generous wit, the frank, manly, human love which he has taught us to feel! Every month of those years has brought us some kind token from this delightful genius. His books may have lost in art, perhaps, but could we afford to wait? Since the days when the 'Spectator' was produced by a man of kindred mind and temper, what books have appeared that have taken so affectionate a hold of the English public as these?

"Who can listen to objections regarding such a book as this? It seems to me a national benefit, and to every man or woman who reads it a personal kindness. The last two people I heard speak of it were women; neither knew the other, or the author, and both said by way of criticism, 'God bless him!' * * * As for Tiny Tim, there is a certain passage in the book regarding that young gentleman about which a man should hardly venture to speak in print or in public, any more than he would of any other affections of his private heart. There is not a reader in England but that little creature will be a bond of union between the author and him; and he will say of Charles Dickens, as the woman just now, 'God bless him!' What a feeling is this for a writer to be able to inspire, and what a reward to reap!"

During six years did Mr. Dickens continue to issue at Christmas these little volumes: "A Christmas Carol" (December, 1843); "The

Chimes" (December, 1844); "The Cricket on the Hearth" (December, 1845); "The Battle of Life" (December, 1846); "The Haunted Man and the Ghost's Bargain" (December, 1848).[*]

Christmas stories are now grown so much the fashion that, whenever the season of holly and mistletoe comes round they greet us at every turn, forcing themselves upon our notice through every species of whimsical and enticing embellishment. Why is it that, amidst such a satiety of novelties, we turn again and again, with an interest as keen as ever, to a perusal of the pages where little Dot Peerybingle chirps as brightly as the cricket on her own hearth; where Trotty Veck listens to the voices of the chimes, striving to comprehend what it is they say to him; and where old Scrooge's heart is softened by his ghostly visitants? It is because Charles Dickens has made such a study of that human nature we all possess in common, that he is able to strike with a practised hand upon the chords of our hearts, and draw forth harmony that vibrates from soul to soul.

It is not, however, our intention here to follow Mr. Dickens through the whole of his long and honorable literary career, far less to undertake the superfluous task of extolling the numerous and brilliant list of writings that have followed each other in rapid and welcome succession from his indefatigable pen. All that remains for us to do now, is to notice briefly two very grave charges that have been made against the general tendency of his writings, and to bring forward some evidence in refutation of them.

These two charges are—1. A willful perversion of facts in describing the political and social condition of our time; 2. An irreverence for and ridicule of sacred things and persons, which (say the objectors) infuses a subtle poison through the whole of his works, and unsettles the belief of the young. We shall take these charges one at a time.

In some of his later novels, such as "Bleak House" and "Little Dorrit," in which he has endeavored to grapple with the great social and political problems of the age, certain critics have accused him of exaggeration, and even of a willful perversion of facts. Against their opinion we are pleased to be able to set that of so good an authority as the author of "Modern Painters:"

"The essential value and truth of Dickens's writings," says Mr. Ruskin, "have been unwisely lost sight of by many thoughtful persons, merely because he presents his truth with some color of caricature. Unwisely, because Dickens's caricature, though often gross, is never mistaken. Allowing for his manner of telling them, the things he tells us are always true. I wish that he could think it right to limit his

* These five volumes were all gracefully illustrated by John Leech, Daniel Maclise, Clarkson Stanfield, Sir Edwin Landseer, Richard Doyle, and others; and a set of the original issue is now much sought after, and not easily met with.

brilliant exaggeration to works written only for public amusement; and when he takes up a subject of high national importance, such as that which he handled in 'Hard Times,' that he would use severer and more accurate analysis. The usefulness of that work (to my mind, in several respects, the greatest he has written), is with many persons seriously diminished, because Mr. Bounderby is a dramatic monster, instead of a characteristic example of a worldly master; and Stephen Blackpool a dramatic perfection, instead of a characteristic example of an honest workman. But let us not lose the use of Dickens's wit and insight because he chooses to speak in a circle of stage fire. He is entirely right in his main drift and purpose in every book he has written; and all of them, but especially 'Hard Times,' should be studied with close and earnest care by persons interested in social questions. They will find much that is partial, and, because partial, apparently unjust; but if they examine all the evidence on the other side, which Dickens seems to overlook, it will appear, after all their trouble, that his view was the finally right one, grossly and sharply told."*

Secondly, Mr. Dickens is accused of an irreverence for, and unseemly ridicule of, sacred things. Any attentive reader of Dickens will have observed that he is not much in the habit of quoting from or alluding to the writings of others; but that when he does quote or allude, it is in the great majority of cases from or to the Holy Scriptures.† Occasionally we come upon a reference to Shakspeare; now and then we meet with one from Swift, or Scott, or Byron; but these occur so seldom, that it may be said, once for all, that the source from which Mr. Dickens is usually in the habit of making quotations is the Bible only. It is very interesting to find that so many of Mr. Dickens's characters are represented as being in the habit either of regularly reading and studying the Bible, or of having it read to them by some one else.

"I ain't much of a hand at reading writing-hand," said Betty Higden, "though I can read my Bible and most print." Little Nell was in the constant habit of taking the Bible with her to read while in her quiet and lonely retreat in the old church, after all her long and weary wanderings were past. In the happy time which Oliver Twist spent with Mrs. Maylie and Rose, he used to read, in the evenings, a chapter or two from the Bible, which he had been studying all the week, and in the performance of which duty he felt more proud and pleased than if he had been the clergyman himself. There was Sarah, in the "Sketches by Boz," who regularly read the Bible to her old mistress; and in the touching Sketch of "Our Next-door Neighbor" in the same book, we find the mother of

the sick boy engaged in reading the Bible to him when the visitor called and interrupted her. This incident reminds us of the poor Chancery prisoner in the Fleet, who, when on his death-bed calmly waiting the release which would set him free forever, had the Bible read to him by an old man in a cobbler's apron. One of David Copperfield's earliest recollections was of a certain Sunday evening, when his mother read aloud to him and Peggotty the story of Our Saviour raising Lazarus from the dead. So deep an impression did the story make upon the boy, taken in connection with all that had been lately told him about his father's funeral, that he requested to be carried up to his bed-room, from the windows of which he could see the quiet church-yard with the dead all lying in their graves at rest below the solemn moon. Pip, too, in "Great Expectations," was not only in the habit of reading the Bible to the convict under sentence of death, but of praying with him as well; and Esther Summerson tells us how she used to come down stairs every evening at nine o'clock to read the Bible to her godmother.

Not a few of the dwellings into which Mr. Dickens conducts us, in the course of some of his best-known stories, have their walls decorated with prints illustrative of familiar scenes from sacred history. Thus when Martin Chuzzlewit went away from Pecksniff's, and was ten good miles on his way to London, he stopped to breakfast in the parlor of a little road-side inn, on the walls of which were two or three highly-colored pictures, representing the Wise Men at the Manger, and the Prodigal Son returning to his Father. On the walls of Peggotty's charming boat-cottage there were prints showing the Sacrifice of Isaac, and the Casting of Daniel into the Den of Lions. When Arthur Clennam came home after his long absence in the East, he found the Plagues of Egypt still hanging, framed and glazed, on the same old place in his mother's parlor. And who has forgotten the fire-place in old Scrooge's house, which "was paved all round with quaint Dutch tiles, designed to illustrate the Scriptures?"

Here are a few comparisons: Mr. Larry, in bestowing a bachelor's blessing on Miss Cross, before "somebody" came to claim her for his own, "held the fair face from him to look at the well-remembered expression on the forehead, and then laid the bright golden hair against his little brown wig, with a genuine tenderness and delicacy which, if such things be old-fashioned, were as old as Adam." Miss Jellyby relieved her mind to Miss Summerson on the subject of Mr. Quale in the following energetic language: "If he were to come with his great shining, lumpy forehead, night after night, till he was as old as Methuselah, I wouldn't have any thing to say to him." And Mr. Filer, in his eminently practical remarks on the lamentable ignorance of political economy on the part of working-people in connection with marriage, observed to Alderman Cute that a man

---

* "Unto this Last," chap. i.
† The following instances are, by kind permission, selected from an admirable article upon this subject, which appeared in the "Temple Bar" Magazine for September, 1869.

may live to be as old as Methuselah, and may labor all his life for the benefit of such people; but there could be no more hope of persuading them that they had no right or business to be married, than he could hope to persuade them that they had no earthly right or business to be born. Miss Betsy Trotwood declared to Mr. Dick that the natural consequence of David Copperfield's mother having married a murderer—or a man with a name very like it—was to set the boy a-prowling and wandering about the country, "like Cain before he was grown up." Joe Gargery's journeyman, on going away from his work at night, used to slouch out of the shop like Cain, or the Wandering Jew, as if he had no idea where he was going, and had no intention of ever coming back. Describing the state of "the thriving City of Eden," when Martin and Mark arrived there, the author of "Martin Chuzzlewit" says— "The waters of the Deluge might have left it but a week before, so choked with slime and matted growth was the hideous swamp which bore that name." The following reference to Noah's Ark is from "Little Dorrit," descriptive of the gradual approach of darkness up among the highest ridges of the Alps: "The ascending night came up the mountains like a rising water. When at last it rose to the walls of the convent of the great St. Bernard, it was as if that weather-beaten structure were another ark, and floated on the shadowy waves." Here is something from the Tower of Babel: "Looming heavy in the black wet night, the tall chimneys of the Coketown factories rose high into the air, and looked as if they were so many competing towers of Babel." When Mortimer Lightwood inquired of Charley Hexam, with reference to the body of the man found in the river, whether or not any means had been employed to restore life, he received this reply: "You wouldn't ask, sir, if you knew his state. Pharaoh's multitude that were drowned in the Red Sea ain't more beyond restoring to life." The boy added, further, "that if Lazarus were only half as far gone, that was the greatest of all the miracles." When the Scotch surgeon was called in professionally to see Mr. Krook's unfortunate lodger, the Scotch tongue pronounced him to be "just as dead as Chairy." Job's poverty is not likely to be forgotten among the comparisons. No, Mr. Mell's mother was as poor as Job. Nor Samson's strength: Dot's mother had so many infallible recipes for the perservation of the baby's health, that had they all been administered, the said baby must have been done for, though strong as an infant Samson. Nor Goliath's importance: John Chivery's chivalrous feeling towards all that belonged to Little Dorrit, made him so very respectable, in spite of his small stature, his weak legs, and his genuine poetic temperament, that a Goliath might have sat in his place demanding less consideration at Arthur Clennam's hands. Nor Solomon's wisdom: Trotty Veck was so delighted when the child kissed him that he couldn't help saying,

"She's as sensible as Solomon." Miss Wade having said farewell to her fellow-travellers in the public room of the hotel at Marseilles, sought her own apartment. As she passed along the gallery, she heard an angry sound of muttering and sobbing. A door stood open and looking into the room, she saw therein Pet's attendant, the maid with the curious name of Tattycoram. Miss Wade asked what was the matter, and received in reply a few short and angry words in a deeply-injured, ill-used tone. Then again commenced the sobs and tears and pinching, tearing fingers, making altogether such a scene as if she were being "rent by the demons of old." Let us close these comparisons by quoting another from the same book, "Little Dorrit," descriptive of the evening stillness after a day of terrific glare and heat at Marseilles: "The sun went down in a red, green, golden glory; the stars came out in the heavens, and the fire-flies mimicked them in the lower air, as men may feebly imitate the goodness of a better order of beings; the long, dusty roads and the interminable plains were in repose, and *so deep a hush was on the sea, that it scarcely whispered of the time when it shall give up its dead.*"

Looking over the familiar pages of "Nicholas Nickleby," our eye lights upon a passage, almost at opening, which refers to God's goodness and mercy. As Nickleby's father lay on his death-bed, he embraced his wife and children, and then "solemnly commended them to One who never deserted the widow or her fatherless children." Towards the close of Esther Summerson's narrative in "Bleak House" we read these touching, tender words regarding Ada's baby: —"The little child who was to have done so much was born before the turf was planted on its father's grave. It was a boy; and I, my husband, and my guardian gave him his father's name. The help that my dear counted on did come to her; though it came in the Eternal Wisdom for another purpose. Though to bless and restore his mother, not his father, was the errand of this baby, its power was mighty to do it. When I saw the strength of the weak little hand, and how its touch could heal my darling's heart and raise up hopes within her, I felt a new sense of the goodness and tenderness of God." After these illustrations of the great lessons of the goodness of God, and that there is mercy in even our hardest trials, we come next upon one which teaches the duty of patience and resignation to God's will. Mrs. Maylie observed to Oliver Twist, with reference to the dangerous illness of Rose, that she had seen and experienced enough to "know that it is not always the youngest and best who are spared to those that love them; but this should give us comfort in our sorrow, for Heaven is just, and such things teach us impressively that there is a brighter world than this, and that the passage to it is speedy. God's will be done!"

Our Saviour's life and teaching afford so many interesting illustrations to Charles Dickens that

our great difficulty, in the limited space to which
we are now confined, is to make a good selection.
Here is a sketch entitled "A Christmas Tree,"
from one of his reprinted pieces, which contains
this simple and beautiful summary of our Lord's
life on earth: "The waits are playing, and they
break my childish sleep! What images do I
associate with the Christmas music as I see
them set forth on the Christmas Tree? Known
before all the others, keeping far apart from all
the others, they gather round my little bed. An
angel speaking to a group of shepherds in a
field; some travellers, with eyes uplifted, following a star; a Baby in a manger; a Child in
a spacious temple talking with grave men; a
solemn figure, with a mild and beautiful face,
raising a dead girl by the hand; again, near a
city gate, calling back the son of a widow, on
his bier, to life; a crowd of people looking
through the opened roof of a chamber where
He sits, and letting down a sick person on a bed
with ropes; the same, in a tempest, walking on
the water to a ship; again, on a sea-shore, teaching a great multitude; again, with a child upon
His knee, and other children round; again, restoring sight to the blind, speech to the dumb,
hearing to the deaf, health to the sick, strength
to the lame, knowledge to the ignorant; again,
dying upon a cross, watched by armed soldiers,
a thick darkness coming on, the earth beginning
to shake, and only one voice heard, 'Forgive
them, for they know not what they do.'"

These passages, which are only a few out of a
very much longer list that might be made, will
be sufficient, we trust, to show how much our
greatest living novelist is in the habit of going
to the sacred narrative for illustrations to many
of his most touching incidents, and how reverent
and respectful always is the spirit in which every
such illustration is employed. To think of
Charles Dickens's writings as containing no religious teaching, is to do them a great injustice.

The first of Mr. Dickens's famous public
Readings was given at Birmingham, during the
Christmas week of 1853. At a meeting held on
Monday, January 10, 1853, in the theatre of the
Philosophical Institution, "for the purpose of
considering the desirableness of establishing in
Birmingham a Scientific and Literary Society
upon a comprehensive plan, having for its object the diffusion," etc., Mr. Arthur Ryland
read a letter from Mr. Charles Dickens, received
by him the day after the Literary and Artistic
Banquet, containing an offer to visit Birmingham
next Christmas, and read his Christmas Carol,
in the Town Hall, for the benefit of the proposed Institution, with the proviso, however,
that as many as possible of the working-class
should be admitted free. "It would," said Mr.
Dickens, "take about two hours, with a pause
of ten minutes half-way through. There would
be some novelty in the thing, as I have never
done it in public, though I have in private, and
(if I may say so) with a great effect on the
hearers. I was so inexpressibly gratified last

night by the warmth and enthusiasm of my
Birmingham friends, that I feel half ashamed
this morning of so poor an offer. But as I had
decided on making it to you before I came down
yesterday, I propose it nevertheless."

The readings—three in number—came off
with great *éclat* during the last week of the year,
and brought in a net sum of £400 to the Institute. Mr. Dickens continued from this time to
give similar readings, for charitable purposes,
both in the provinces and in London; but it
was not till five years later (1858) that he began to read on his own account.

As we are writing, that long series of readings—continued through sixteen years, in both
hemispheres—is drawing to a close, and the
voice and figure of Charles Dickens, that have
grown so familiar to us all, will dwell henceforth
in the memory alone, but in one of its most honored niches.

We ought not to omit to mention what any
reader may well surmise, that Charles Dickens
is inimitable in enlivening correspondence or
table-talk with humorous anecdote, appropriate
to the occasion. We subjoin a few specimens.
The first is from one of his letters to Douglas
Jerrold, and is dated Paris, 14th February,
1847:—"I am somehow reminded of a good
story I heard the other night from a man who
was a witness of it, and an actor in it. At a
certain German town last autumn there was a
tremendous *furore* about Jenny Lind, who, after
driving the whole place mad, left it, on her travels, early one morning. The moment her carriage was outside the gates, a party of rampant
students, who had escorted it, rushed back to
the inn, demanded to be shown to her bedroom,
swept like a whirlwind up stairs into the room
indicated to them, tore up the sheets, and wore
them in strips as decorations. An hour or two
afterwards a bald old gentleman, of amiable appearance, an Englishman, who was staying in
the hotel, came to breakfast at the *table d'hôte*,
and was observed to be much disturbed in his
mind, and to show great terror whenever a student come near him. At last he said, in a low
voice, to some people who were near him at the
table, 'You are English gentlemen, I observe.
Most extraordinary people, these Germans!
Students, as a body, raving mad, gentlemen!'
'Oh no!' said somebody else; 'excitable, but
very good fellows, and very sensible.' 'By
God, sir!' returned the old gentleman, still
more disturbed, 'then there's something political in it, and I am a marked man. I went out
for a little walk this morning after shaving, and
while I was gone'—he fell into a terrible per-
spiration as he told it—'they burst into my bedroom, tore up my sheets, and are now patrolling
the town in all directions with bits of 'em in
their button-holes!' I needn't wind up by adding that they had gone to the wrong chamber."

Dickens now and then administers a little
gentle rebuke to affectation, in a pleasant but
unmistakable manner. Here is an instance of
how he silenced a bilious young writer, who

was inveighing against the world in a very "forcible feeble manner." During a pause in this philippic against the human race, Dickens said across the table, in the most self-congratulatory of tones: "I say—what a lucky thing it is you and I don't belong to it? It reminds me," continued the author of Pickwick, "of the two men, who on a *raised* scaffold were awaiting the final delicate attention of the hangman; the notice of one was aroused by observing that a bull had got into the crowd of spectators, and was busily employed in tossing one here, and another there; whereupon one of the criminals said to the other—'I say, Bill, how *lucky it is* for us that we *are up here.*'"

But the thing which, above all others, has characterized Dickens throughout his career, that has made his world-wide fame, and rendered his name a household name, is his broad, genial sympathy with life in all its phases, and with those most who are manfully toiling towards a better day. To this "enthusiasm of humanity" John Forster has alluded in the Dedicatory Sonnet to Charles Dickens, prefixed to his "Life of Goldsmith" (March, 1848), when he says:

> "Come with me and behold,
> O friend with heart as gentle for distress,
> As resolute with wise true thoughts to bind
> The happiest to the unhappiest of our kind,
> That there is fiercer crowded misery
> In garret-toil and London loneliness
> Than in cruel islands 'mid the far-off sea."

The great heart of Dickens has beat in unison with his age and with the people, and his name will be dear to all English-speaking races long after this little island of ours, the old home, shall have become a summer resort—a curiosity to visit—for the children of the great Anglo-Saxon Republics that are now growing up in the New and Southern Worlds.

December, 1869.

CHARLES DICKENS died on the 9th of June, at his residence at Gadshill. He fell in harness. The previous Saturday he was present at a neighboring *fête champetre*, and during the early part of the week of his death he was engaged upon the "Mystery of Edwin Drood." On Wednesday, the 8th of June, he was employed at his literary labors until dinner-time. While at dinner, his sister-in-law, Miss Hogarth, observed an unusual appearance in his face, and, becoming alarmed, said she feared he was ill, proposing, in the same breath, to telegraph for medical assistance. Mr. Dickens replied, "No, no; I have got the toothache, and shall be better presently." He then asked that the windows might be shut; and almost immediately he lapsed into unconsciousness, from which state he never recovered. Medical assistance was at once procured, but the case was pronounced a hopeless one from the very first. He died about a quarter after six, Thursday evening. His son Charles, his two daughters, and his sister-in-law, were present at the death-bed.

The day of the great novelist's death was the anniversary of the Staplehurst accident, in which he was in great peril, and from which some of those nearest to him consider he received a physical shock from which he never recovered. The friends who were in the habit of meeting Mr. Dickens privately recall now the energy with which he depicted that dreadful scene, and how, as the climax of his story came, and its dread interest grew, he would rise from the table and literally act the parts of the several sufferers to whom he had lent a helping hand. It is remembered, too, that one of the first surgeons of the day, who was present when this Staplehurst story was told, soon after its occurrence, remarked that "the worst of these railway accidents was the difficulty of determining the period at which the system could be said to have survived the shock, and that instances were on record of two or three years having gone by before the life-sufferer knew that he was seriously hurt."

But medical testimony is clear and precise as to the immediate cause of his death. He was carried away by apoplexy—an effusion of blood on the brain—the cause an overstrained system, and the result one which was only staved off twelve months ago, when he was induced to obey his doctor's injunctions, and to suspend his reading in public.

Mr. Dickens, it is said, often expressed the wish that he might be buried in the quiet cemetery at Kensal Green, where lie the remains of some who were very dear to him in life; and it is well known that he felt a repugnance to public funerals. But on the day on which his death became known, the Dean of Westminster had an interview with Mr. Charles Dickens, Jr., and proposed that he should be buried in Westminster Abbey. On consultation with some of Mr. Dickens's dearest and oldest friends, and finding that his written instructions regarding his funeral, contained in his will, could be complied with, the family consented to the Dean's request.

The funeral ceremonies were very simple. The body was conveyed early on Tuesday morning, June 14, from the house at Gadshill by special train to the Charing Cross Station, where it was received by a plain hearse attended by three plain mourning coaches without trappings of any kind, and was carried to Westminster Abbey about half-past nine. It was met in Dean's Yard by Dean Stanley and the clergy of the Abbey, and conveyed along the western cloisters to the Poet's Corner, where a grave had been prepared. The service was the plain, unadorned ritual of the Prayer-book, the only embellishment being a low and soft voluntary on the organ between the prayers. The coffin was of plain oak, and bore on a brass plate the simple inscription—

CHARLES DICKENS,
BORN FEBRUARY 7TH, 1812,
DIED JUNE 9TH, 1870.

Flowers were thrown into the grave by the female mourners, and the solemn assembly separated in silence. Owing to the secrecy preserved no spectators were present, and the proceedings, in accordance with the well-known wishes of the deceased, were of the most private and unostentatious character.

The grave of Charles Dickens is situated at the foot of the coffin of Handel and at the head of the coffin of Sheridan, and between the coffins of Lord Macaulay and Cumberland, the dramatic poet. Only a few feet removed, and near to the side of Dickens, but towards his feet, lie Johnson and Garrick; while near them repose the remains of Campbell. The statue of Addison and the bust of Thackeray overlook the grave at its head. Shakspeare's monument is not far from its foot. Goldsmith's monument and that of the great Duke of Argyll are on the left.

SPEECHES AND SAYINGS

OF

CHARLES DICKENS.

I.

EDINBURGH, JUNE 25, 1841.

[At a public dinner, given in honor of Mr. Dickens, and presided over by the late Professor Wilson, the Chairman having proposed his health in a long and eloquent speech, Mr. Dickens returned thanks as follows:]

IF I felt your warm and generous welcome less, I should be better able to thank you. If I could have listened as you have listened to the glowing language of your distinguished Chairman, and if I could have heard as you heard the "thoughts that breathe and words that burn" which he has uttered, it would have gone hard but I should have caught some portion of his enthusiasm, and kindled at his example. But every word which fell from his lips, and every demonstration of sympathy and approbation with which you received his eloquent expressions, renders me unable to respond to his kindness, and leaves me at last all heart and no lips, yearning to respond as I would do to your cordial greeting—possessing, Heaven knows, the will, and desiring only to find the way.

The way to your good opinion, favor, and support has been to me very pleasing—a path strewn with flowers and cheered with sunshine. I feel as if I stood amongst old friends, whom I had intimately known and highly valued. I feel as if the deaths of the fictitious creatures in which you have been kind enough to express an interest, had endeared us to each other as real afflictions deepen friendships in actual life; I feel as if they had been real persons, whose fortunes we had pursued together in inseparable connection, and that I had never known them apart from you.

It is a difficult thing for a man to speak of himself or of his works. But perhaps on this occasion I may, without impropriety, venture to say a word on the spirit in which mine were conceived. I felt an earnest and humble desire, and shall do till I die, to increase the stock of harmless cheerfulness. I felt that the world was not utterly to be despised; that it was worthy of living in, for many reasons. I was anxious to find, as the Professor has said, if I could, in evil things, that soul of goodness which the Creator has put in them. I was anxious to show that virtue may be found in the by-ways of the world, that it is not incompatible with poverty and even with rags, and to keep steadily through life the motto, expressed in the burning words of your Northern poet—

"The rank is but the guinea stamp,
     The man's the gowd for a' that."

And in following this track, where could I have better assurance that I was right, or where could I have stronger assurance to cheer me on than in your kindness on this to me memorable night?

I am anxious and glad to have an opportunity of saying a word in reference to one incident in which I am happy to know you were interested, and still more happy to know, though it may sound paradoxical, that you were disappointed—I mean the death of the little heroine. When I first conceived the idea of conducting that simple story to its termination, I determined rigidly to adhere to it, and never to forsake the end I had in view. Not untried in the school of affliction, in the death of those we love, I thought what a good thing it would be if, in my little work of pleasant amusement, I could substitute a garland of fresh flowers for the sculptured horrors which disgrace the tomb If I have put into my book any thing which can fill the young mind with better thoughts of death, or soften the grief of older hearts; if I have written one word which can afford pleasure or consolation to old or young in time of trial, I shall consider it as something achieved

—something which I shall be glad to look back upon in after-life. Therefore I kept to my purpose, notwithstanding that, toward the conclusion of the story, I daily received letters of remonstrance, especially from the ladies. God bless them for their tender mercies! The Professor was quite right when he said that I had not reached to an adequate delineation of their virtues; and I fear that I must go on blotting their characters in endeavoring to reach the ideal in my mind. These letters were, however, combined with others from the sterner sex, and some of them were not altogether free from personal invective. But, notwithstanding, I kept to my purpose, and I am happy to know that many of those who at first condemned me are now foremost in their approbation.

If I have made a mistake in detaining you with this little incident, I do not regret having done so; for your kindness has given me such a confidence in you, that the fault is yours and not mine. I come once more to thank you, and here I am in a difficulty again. The distinction you have conferred upon me is one which I never hoped for, and of which I never dared to dream. That it is one which I shall never forget, and that while I live I shall be proud of its remembrance, you must well know. I believe I shall never hear the name of this capital of Scotland without a thrill of gratitude and pleasure. I shall love while I have life her people, her hills, and her houses, and even the very stones of her streets. And if in the future works which may lie before me you should discern—God grant you may!—a brighter spirit and a clearer wit, I pray you to refer it back to this night, and point to that as a Scottish passage for evermore. I thank you again and again, with the energy of a thousand thanks in each one, and I drink to you with a heart as full as my glass, and far easier emptied, I do assure you.

[Later in the evening, in proposing the health of Professor Wilson, Mr. Dickens said:]

I have the honor to be intrusted with a toast, the very mention of which will recommend itself to you, I know, as one possessing no ordinary claims to your sympathy and approbation, and the proposing of which is as congenial to my wishes and feelings as its acceptance must be to yours. It is the health of our Chairman, and coupled with his name I have to propose the literature of Scotland—a literature which he has done much to render famous through the world, and of which he has been for many years —as I hope and believe he will be for many more—a most brilliant and distinguished orna-

ment. Who can revert to the literature of the land of Scott and of Burns without having directly in his mind, as inseparable from the subject and foremost in the picture, that old man of might, with his lion heart and sceptred crutch —Christopher North. I am glad to remember the time when I believed him to be a real, actual, veritable old gentleman, that might be seen any day hobbling along the High Street with the most brilliant eye—but that is no fiction—and the grayest hair in all the world—who wrote not because he cared to write, not because he cared for the wonder and admiration of his fellow-men, but who wrote because he could not help it, because there was always springing up in his mind a clear and sparkling stream of poetry which must have vent, and like the glittering fountain in the fairy tale, draw what you might, was ever at the full, and never languished even by a single drop or bubble. I had so figured him in my mind, and when I saw the Professor two days ago, striding along the Parliament House, I was disposed to take it as a personal offense—I was vexed to see him look so hearty. I drooped to see twenty Christophers in one. I began to think that Scottish life was all light and no shadows, and I began to doubt that beautiful book to which I have turned again and again, always to find new beauties and fresh sources of interest.

[In proposing the memory of the late Sir David Wilkie, Mr. Dickens said:]

Less fortunate than the two gentlemen who have preceded me, it is confided to me to mention a name which can not be pronounced without sorrow, a name in which Scotland had a great triumph, and which England delighted to honor. One of the gifted of the earth has passed away, as it were, yesterday; one who was devoted to his art, and his art was nature— I mean David Wilkie.* He was one who made the cottage hearth a graceful thing—of whom it might truly be said that he found " books in the running brooks," and who has left in all he did some breathing of the air which stirs the heather. But however desirous to enlarge on his genius as an artist, I would rather speak of him now as a friend who has gone from among us. There is his deserted studio—the empty easel lying idly by—the unfinished picture with its face turned to the wall, and there is that bereaved sister, who loved him with an affection which death can not quench. He has left a

---

* Sir David Wilkie died at sea, on board the *Oriental*, off Gibraltar, on the 1st of June, 1841, while on his way back to England. During the evening of the same day his body was committed to the deep.—ED.

name in fame clear as the bright sky ; he has filled our minds with memories pure as the blue waves which roll over him. Let us hope that she who more than all others mourns his loss, may learn to reflect that he died in the fullness of his fame, before age or sickness had dimmed his powers—and that she may yet associate with feelings as calm and pleasant as we do now the memory of Wilkie.

~~~~~~~~~

II.

JANUARY, 1842.

[In presenting Captain Hewett, of the *Britannia*,* with a service of plate on behalf of the passengers, Mr. Dickens addressed him as follows:]

CAPTAIN HEWETT,—I am very proud and happy to have been selected as the instrument of conveying to you the heartfelt thanks of my fellow-passengers on board the ship intrusted to your charge, and of entreating your acceptance of this trifling present. The ingenious artists who work in silver do not always, I find, keep their promises, even in Boston. I regret that, instead of two goblets, which there should be here, there is, at present, only one. The deficiency, however, will soon be supplied ; and, when it is, our little testimonial will be, so far, complete.

You are a sailor, Captain Hewett, in the truest sense of the word ; and the devoted admiration of the ladies, God bless them ! is a sailor's first boast. I need not enlarge upon the honor they have done you, I am sure, by their presence here. Judging of you by myself, I am certain that the recollection of their beautiful faces will cheer your lonely vigils upon the ocean for a long time to come.

In all time to come, and in all your voyages upon the sea, I hope you will have a thought for those who wish to live in your memory by the help of these trifles. As they will often connect you with the pleasure of those homes and firesides from which they once wandered, and which, but for you, they might never have regained, so they trust that you will sometimes associate them with your hours of festive enjoyment ; and that, when you drink from these cups, you will feel that the draught is commended to your lips by friends whose best wishes you have ; and who earnestly and truly hope for your success, happiness, and prosperity, in all the undertakings of your life.

* The *Britannia* was the vessel that conveyed Mr. Dickens across the Atlantic on his first visit to America.—ED.

III.

FEBRUARY 1, 1842.

[At a dinner given to Mr. Dickens by the young men of Boston. The company consisted of about two hundred, among whom were George Bancroft, Washington Allston, and Oliver Wendell Holmes. The toast of "Health, happiness, and a hearty welcome to Charles Dickens," having been proposed by the Chairman, Mr. Quincy, and received with great applause, Mr. Dickens responded with the following address:]

GENTLEMEN,—If you had given this splendid entertainment to any one else in the whole wide world—if I were to-night to exult in the triumph of my dearest friend—if I stood here upon my defense, to repel any unjust attack—to appeal as a stranger to your generosity and kindness as the freest people on the earth—I could, putting some restraint upon myself, stand among you as self-possessed and unmoved as I should be alone in my own room in England. But when I have the echoes of your cordial greeting ringing in my ears ; when I see your kind faces beaming a welcome so warm and earnest as never man had —I feel, it is my nature, so vanquished and subdued, that I have hardly fortitude enough to thank you. If your President, instead of pouring forth that delightful mixture of humor and pathos which you have just heard, had been but a caustic, ill-natured man—if he had only been a dull one—if I could only have doubted or distrusted him or you, I should have had my wits at my fingers' ends, and, using them, could have held you at arm's-length. But you have given me no such opportunity ; you take advantage of me in the tenderest point ; you give me no chance of playing at company, or holding you at a distance, but flock about me like a host of brothers, and make this place like home. Indeed, gentlemen, indeed, if it be natural and allowable for each of us, on his own hearth, to express his thoughts in the most homely fashion, and to appear in his plainest garb, I have a fair claim upon you to let me do so to-night, for you have made my home an Aladdin's Palace. You fold so tenderly within your breasts that common household lamp in which my feeble fire is all enshrined, and at which my flickering torch is lighted up, that straight my household gods take wing and are transported there. And whereas it is written of that fairy structure that it never moved without two shocks —one when it rose, and one when it settled down—I can say of mine that, however sharp a tug it took to pluck it from its native ground, it struck at once an easy, and a deep and lasting root into this soil, and loved it as its own. I can say more of it, and say with truth, that long before it moved, or had a chance of moving, its master—perhaps from some secret sympathy between its timbers and a certain stately tree that has its being hereabout, and spreads its broad branches far and wide—dreamed by day and night, for years, of setting foot upon this shore, and breathing this pure air. And, trust me, gentlemen, that, if I had wandered here, unknowing and unknown, I would—if I know my own heart—have come with all my sympathies clustering as richly about this land and people —with all my sense of justice as keenly alive to their high claims on every man who loves God's image—with all my energies as fully bent on judging for myself, and speaking out, and telling in my sphere the truth, as I do now, when you rain down your welcomes on my head.

Our President has alluded to those writings which have been my occupation for some years past; and you have received his allusions in a manner which assures me—if I needed any such assurance—that we are old friends in the spirit, and have been in close communion for a long time.

It is not easy for a man to speak of his own books. I dare say that few persons have been more interested in mine than I; and if it be a general principle in nature that a lover's love is blind, and that a mother's love is blind, I believe it may be said of an author's attachment to the creatures of his own imagination, that it is a perfect model of constancy and devotion, and is the blindest of all. But the objects and purposes I have had in view are very plain and simple, and may be easily told. I have always had, and always shall have, an earnest and true desire to contribute, as far as in me lies, to the common stock of healthful cheerfulness and enjoyment. I have always had, and always shall have, an invincible repugnance to that mole-eyed philosophy which loves the darkness, and winks and scowls in the light. I believe that Virtue shows quite as well in rags and patches as she does in purple and fine linen. I believe that she and every beautiful object in external nature claims some sympathy in the breast of the poorest man who breaks his scanty loaf of daily bread. I believe that she goes barefoot as well as shod. I believe that she dwells rather oftener in alleys and by-ways than she does in courts and palaces, and that it is good, and pleasant, and profitable to track her out and follow her. I believe that to lay one's hand upon some of those rejected ones whom the world has too long forgotten and too often misused, and to say to the proudest and most thoughtless—"These creatures have the same elements and capacities of goodness as yourselves, they are moulded in the same form, and made of the same clay; and

though ten times worse than you, may, in having retained any thing of their original nature amidst the trials and distresses of their condition, be really ten times better;" I believe that to do this is to pursue a worthy and not useless vocation. Gentlemen, that you think so too, your fervent greeting sufficiently assures me. That this feeling is alive in the Old World as well as the New, no man should know better than I—I, who have found such wide and ready sympathy in my own dear land. That in expressing it, we are but treading in the steps of those great master-spirits who have gone before, we know by reference to all the bright examples in our literature, from Shakspeare downward.

There is one other point connected with the labors (if I may call them so) that you hold in such generous esteem, to which I can not help adverting. I can not help expressing the delight, the more than happiness it was to me to find so strong an interest awakened on this side of the water, in favor of that little heroine of mine, to whom your President has made allusion, who died in her youth. I had letters about that child, in England, from the dwellers in log-houses among the morasses, and swamps, and densest forests, and deep solitudes of the Far West. Many a sturdy hand, hard with the axe and spade, and browned by the summer's sun, has taken up the pen, and written to me a little history of domestic joy or sorrow, always coupled, I am proud to say, with something of interest in that little tale, or some comfort or happiness derived from it; and my correspondent has always addressed me, not as a writer of books for sale, resident some four or five thousand miles away, but as a friend to whom he might freely impart the joys and sorrows of his own fireside. Many a mother—I could reckon them now by dozens, not by units—has done the like, and has told me how she lost such a child at such a time, and where she lay buried, and how good she was, and how, in this or that respect, she resembles Nell. I do assure you that no circumstance of my life has given me one-hundredth part of the gratification I have derived from this source. I was wavering at the time whether or not to wind up my Clock,* and come and see this country, and this decided me. I felt as if it were a positive duty, as if I were bound to pack up my clothes, and come and see my friends; and even now I have such an odd sensation in connection with these things, that you have no chance of spoiling me. I feel as

* "Master Humphrey's Clock," under which title the two novels of "Barnaby Rudge" and "The Old Curiosity Shop" originally appeared.—ED.

though we were agreeing—as indeed we are, if we substitute for fictitious characters the classes from which they are drawn—about third parties, in whom we had a common interest. At every new act of kindness on your part, I say to myself, " That's for Oliver; I should not wonder if that was meant for Smike; I have no doubt that is intended for Nell;" and so I become a much happier, certainly, but a more sober and retiring man than ever I was before.

Gentlemen, talking of my friends in America brings me back, naturally and of course, to you. Coming back to you, and being thereby reminded of the pleasure we have in store in hearing the gentlemen who sit about me, I arrive by the easiest, though not by the shortest course in the world, at the end of what I have to say. But before I sit down, there is one topic on which I am desirous to lay particular stress. It has, or should have, a strong interest for us all, since to its literature every country must look for one great means of refining and improving its people, and one great source of national pride and honor. You have in America great writers—great writers—who will live in all time, and are as familiar to our lips as household words. Deriving (as they all do in a greater or less degree, in their several walks) their inspiration from the stupendous country that gave them birth, they diffuse a better knowledge of it, and a higher love for it, all over the civilized world. I take leave to say, in the presence of some of those gentlemen, that I hope the time is not far distant when they, in America, will receive of right some substantial profit and return in England from their labors; and when we, in England, shall receive some substantial profit and return in America for ours. Pray do not misunderstand me. Securing to myself from day to day the means of an honorable subsistence, I would rather have the affectionate regard of my fellow-men, than I would have heaps and mines of gold. But the two things do not seem to me incompatible. They can not be, for nothing good is incompatible with justice; there must be an international arrangement in this respect: England has done her part, and I am confident that the time is not far distant when America will do hers. It becomes the character of a great country; *firstly*, because it is justice; *secondly*, because without it you never can have, and keep, a literature of your own.

Gentlemen, I thank you with feelings of gratitude, such as are not often awakened, and can never be expressed. As I understand it to be the pleasant custom here to finish with a toast, I would beg to give you: AMERICA AND ENGLAND; and may they never have any division but the Atlantic between them.

IV.

FEBRUARY 7, 1842.

GENTLEMEN,—To say that I thank you for the earnest manner in which you have drunk the toast just now so eloquently proposed to you—to say that I give you back your kind wishes and good feelings with more than compound interest; and that I feel how dumb and powerless the best acknowledgments would be beside such genial hospitality as yours, is nothing. To say that in this winter season flowers have sprung up in every footstep's length of the path which has brought me here; that no country ever smiled more pleasantly than yours has smiled on me, and that I have rarely looked upon a brighter summer prospect than that which lies before me now,* is nothing.

But it is something to be no stranger in a strange place—to feel, sitting at a board for the first time, the ease and affection of an old guest, and to be at once on such intimate terms with the family as to have a homely, genuine interest in its every member—it is, I say, something to be in this novel and happy frame of mind. And, as it is of your creation, and owes its being to you, I have no reluctance in urging it as a reason why, in addressing you, I should not so much consult the form and fashion of my speech, as I should employ that universal language of the heart, which you, and such as you, best teach, and best can understand. Gentlemen, in that universal language—common to you in America and to us in England, as that younger mother-tongue, which, by the means of, and through the happy union of our two great countries, shall be spoken ages hence, by land and sea, over the wide surface of the globe—I thank you.

I had occasion to say the other night in Boston, as I have more than once had occasion to remark before, that it is not easy for an author to speak of his own books. If the task be a difficult one at any time, its difficulty, certainly, is not diminished when a frequent recurrence to the same theme has left one nothing new to say. Still, I feel that in a company like this, and especially after what has been said by the President, that I ought not to pass lightly over those

* " I shall always entertain a very pleasant and grateful recollection of Hartford. It is a lovely place, and I had many friends there, whom I can never remember with indifference. We left it with no little regret."—" American Notes " (Lond. 1842), vol i. p. 182

labors of love, which, if they had no other merit, have been the happy means of bringing us together.

It has been often observed, that you can not judge of an author's personal character from his writings. It may be that you can not. I think it very likely, for many reasons, that you can not. But, at least, a reader will rise from the perusal of a book with some defined and tangible idea of the writer's moral creed and broad purposes, if he has any at all; and it is probable enough that he may like to have this idea confirmed from the author's lips, or dissipated by his explanation. Gentlemen, my moral creed—which is a very wide and comprehensive one, and includes all sects and parties—is very easily summed up. I have faith, and I wish to diffuse faith, in the existence—yes, of beautiful things, even in those conditions of society which are so degenerate, degraded, and forlorn, that, at first sight, it would seem as though they could not be described but by a strange and terrible reversal of the words of Scripture, "God said, Let there be light, and there was none." I take it that we are born, and that we hold our sympathies, hopes, and energies, in trust for the many, and not for the few. That we can not hold in too strong a light of disgust and contempt, before the view of others, all meanness, falsehood, cruelty, and oppression, of every grade and kind. Above all, that nothing is high because it is in a high place ; and that nothing is low because it is in a low one. This is the lesson taught us in the great book of nature. This is the lesson which may be read, alike in the bright track of the stars, and in the dusty course of the poorest thing that drags its tiny length upon the ground. This is the lesson ever uppermost in the thoughts of that inspired man, who tells us that there are

"Tongues in the trees, books in the running brooks,
Sermons in stones, and good in every thing."

Gentlemen, keeping these objects steadily before me, I am at no loss to refer your favor and your generous hospitality back to the right source. While I know, on the one hand, that if, instead of being what it is, this were a land of tyranny and wrong, I should care very little for your smiles or frowns, so I am sure, upon the other, that if, instead of being what I am, I were the greatest genius that ever trod the earth, and had diverted myself for the oppression and degradation of mankind, you would despise and reject me. I hope you will, whenever, through such means, I give you the opportunity. Trust me, that whenever you give me the like occasion, I will return the compliment with interest.

Gentlemen, as I have no secrets from you, in the spirit of confidence you have engendered between us, and as I have made a kind of compact with myself that I never will, while I remain in America, omit an opportunity of referring to a topic in which I and all others of my class on both sides of the water are equally interested—equally interested, there is no difference between us, I would beg leave to whisper in your ear two words : *International Copyright.* I use them in no sordid sense, believe me, and those who know me best, best know that. For myself, I would rather that my children, coming after me, trudged in the mud, and knew by the general feeling of society that their father was beloved and had been of some use, than I would have them ride in their carriages, and know by their banker's books that he was rich. But I do not see, I confess, why one should be obliged to make the choice, or why fame, besides playing that delightful *reveil* for which she is so justly celebrated, should not blow out of her trumpet a few notes of a different kind from those with which she has hitherto contented herself.

It was well observed the other night by a beautiful speaker, whose words went to the heart of every man who heard him, that, if there had existed any law in this respect, Scott might not have sunk beneath the mighty pressure on his brain, but might have lived to add new creatures of his fancy to the crowd which swarm about you in your summer walks, and gather round your winter evening hearths.

As I listened to his words there came back fresh upon me that touching scene in the great man's life, when he lay upon his couch, surrounded by his family, and listened for the last time to the rippling of the river he had so well loved, over its stony bed. I pictured him to myself faint, wan, dying, crushed both in mind and body by his honorable struggle, and hovering round him the phantoms of his own imagination —Waverley, Ravenswood, Jeanie Deans, Rob Roy, Caleb Balderstone, Dominie Sampson—all the familiar throng—with cavaliers, and Puritans, and Highland chiefs innumerable overflowing the chamber, and fading away in the dim distance beyond. I pictured them fresh from traversing the world, and hanging down their heads in shame and sorrow, that, from all those lands into which they had carried gladness, instruction, and delight for millions, they brought him not one friendly hand to help to raise him from that sad, sad bed. No, nor brought him from that land in which his own language was spoken, and in every house and hut of which his own books were read in his own tongue, one grateful dollar-piece to buy a garland for his grave. Oh! if every man who goes from here, as many do, to look upon the tomb in Dryburgh Abbey, would but remember this, and bring the recollection home!

Gentlemen, I thank you again, and once again, and many times to that. You have given me a new reason for remembering this day, which is already one of mark in my calendar, it being my birthday; and you have given those who are nearest and dearest to me a new reason for recollecting it with pride and interest. Heaven knows that, although I should grow ever so gray, I shall need nothing to remind me of this epoch in my life. But I am glad to think that from this time you are inseparably connected with every recurrence of this day; and that, on its periodical return, I shall always, in imagination, have the unfading pleasure of entertaining you as my guests, in return for the gratification you have afforded me to-night.

V.

NEW YORK, FEBRUARY 18, 1842.

[At a dinner presided over by Washington Irving, when nearly eight hundred of the most distinguished citizens of New York were present, "Charles Dickens, the Literary Guest of the Nation," having been "proffered as a sentiment" by the Chairman, Mr. Dickens rose, and spoke as follows·]

GENTLEMEN,—I don't know how to thank you—I really don't know how. You would naturally suppose that my former experience would have given me this power, and that the difficulties in my way would have been diminished; but I assure you the fact is exactly the reverse, and I have completely balked the ancient proverb that "a rolling stone gathers no moss;" and in my progress to this city I have collected such a weight of obligations and acknowledgment—I have picked up such an enormous mass of fresh moss at every point, and was so struck by the brilliant scenes of Monday night, that I thought I could never by any possibility grow any bigger. I have made, continually, new accumulations to such an extent that I am compelled to stand still, and can roll no more!

Gentlemen, we learn from the authorities that, when fairy stones, or balls, or rolls of thread, stopped of their own accord—as I do not—it presaged some great catastrophe near at hand. The precedent holds good in this case. When I have remembered the short time I have before me to spend in this land of mighty interests, and the poor opportunity I can at best have of acquiring a knowledge of, and forming an acquaintance with it, I have felt it almost a duty to decline the honors you so generously heap upon me, and pass more quietly among you. For Argus himself, though he had but one mouth for his hundred eyes, would have found the reception of a public entertainment once a week too much for his greatest activity; and, as I would lose no scrap of the rich instruction and the delightful knowledge which meet me on every hand (and already I have gleaned a great deal from your hospitals and common jails), I have resolved to take up my staff and go my way rejoicing, and for the future to shake hands with America, not at parties but at home; and, therefore, gentlemen, I say to-night, with a full heart, and an honest purpose, and grateful feelings, that I bear, and shall ever bear, a deep sense of your kind, your affectionate, and your noble greeting, which it is utterly impossible to convey in words. No European sky without, and no cheerful home or well-warmed room within, shall ever shut out this land from my vision. I shall often hear your words of welcome in my quiet room, and oftenest when most quiet; and shall see your faces in the blazing fire. If I should live to grow old, the scenes of this and other evenings will shine as brightly to my dull eyes fifty years hence as now; and the honors you bestow upon me shall be well remembered and paid back in my undying love, and honest endeavors for the good of my race.

Gentlemen, one other word with reference to this first person singular, and then I shall close. I came here in an open, honest, and confiding spirit, if ever man did, and because I felt a deep sympathy in your land; had I felt otherwise, I should have kept away. As I came here, and am here, without the least admixture of one-hundredth part of one grain of base alloy, without one feeling of unworthy reference to self in any respect, I claim, in regard to the past, for the last time, my right in reason, in truth, and in justice, to approach, as I have done on two former occasions, a question of literary interest. I claim that justice be done; and I prefer this claim as one who has a right to speak and be heard. I have only to add that I shall be as true to you as you have been to me. I recognize in your enthusiastic approval of the creatures of my fancy, your enlightened care for the happiness of the many, your tender regard for the afflicted, your sympathy for the downcast, your plans for correcting and improving the bad, and for encouraging the good; and to advance these great objects shall be, to the end of my life, my earnest endeavor, to the extent of my humble ability. Having said thus much with reference to myself, I shall have the pleasure of saying a few words with reference to somebody else. There is in this city a gentleman who, at the reception of one of my books—I well remember it was the Old Curiosity Shop—wrote to me in England a letter so generous, so affectionate, and so manly, that if I had written the book under every circumstance of disappointment, of discouragement, and difficulty, instead of the reverse, I should have found in the receipt of that letter my best and most happy reward. I answered him,* and he answered me, and so we kept shaking hands autographically, as if no ocean rolled between us. I came here to this city eager to see him, and [*laying his hand upon Irving's shoulder*] here he sits! I need not tell you how happy and delighted I am to see him here to-night in this capacity.

Washington Irving! Why, gentlemen, I don't go up stairs to bed two nights out of the seven—as a very creditable witness near at hand can testify—I say I do not go to bed two nights out of the seven without taking Washington Irving under my arm; and, when I don't take him, I take his own brother, Oliver Goldsmith. Washington Irving! Why, of whom but him was I thinking the other day when I came up by the Hog's Back, the Frying Pan, Hell Gate, and all these places? Why, when, not long ago, I visited Shakspeare's birthplace, and went beneath the roof where he first saw light, whose name but *his* was pointed out to me upon the wall? Washington Irving—Diedrich Knickerbocker—Geoffrey Crayon—why, where can you go that they have not been there before? Is there an English farm—is there an English stream, an English city, or an English country-seat, where they have not been? Is there no Bracebridge Hall in existence? Has it no ancient shades or quiet streets?

In by-gone times, when Irving left that Hall, he left sitting in an old oak chair, in a small parlor of the Boar's Head, a little man with a red nose and an oil-skin hat. When I came away he was sitting there still!—not a man *like* him, but the same man—with the nose of immortal redness and the hat of an undying glaze! Crayon, while there, was on terms of intimacy with a certain radical fellow, who used to go about, with a hatful of newspapers, woefully out at elbows, and with a coat of great antiquity. Why, gentlemen, I know that man—Tibbles

* See the "Life and Letters of Washington Irving" (Lond., 1863), p. 644, where Irving speaks of a letter he has received "from that glorious fellow, Dickens, in reply to the one I wrote, expressing my heartfelt delight with his writings, and my yearnings toward himself." See also the letter itself, in the second division of this volume.—Ed.

the elder, and he has not changed a hair; and, when I came away, he charged me to give his best respects to Washington Irving!

Leaving the town and the rustic life of England—forgetting this man, if we can—putting out of mind the country church-yard and the broken heart—let us cross the water again, and ask who has associated himself most closely with the Italian peasantry and the bandits of the Pyrenees? When the traveller enters his little chamber beyond the Alps—listening to the dim echoes of the long passages and spacious corridors—damp, and gloomy, and cold—as he hears the tempest beating with fury against his window, and gazes at the curtains, dark, and heavy, and covered with mould—and when all the ghost-stories that ever were told come up before him—amidst all his thick-coming fancies, whom does he think of? Washington Irving.

Go farther still: go to the Moorish fountains, sparkling full in the moonlight—go among the water-carriers and the village gossips, living still as in days of old—and who has travelled among them before you, and peopled the Alhambra and made eloquent its shadows? Who awakes there a voice from every hill and in every cavern, and bids legends, which for centuries have slept a dreamless sleep, or watched unwinkingly, start up and pass before you in all their life and glory?

But leaving this again, who embarked with Columbus upon his gallant ship, traversed with him the dark and mighty ocean, leaped upon the land and planted there the flag of Spain, but this same man, now sitting by my side? And being here at home again, who is a more fit companion for money-diggers? and what pen but his has made Rip Van Winkle, playing at nine-pins on that thundering afternoon, as much part and parcel of the Catskill Mountains as any tree or crag that they can boast?

But these are topics familiar from my boyhood, and which I am apt to pursue; and lest I should be tempted now to talk too long about them, I will, in conclusion, give you a sentiment, most appropriate, I am sure, in the presence of such writers as Bryant, Halleck, and—but I suppose I must not mention the ladies here—

THE LITERATURE OF AMERICA:

She well knows how to do honor to her own literature and to that of other lands, when she chooses Washington Irving for her representative in the country of Cervantes.

VI.

MANCHESTER, OCTOBER 5, 1843.

[This address was delivered at a soirée of the members of the Manchester Athenæum, at which Mr. Dickens presided. Among the other speakers on the occasion were Mr. Cobden and Mr. Disraeli.]

LADIES AND GENTLEMEN,—I am sure I need scarcely tell you that I am very proud and happy; and that I take it as a great distinction to be asked to come amongst you on an occasion such as this, when, even with the brilliant and beautiful spectacle which I see before me, I can hail it as the most brilliant and beautiful circumstance of all, that we assemble together here, even here, upon neutral ground, where we have no more knowledge of party difficulties, or public animosities between side and side, or between man and man, than if we were a public meeting in the commonwealth of Utopia.

Ladies and gentlemen, upon this, and upon a hundred other grounds, this assembly is not less interesting to me, believe me—although, personally, almost a stranger here—than it is interesting to you; and I take it, that it is not of greater importance to all of us than it is to every man who has learned to know that he has an interest in the moral and social elevation, the harmless relaxation, the peace, happiness, and improvement, of the community at large. Not even those who saw the first foundation of your Athenæum laid, and watched its progress, as I know they did, almost as tenderly as if it were the progress of a living creature, until it reared its beautiful front, an honor to the town—not even they, nor even you who, within its walls, have tasted its usefulness, and put it to the proof, have greater reason, I am persuaded, to exult in its establishment, or to hope that it may thrive and prosper, than scores of thousands at a distance, who — whether consciously or unconsciously, matters not—have, in the principle of its success and bright example, a deep and personal concern.

It well becomes, particularly well becomes, this enterprising town, this little world of labor, that she should stand out foremost in the foremost rank in such a cause. It well becomes her, that, among her numerous and noble public institutions, she should have a splendid temple sacred to the education and improvement of a large class of those who, in their various useful stations, assist in the production of our wealth, and in rendering her name famous through the world. I think it is grand to know, that, while her factories re-echo with the clanking of stupendous engines, and the whirl and rattle of machinery, the immortal mechanism of God's own hand, the mind, is not forgotten in the din and uproar, but is lodged and tended in a palace of its own. That it is a structure deeply fixed and rooted in the public spirit of this place, and built to last, I have no more doubt, judging from the spectacle I see before me, and from what I know of its brief history, than I have of the reality of these walls that hem us in, and the pillars that spring up about us.

You are perfectly well aware, I have no doubt, that the Athenæum was projected at a time when commerce was in a vigorous and flourishing condition, and when those classes of society to which it particularly addresses itself were fully employed, and in the receipt of regular incomes. A season of depression almost without a parallel ensued, and large numbers of young men employed in warehouses and offices suddenly found their occupation gone, and themselves reduced to very straitened and penurious circumstances. This altered state of things led, as I am told, to the compulsory withdrawal of many of the members, to a proportionate decrease in the expected funds, and to the incurrence of a debt of £3000. By the very great zeal and energy of all concerned, and by the liberality of those to whom they applied for help, that debt is now in rapid course of being discharged. A little more of the same indefatigable exertion on the one hand, and a little more of the same community of feeling upon the other, and there will be no such thing; the figures will be blotted out for good and all, and, from that time, the Athenæum may be said to belong to you and to your heirs forever.

But, ladies and gentlemen, at all times, now in its most thriving, and in its least flourishing condition—here, with its cheerful rooms, its pleasant and instructive lectures, its improving library of 6000 volumes, its classes for the study of the foreign languages, elocution, music; its opportunities of discussion and debate, of healthful bodily exercise, and, though last not least—for by this I set great store, as a very novel and excellent provision—its opportunities of blameless, rational enjoyment, here it is, open to every youth and man in this great town, accessible to every bee in this vast hive, who, for all these benefits, and the inestimable ends to which they lead, can set aside one sixpence weekly. I do look upon the reduction of the subscription, and upon the fact that the number of members has considerably more than doubled within the last twelve months, as strides in the path of the very best civilization and chapters of rich promise in the history of mankind.

I do not know whether, at this time of day, and with such a prospect before us, we need trouble ourselves very much to rake up the ashes of the dead-and-gone objections that were wont to be urged by men of all parties against institutions such as this, whose interests we are met to promote; but their philosophy was always to be summed up in the unmeaning application of one short sentence. How often have we heard from a large class of men wise in their generation, who would really seem to be born and bred for no other purpose than to pass into currency counterfeit and mischievous scraps of wisdom, as it is the sole pursuit of some other criminals to utter base coin—how often have we heard from them, as an all-convincing argument, that "a little learning is a dangerous thing?" Why, a little hanging was considered a very dangerous thing, according to the same authorities, with this difference, that, because a little hanging was dangerous, we had a great deal of it; and, because a little learning was dangerous, we were to have none at all. Why, when I hear such cruel absurdities gravely reiterated, I do sometimes begin to doubt whether the parrots of society are not more pernicious to its interests than its birds of prey. I should be glad to hear such people's estimate of the comparative danger of "a little learning" and a vast amount of ignorance; I should be glad to know which they consider the most prolific parent of misery and crime. Descending a little lower in the social scale, I should be glad to assist them in their calculations, by carrying them into certain jails and nightly refuges I know of, where my own heart dies within me, when I see thousands of immortal creatures condemned, without alternative or choice, to tread, not what our great poet calls the "primrose path" to the everlasting bonfire, but one of jagged flints and stones, laid down by brutal ignorance, and held together, like the solid rocks, by years of this most wicked axiom.

Would we know from any honorable body of merchants, upright in deed and thought, whether they would rather have ignorant or enlightened persons in their own employment? Why, we have had their answer in this building; we have it in this company; we have it emphatically given in the munificent generosity of your own merchants of Manchester, of all sects and kinds, when this establishment was first proposed. But are the advantages derivable by the people from institutions such as this only of a negative character? If a little learning be an innocent thing, has it no distinct, wholesome, and immediate influence upon the mind? The old doggerel rhyme, so often written in the beginning of books, says that

"When house and lands are gone and spent,
     Then learning is most excellent;"

but I should be strongly disposed to reform the adage, and say that

"Though house and lands be never got,
     Learning can give what they can *not*."

And this I know, that the first unpurchasable blessing earned by every man who makes an effort to improve himself in such a place as the Athenæum, is self-respect—an inward dignity of character, which, once acquired and righteously maintained, nothing—no, not the hardest drudgery, nor the direst poverty—can vanquish. Though he should find it hard for a season even to keep the wolf—hunger—from his door, let him but once have chased the dragon—ignorance—from his hearth, and self-respect and hope are left him. You could no more deprive him of those sustaining qualities by loss or destruction of his worldly goods, than you could, by plucking out his eyes, take from him an internal consciousness of the bright glory of the sun.

The man who lives from day to day by the daily exercise in his sphere of hands or head, and seeks to improve himself in such a place as the Athenæum, acquires for himself that property of soul which has in all times upheld struggling men of every degree, but self-made men especially and always. He secures to himself that faithful companion which, while it has ever lent the light of its countenance to men of rank and eminence who have deserved it, has ever shed its brightest consolations on men of low estate and almost hopeless means. It took its patient seat beside Sir Walter Raleigh in his dungeon-study in the Tower; it laid its head upon the block with More; but it did not disdain to watch the stars with Ferguson, the shepherd's boy; it walked the streets in mean attire with Crabbe; it was a poor barber here in Lancashire with Arkwright; it was a tallow-chandler's son with Franklin; it worked at shoemaking with Bloomfield in his garret; it followed the plough with Burns; and, high above the noise of loom and hammer, it whispers courage even at this day in ears I could name in Sheffield and in Manchester.

The more the man who improves his leisure in such a place learns, the better, gentler, kinder man he must become. When he knows how much great minds have suffered for the truth in every age and time, and to what dismal persecutions opinion has been exposed, he will become more tolerant of other men's beliefs in all matters, and will incline more leniently to their sentiments when they chance to differ from his own. Understanding that the relations between himself and his employer involve a mutual duty and responsibility, he will discharge his part of the implied contract cheerfully, satisfactorily, and honorably; for the history of every useful life warns him to shape his course in that direction.

The benefits he acquires in such a place are not of a selfish kind, but extend themselves to his home, and to those whom it contains. Something of what he hears or reads within such walls can scarcely fail to become at times a topic of discourse by his own fireside, nor can it ever fail to lead to larger sympathies with man, and to a higher veneration for the great Creator of all the wonders of this universe. It appeals to his home and his homely feeling in other ways; for at certain times he carries there his wife and daughter, or his sister, or, possibly, some bright-eyed acquaintance of a more tender description. Judging from what I see before me, I think it is very likely; I am sure I would if I could. He takes her there to enjoy a pleasant evening, to be gay and happy. Sometimes it may possibly happen that he dates his tenderness from the Athenæum. I think that is a very excellent thing, too, and not the least among the advantages of the institution. In any case, I am sure the number of bright eyes and beaming faces which grace this meeting to-night by their presence will never be among the least of its excellences in my recollection.

Ladies and gentlemen, I shall not easily forget this scene, the pleasing task your favor has devolved upon me, or the strong and inspiring confirmation I have to-night, of all the hopes and reliances I have ever placed upon institutions of this nature. In the latter point of view in their bearing upon this latter point—I regard them as of great importance, deeming that the more intelligent and reflective society in the mass becomes, and the more readers there are, the more distinctly writers of all kinds will be able to throw themselves upon the truthful feeling of the people, and the more honored and the more useful literature must be. At the same time, I must confess that, if there had been an Athenæum, and if the people had been readers, years ago, some leaves of dedication in your library, of praise of patrons which was very cheaply bought, very dearly sold, and very marketably haggled for by the groat, would be blank leaves, and posterity might probably have lacked the information that certain monsters of virtue ever had existence. But it is upon a much better and wider scale, let me say it once

again—it is in the effect of such institutions upon the great social system, and the peace and happiness of mankind, that I delight to contemplate them; and, in my heart, I am quite certain that long after your institution, and others of the same nature, have crumbled into dust, the noble harvest of the seed sown in them will shine out brightly in the wisdom, the mercy, and the forbearance of another race.

VII.

LIVERPOOL, FEBRUARY 26, 1844.

[The following address was delivered at a soirée of the Liverpool Mechanics' Institution, at which Mr. Dickens presided.]

LADIES AND GENTLEMEN,—It was rather hard of you to take away my breath before I spoke a word; but I would not thank you, even if I could, for the favor which has set me in this place, or for the generous kindness which has greeted me so warmly, because my first strong impulse still would be, although I had that power, to lose sight of all personal considerations in the high intent and meaning of this numerous assemblage, in the contemplation of the noble objects to which this building is devoted, of its brilliant and inspiring history, of that rough, upward track, so bravely trodden, which it leaves behind, and that bright path of steadily-increasing usefulness which lies stretched out before it. My first strong impulse still would be to exchange congratulations with you, as the members of one united family, on the thriving vigor of this strongest child of a strong race. My first strong impulse still would be, though every body here had twice as many hundreds of hands as there are hundreds of persons present, to shake them in the spirit, every one; always, allow me to say, excepting those hands (and there are a few such here), which, with the constitutional infirmity of human nature, I would rather salute in some more tender fashion.

When I first had the honor of communicating with your Committee with reference to this celebration, I had some selfish hopes that the visit proposed to me might turn out to be one of congratulation, or, at least, of solicitous inquiry; for they who receive a visitor in any season of distress are easily touched and moved by what he says, and I entertained some confident expectation of making a mighty strong impression on you. But, when I came to look over the printed documents which were forwarded to me at the same time, and with which you are all tolerably familiar, these anticipations very speedily vanished, and left me bereft of all consolation but the triumphant feeling to which I have referred. For what do I find, on looking over those brief chronicles of this swift conquest over ignorance and prejudice, in which no blood has been poured out, and no treaty signed but that one sacred compact which recognizes the just right of every man, whatever his belief, or however humble his degree, to aspire, and to have some means of aspiring, to be a better and a wiser man? I find that, in 1825, certain misguided and turbulent persons proposed to erect in Liverpool an unpopular, dangerous, irreligious, and revolutionary establishment, called a Mechanics' Institution; that, in 1835—Liverpool having, somehow or other, got on pretty comfortably in the mean time, in spite of it—the first stone of a new and spacious edifice was laid; that, in 1837, it was opened; that it was afterwards, at different periods, considerably enlarged; that, in 1844, conspicuous among the public beauties of a beautiful town, here it stands triumphant, its enemies lived down, its former students attesting, in their various useful callings and pursuits, the sound, practical information it afforded them; its members numbering considerably more than 3000, and setting in rapidly for 6000 at least; its library comprehending 11,000 volumes, and daily sending forth its hundreds of books into private homes; its staff of masters and officers, amounting to half a hundred in themselves; its schools conveying every sort of instruction, high and low, adapted to the labor, means, exigencies, and convenience of nearly every class and grade of persons. I was here this morning, and in its spacious halls I found stores of the wonders worked by nature in the air, in the forest, in the cavern, and in the sea—stores of the surpassing engines devised by science for the better knowledge of other worlds, and the greater happiness of this—stores of those gentler works of art, which, though achieved in perishable stone, by yet more perishable hands of dust, are in their influence immortal. With such means at their command, so well-directed, so cheaply shared, and so extensively diffused, well may your Committee say, as they have done in one of their Reports, that the success of this establishment has far exceeded their most sanguine expectations.

But, ladies and gentlemen, as that same philosopher whose words they quote, as Bacon tells us, instancing the wonderful effects of little things and small beginnings, that the influence of the loadstone was first discovered in particles of iron, and not in iron bars, so they may lay it to their hearts, that when they combined together to form the institution which has risen to this majestic height, they issued on a field of enterprise, the glorious end of which they can

not even now discern. Every man who has felt the advantages of, or has received improvement in this place, carries its benefits into the society in which he moves, and puts them out at compound interest; and what the blessed sum may be at last, no man can tell. Ladies and gentlemen, with that Christian prelate whose name appears on your list of honorary members—that good and liberal man who once addressed you within these walls, in a spirit worthy of his calling and of his High Master— I look forward from this place, as from a tower, to the time when high and low, and rich and poor, shall mutually assist, improve, and educate each other.

I feel, ladies and gentlemen, that this is not a place, with its 3200 members, and at least 3200 arguments in every one, to enter on any advocacy of the principle of Mechanics' Institutions, or to discuss the subject with those who do or ever did object to them. I should as soon think of arguing the point with those untutored savages whose mode of life you last year had the opportunity of witnessing; indeed, I am strongly inclined to believe them by far the more rational class of the two. Moreover, if the institution itself be not a sufficient answer to all such objections, then there is no such thing in fact or reason, human or divine. Neither will I venture to enter into those details of the management of this place which struck me most on the perusal of its papers; but I can not help saying how much impressed and gratified I was, as every body must be who comes to their perusal for the first time, by the extraordinary munificence with which this institution has been endowed by certain gentlemen.

Amongst the peculiar features of management which made the greatest impression on me, I may observe that that regulation which empowers fathers, being annual subscribers of one guinea, to introduce their sons who are minors; and masters, on payment of the astoundingly small sum of five shillings annually, in like manner their apprentices, is not the least valuable of its privileges; and certainly not the one least valuable to society. And, ladies and gentlemen, I can not say to you what pleasure I derived from the perusal of an apparently excellent report in your local papers of a meeting held here, some short time since, in aid of the formation of a girls' school in connection with this institution. This is a new and striking chapter in the history of these institutions; it does equal credit to the gallantry and policy of this, and disposes one to say of it, with a slight parody on the words of Burns, that

"Its 'prentice han' it tried on man,
And then it *taught* the lasses, O."

That those who are our best teachers, and whose lessons are oftenest heeded in after-life, should be well taught themselves, is a proposition few reasonable men will gainsay; and, certainly, to breed up good husbands on the one hand, and good wives on the other, does appear as reasonable and straightforward a plan as could well be devised for the improvement of the next generation.

This, and what I see before me, naturally brings me to our fairer members, in respect of whom I have no doubt you will agree with me, that they ought to be admitted to the widest possible extent, and on the lowest possible terms; and, ladies, let me venture to say to you, that you never did a wiser thing in all your lives then when you turned your favorable regard on such an establishment as this; for wherever the light of knowledge is diffused, wherever the humanizing influence of the arts and sciences extends itself, wherever there is the clearest perception of what is beautiful, and good, and most redeeming, amid all the faults and vices of mankind, there your character, your virtues, your graces, your better nature, will be the best appreciated, and there the truest homage will be proudly paid to you. You show best, trust me, in the clearest light; and every ray that falls upon you at your own firesides, from any book or thought communicated within these walls, will raise you nearer to the angels in the eyes you care for most.

I will not longer interpose myself, ladies and gentlemen, between you and the pleasure we all anticipate in hearing other gentlemen, and in enjoying those social pleasures with which it is a main part of the wisdom of this society to adorn and relieve its graver pursuits. We all feel, I am sure, being here, that we are truly interested in the cause of human improvement and rational education, and that we pledge ourselves, every one as far as in him lies, to extend the knowledge of the benefits afforded in this place, and to bear honest witness in its favor. To those who yet remain without its walls, but have the means of purchasing its advantages, we make appeal, and in a friendly and forbearing spirit say, "Come in, and be convinced—

'Who enters here, leaves *doubt* behind.'"

If you, happily, have been well taught yourself, and are superior to its advantages, so much the more should you make one in sympathy with those who are below you. Beneath this roof we breed the men who, in the time to come,

must be found working for good or evil, in every quarter of society. If mutual respect and forbearance among various classes be not found here, where so many men are trained up in so many grades, to enter on so many roads of life, dating their entry from one common starting-point, as they are all approaching, by various paths, one common end, where else can that great lesson be imbibed? Differences of wealth, of rank, of intellect, we know there must be, and we respect them; but we would give to all the means of taking out one patent of nobility, and we define it, in the words of a great living poet, who is one of us, and who uses his great gifts, as he holds them in trust, for the general welfare—

"Howe'er it be, it seems to me
'Tis only noble to be good:
True hearts are more than coronets,
And simple faith than Norman blood."[*]

~~~~~~~

VIII.

BIRMINGHAM, FEBRUARY 28, 1844.

[The following speech was delivered at a Conversazione, in aid of the funds of the Birmingham Polytechnic Institution, at which Mr. Dickens presided:]

You will think it very unwise, or very self-denying in me, in such an assembly, in such a splendid scene, and after such a welcome, to congratulate myself on having nothing new to say to you; but I do so, notwithstanding. To say nothing of places nearer home, I had the honor of attending at Manchester, shortly before Christmas, and at Liverpool only the night before last, for a purpose similar to that which brings you together this evening; and looking down a short perspective of similar engagements, I feel gratification at the thought that I shall very soon have nothing at all to say; in which case, I shall be content to stake my reputation, like the Spectator of Addison, and that other great periodical speaker, the Speaker of the House of Commons, on my powers of listening.

This feeling, and the earnest reception I have met with, are not the only reasons why I feel a genuine, cordial, and peculiar interest in this night's proceedings. The Polytechnic Institution of Birmingham is in its infancy—struggling into life under all those adverse and disadvantageous circumstances which, to a greater or less extent, naturally beset all infancy; but I would much rather connect myself with it now, however humble, in its days of difficulty

---

[*] Tennyson, "Lady Clara Vere de Vere," then newly published in the collection of 1842.—ED.

and of danger, than look back on its origin when it may have become strong, and rich, and powerful. I should prefer an intimate association with it now, in its early days and apparent struggles, to becoming its advocate and acquaintance, its fair-weather friend, in its high and palmy days. I would rather be able to say I knew it in its swaddling-clothes, than in maturer age. Its two elder brothers have grown old and died: their chests were weak—about their cradles nurses shook their heads, and gossips groaned; but the present institution shot up, amidst the ruin of those which have fallen, with an indomitable constitution, with vigorous and with steady pulse; temperate, wise, and of good repute; and by perseverance it has become a very giant. Birmingham is, in my mind and in the minds of most men, associated with many giants; and I no more believe that this young institution will turn out sickly, dwarfish, or of stunted growth, than I do that when the glass-slipper of my chairmanship shall fall off, and the clock strike twelve tonight, this hall will be turned into a pumpkin. I found that strong belief upon the splendid array of grace and beauty by which I am surrounded, and which, if it only had one-hundredth part of the effect upon others it has upon me, could do any thing it pleased with any thing and any body. I found my strong conviction, in the second place, upon the public spirit of the town of Birmingham—upon the name and fame of its capitalists and workingmen; upon the greatness and importance of its merchants and manufacturers; upon its inventions, which are constantly in progress; upon the skill and intelligence of its artisans, which are daily developed; and the increasing knowledge of all portions of the community. All these reasons lead me to the conclusion that your institution will advance—that it will and must progress, and that you will not be content with lingering leagues behind.

I have another peculiar ground of satisfaction in connection with the object of this assembly; and it is, that the resolutions about to be proposed do not contain in themselves any thing of a sectarian or class nature; that they do not confine themselves to any one single institution, but assert the great and omnipotent principles of comprehensive education everywhere and under every circumstance. I beg leave to say that I concur, heart and hand, in those principles, and will do all in my power for their advancement; for I hold, in accordance with the imperfect knowledge which I possess, that it is impossible for any fabric of society to go on day after day, and year after year, from father to son, and from grandfather to grandson, punishing men for not engaging in the pursuit of virtue and for the practice of crime, without showing them what virtue is, and where it best can be found—in justice, religion, and truth. The only reason that can possibly be adduced against it is one founded on fiction—namely, the case where an obdurate old genie, in the "Arabian Nights," was bound upon taking the life of a merchant, because he had struck out the eye of his invisible son. I recollect, likewise, a tale in the same book of charming fancies, which I consider not inappropriate: it is a case where a powerful spirit has been imprisoned at the bottom of the sea, in a casket with a leaden cover, and the seal of Solomon upon it; there he had lain neglected for many centuries, and during that period had made many different vows: at first, that he would reward magnificently those who should release him; and at last, that he would destroy them. Now, there is a spirit of great power—the Spirit of Ignorance—which is shut up in a vessel of leaden composition, and sealed with the seal of many, many Solomons, and which is effectually in the same position: release it in time, and it will bless, restore, and reanimate society; but let it lie under the rolling waves of years, and its blind revenge is sure to lead to certain destruction. That there are classes which, if rightly treated, constitute strength, and if wrongly, weakness, I hold it impossible to deny—by these classes I mean industrious, intelligent, and honorably independent men, in whom the higher classes of Birmingham are especially interested, and bound to afford them the means of instruction and improvement, and to ameliorate their mental and moral condition. Far be it from me (and I wish to be most particularly understood) to attempt to depreciate the excellent Church Instruction Societies, or the worthy, sincere, and temperate zeal of those reverend gentlemen by whom they are usually conducted; on the contrary, I believe that they have done, and are doing, much good, and are deserving of high praise; but I hope that, without offense, in a community such as Birmingham, there are other objects not unworthy in the sight of heaven, and objects of recognized utility which are worthy of support—principles which are practised in word and deed in Polytechnic Institutions—principles for the diffusion of which honest men of all degrees and of every creed might associate together, on an independent footing and on neutral ground, and at a small expense, for the better understanding and the greater consideration of each other, and for the better cultivation of the happiness of all: for it surely can not be allowed that those who labor day by day, surrounded by machinery, shall be permitted to degenerate into machines themselves, but, on the contrary, they should assert their common origin from their Creator, at the hands of those who are responsible and thinking men. There is, indeed, no difference in the main, with respect to the dangers of ignorance and the advantages of knowledge, between those who hold different opinions; for it is to be observed, that those who are most distrustful of the advantages of education, are always the first to exclaim against the results of ignorance. This fact was pleasantly illustrated on the railway, as I came here. In the same carriage with me there sat an ancient gentleman (I feel no delicacy in alluding to him, for I know that he is not in the room, having got out far short of Birmingham), who expressed himself most mournfully as to the ruinous effects and rapid spread of railways, and was most pathetic upon the virtues of the slow-going old stage-coaches. Now I, entertaining some little lingering kindness for the road, made shift to express my concurrence with the old gentleman's opinion, without any great compromise of principle. Well, we got on tolerably comfortably together, and when the engine, with a frightful screech, dived into some dark abyss, like some strange aquatic monster, the old gentleman said it would never do, and I agreed with him. When it parted from each successive station, with a shock and a shriek as if it had had a double-tooth drawn, the old gentleman shook his head, and I shook mine. When he burst forth against such new-fangled notions, and said no good could come of them, I did not contest the point. But I found that when the speed of the engine was abated, or there was a prolonged stay at any station, up the old gentleman was at arms, and his watch was instantly out of his pocket, denouncing the slowness of our progress. Now I could not help comparing this old gentleman to that ingenious class of persons who are in the constant habit of declaiming against the vices and crimes of society, and at the same time are the first and foremost to assert that vice and crime have not their common origin in ignorance and discontent.

The good work, however, in spite of all political and party differences, has been well begun; we are all interested in it; it is advancing, and can not be stopped by any opposition, although it may be retarded in this place or in that, by the indifference of the middle classes, with whom its successful progress chiefly rests. Of this success I can not entertain a doubt; for whenever the working-classes have enjoyed an opportunity of effectually rebutting accusations which false-hood or thoughtlessness have brought against them, they always avail themselves of it, and show themselves in their true characters; and it was this which made the damage done to a single picture in the National Gallery of London, by some poor lunatic or cripple, a mere matter of newspaper notoriety and wonder for some few days. This, then, establishes a fact evident to the meanest comprehension — that any given number of thousands of individuals, in the humblest walks of life in this country, can pass through the national galleries or museums in seasons of holiday-making, without damaging, in the slightest degree, those choice and valuable collections. I do not myself believe that the working-classes ever were the wanton or mischievous persons they were so often and so long represented to be; but I rather incline to the opinion that some men take it into their heads to lay it down as a matter of fact, without being particular about the premises; and that the idle and the prejudiced, not wishing to have the trouble of forming opinions for themselves, take it for granted—until the people have an opportunity of disproving the stigma and vindicating themselves before the world.

Now this assertion is well illustrated by what occurred respecting an equestrian statue in the metropolis, with respect to which a legend existed that the sculptor hanged himself, because he had neglected to put a girth to the horse. This story was currently believed for many years, until it was inspected for altogether a different purpose, and it was found to have had a girth all the time.

But surely if, as is stated, the people are ill-disposed and mischievous, that is the best reason that can be offered for teaching them better; and if they are not, surely that is a reason for giving them every opportunity of vindicating their injured reputation; and no better opportunity could possibly be afforded than that of associating together voluntarily for such high purposes as it is proposed to carry out by the establishment of the Birmingham Polytechnic Institution. In any case—nay, in every case— if we would reward honesty, if we would hold out encouragement to good, if we would eradicate that which is evil or correct that which is bad, education—comprehensive, liberal education—is the one thing needful, and the only effective end. If I might apply to my purpose and turn into plain prose some words of Hamlet —not with reference to any government or party (for party, being, for the most part, an irrational sort of thing, has no connection with the object we have in view)—if I might apply those words to education as Hamlet applied them to the skull of Yorick, I would say—"Now hie thee to the council-chamber, and tell them, though they lay it on in sounding thoughts and learned words an inch thick, to this complexion they must come at last."

[In answer to a vote of thanks,* Mr. Dickens said, at the close of the meeting:]

LADIES AND GENTLEMEN,— We are now quite even—for every effect which I may have made upon you, the compliment has been amply returned to me; but at the same time I am as little disposed to say to you, "Go and sin no more," as I am to promise for myself that "I will never do so again." So long as I can make you laugh and cry, I will; and you will readily believe me, when I tell you, you can not do too much on your parts to show that we are still cordial and loving friends. To you, ladies of the Institution, I am deeply and especially indebted. I sometimes [*pointing to the word "Boz," in front of the great gallery*] think there is some small quantity of magic in that very short name, and that it must consist in its containing as many letters as the three graces, and they, every one of them, being of your fair sisterhood.

A story is told of an Eastern potentate of modern times, who, for an Eastern potentate, was a tolerably good man, sometimes bowstringing his dependents indiscriminately in his moments of anger, but burying them in great splendor in his moments of penitence, that whenever intelligence was brought him of a new plot or turbulent conspiracy, his first inquiry was, "Who is she?" meaning that a woman was at the bottom. Now, in my small way, I differ from that potentate; for when there is any good to be attained, the services of any ministering angel required, my first inquiry is, "Where is she?" and the answer invariably is, "Here." Proud and happy am I indeed to thank you for your generosity—

"A thousand times, good-night:
A thousand times the worse to want your light."

* "That this meeting, while conveying its cordial thanks to Charles Dickens, Esq., for his presence this evening, and for his able and courteous conduct as President, can not separate without tendering the warmest expression of its gratitude and admiration to one whose writings have so loyally inculcated the lessons of benevolence and virtue, and so richly contributed to the stores of public pleasure and instruction."

IX.

GARDENERS AND GARDENING.

LONDON, JUNE 14, 1852.

[The Ninth Anniversary Dinner of the Gardeners' Benevolent Institution was held on the above date at the London Tavern. The company numbered more than 150. The dessert was worthy of the occasion, and an admirable effect was produced by a profuse display of natural flowers upon the tables and in the decoration of the room The chair was taken by Mr. Charles Dickens, who, in proposing the toast of the evening, spoke as follows :]

FOR three times three years the Gardeners' Benevolent Institution has been stimulated and encouraged by meetings such as this, and by three times three cheers we will urge it onward in its prosperous career. [*The cheers were warmly given.*]

Occupying the post I now do, I feel something like a counsel for the plaintiff with nobody on the other side; but even if I had been placed in that position ninety times nine, it would still be my duty to state a few facts from the very short brief with which I have been provided.

This Institution was founded in the year 1838. During the first five years of its existence, it was not particularly robust, and seemed to have been placed in rather a shaded position, receiving somewhat more than its needful allowance of cold water. In 1843 it was removed into a more favorable position, and grafted on a nobler stock, and it has now borne fruit, and become such a vigorous tree that at present thirty-five old people daily sit within the shelter of its branches, and all the pensioners upon the list have been veritable gardeners, or the wives of gardeners. It is managed by gardeners, and it has upon its books the excellent rule that any gardener who has subscribed to it for fifteen years, and conformed to the rules, may, if he will, be placed upon the pensioners' list without election, without canvass, without solicitation, and as his independent right. I lay very great stress upon that honorable characteristic of the charity, because the main principle of any such institution should be to help those who help themselves. That the Society's pensioners do not become such so long as they are able to support themselves, is evinced by the significant fact that the average age of those now upon the list is seventy-seven; that they are not wasteful is proved by the fact that the whole sum expended on their relief is but £500 a year; that the Institution does not restrict itself to any narrow confines, is shown by the circumstance that the pensioners come from all parts of England; whilst all the expenses are paid from the annual income and interest on stock, and therefore are not disproportionate to its means.

Such is the Institution which appeals to you through me, as a most unworthy advocate, for sympathy and support—an Institution which has for its President a nobleman* whose whole possessions are remarkable for taste and beauty, and whose gardener's laurels are famous throughout the world. In the list of its vice-presidents there are the names of many noblemen and gentlemen of great influence and station, and I have been struck, in glancing through the list of its supporters, with the sums written against the names of the numerous nurserymen and seedsmen therein comprised. I hope the day will come when every gardener in England will be a member of the charity.

The gardener particularly needs such a provision as this Institution affords. His gains are not great; he knows gold and silver more as being of the color of fruits and flowers than by its presence in his pockets; he is subjected to that kind of labor which renders him peculiarly liable to infirmity; and when old age comes upon him, the gardener is, of all men, perhaps best able to appreciate the merits of such an institution.

To all, indeed, present and absent, who are descended from the first

"Gardener Adam and his wife,"

the benefits of such a society are obvious. In the culture of flowers there can not, by their very nature, be any thing solitary or exclusive. The wind that blows over the cottager's porch sweeps also over the grounds of the nobleman; and as the rain descends on the just and on the unjust, so it communicates to all gardeners, both rich and poor, an interchange of pleasure and enjoyment, and the gardener of the rich man, in developing and enhancing a fruitful flavor or a delightful scent, is, in some sort, the gardener of every body else.

The love of gardening is associated with all conditions of men, and all periods of time. The scholar and the statesman, men of peace and men of war, have agreed in all ages to delight in gardens. The most ancient people of the earth had gardens where there is now nothing but solitary heaps of earth. The poor man in crowded cities gardens still in jugs and basins and bottles: in factories and workshops people garden; and even the prisoner is found gardening in his lonely cell, after years and years of solitary confinement. Surely, then, the gardener, who produces shapes and objects so lovely and so comforting, should have some hold upon the world's remembrance when he himself becomes in need of comfort.

* The Duke of Devonshire.

I will call upon you to drink " Prosperity to the Gardeners' Benevolent Institution;" and I beg to couple with that toast the name of its noble President, the Duke of Devonshire, whose worth is written in all his deeds, and who has communicated to his title and his riches a lustre which no title and no riches could confer.

[Later in the evening, Mr. Dickens said:]

My office has compelled me to burst into bloom so often that I could wish there were a closer parallel between myself and the American aloe. It is particularly agreeable and appropriate to know that the parents of this Institution are to be found in the seed and nursery trade; and the seed having yielded such good fruit, and the nursery having produced such a healthy child, I have the greatest pleasure in proposing the health of the parents of the Institution.

[In proposing the health of the Treasurers, Mr. Dickens said:]

My observation of the signboards of this country has taught me that its conventional gardeners are always jolly, and always three in number. Whether that conventionality has reference to the Three Graces, or to those very significant letters, L., S., D., I do not know. Those mystic letters are, however, most important, and no society can have officers of more importance than its Treasurers, nor can it possibly give them too much to do.

X.

BIRMINGHAM, JANUARY 6, 1853.

[On Thursday, January 6, 1853, at the rooms of the Society of Artists, in Temple Row, Birmingham, a large company assembled to witness the presentation of a testimonial to Mr. Charles Dickens, consisting of a silver-gilt salver and a diamond ring. Mr. Dickens acknowledged the tribute, and the address which accompanied it, in the following words:]

GENTLEMEN.—I feel it very difficult, I assure you, to tender my acknowledgments to you, and through you, to those many friends of mine whom you represent, for this honor and distinction which you have conferred upon me. I can most honestly assure you that it is in the power of no great representative of numbers of people to awaken such happiness in me as is inspired by this token of good-will and remembrance, coming to me direct and fresh from the numbers themselves. I am truly sensible, gentlemen, that my friends who have united in address are partial in their kindness, and what I have done with too great favor. may say, with reference to one class—s bers of which, I presume, are included there—that I should, in my own eyes, be very unworthy both of the generous gift and the generous feeling which has been evinced, and this occasion, instead of pleasure, would give me nothing but pain, if I was unable to assure them, and those who are in front of this assembly, that what the working people have found me towards them in my books, I am throughout my life. Gentlemen, whenever I have tried to hold up to admiration their fortitude, patience, gentleness, the reasonableness of their nature, so accessible to persuasion, and their extraordinary goodness one towards another, I have done so because I have first genuinely felt that admiration myself, and have been thoroughly imbued with the sentiment which I sought to communicate to others.

Gentlemen, I accept this salver and this ring as far above all price to me, as very valuable in themselves, and as beautiful specimens of the workmanship of this town, with great emotion, I assure you, and with the liveliest gratitude. You remember something, I dare say, of the old romantic stories of those charmed rings which would lose their brilliance when their wearer was in danger, or would press his finger reproachfully when he was going to do wrong. In the very improbable event of my being in the least danger of deserting the principles which have won me these tokens, I am sure the diamond in that ring would assume a clouded aspect to my faithless eye, and would, I know, squeeze a throb of pain out of my treacherous heart. But I have not the least misgiving on that point; and, in this confident expectation, I shall remove my own old diamond ring from my left hand, and in future wear the Birmingham ring on my right, where its grasp will keep me in mind of the good friends I have here, and in vivid remembrance of this happy hour.

Gentlemen, in conclusion, allow me to thank you and the Society to whom these rooms belong, that the presentation has taken place in an atmosphere so congenial to me, and in an apartment decorated with so many beautiful works of art, among which I recognize before me the productions of friends of mine, whose labors and triumphs will never be subjects of indifference to me. I thank those gentlemen for giving me the opportunity of meeting them here on an occasion which has some connection with their own proceedings; and, though last not least, I tender my acknowledgments to that charming presence, without which nothing beautiful can be complete, and which is endearingly associated with rings of a plainer description, and which, I must confess, awakens in my mind

at the present moment a feeling of regret that I am not in a condition to make an offer of these testimonials. I beg you, gentlemen, to commend me very earnestly and gratefully to our absent friends, and to assure them of my affectionate and heartfelt respect.

[The company then adjourned to Dee's Hotel, where a banquet took place, at which about two hundred and twenty persons were present, among whom were some of the most distinguished of the Royal Academicians. To the toast of "The Literature of England," Mr. Dickens responded as follows:]

MR. MAYOR AND GENTLEMEN,—I am happy, on behalf of many laborers in that great field of literature to which you have pledged the toast, to thank you for the tribute you have paid to it. Such an honor, rendered by acclamation in such a place as this, seems to me, if I may follow on the same side as the venerable Archdeacon (Sandford) who lately addressed you, and who has inspired me with a gratification I can never forget—such an honor, gentlemen, rendered here, seems to me a two-sided illustration of the position that literature holds in these latter and, of course, "degenerate" days. To the great compact phalanx of the people, by whose industry, perseverance, and intelligence, and their result in money-wealth, such places as Birmingham, and many others like it, have arisen—to that great centre of support, that comprehensive experience, and that beating heart, literature has turned happily from individual patrons—sometimes munificent, often sordid, always few—and has there found at once its highest purpose, its natural range of action, and its best reward. Therefore it is right, also, as it seems to me, not only that literature should receive honor here, but that it should render honor, too, remembering that if it has undoubtedly done good to Birmingham, Birmingham has undoubtedly done good to it. From the shame of the purchased dedication, from the scurrilous and dirty work of Grub Street, from the dependent seat on sufferance at my Lord Duke's table to-day, and from the sponging-house or Marshalsea to-morrow—from that venality which, by a fine moral retribution, has degraded statesmen even to a greater extent than authors, because the statesman entertained a low belief in the universality of corruption, while the author yielded only to the dire necessity of his calling—from all such evils the people have set literature free. And my creed, in the exercise of that profession is, that literature can not be too faithful to the people in return—can not too ardently advocate the cause of their advancement, happiness, and prosperity. I have heard it sometimes said—and what is worse, as expressing something more cold-blooded, I have sometimes seen it written—that literature has suffered by this change, that it has degenerated by being made cheaper. I have not found that to be the case; nor do I believe that you have made the discovery either. But let a good book in these "bad" times be made accessible—even upon an abstruse and difficult subject, so that it be one of legitimate interest to mankind—and my life on it, it shall be extensively bought, read, and well considered.

Why do I say this? Because I believe there are in Birmingham at this moment many working-men infinitely better versed in Shakspeare and in Milton than the average of fine gentlemen in the days of bought-and-sold dedications and dear books. I ask any one to consider for himself who, at this time, gives the greatest relative encouragement to the dissemination of such useful publications as "Macaulay's History," "Layard's Researches," "Tennyson's Poems," "The Duke of Wellington's published Dispatches," or the minutest truths (if any truth can be called minute) discovered by the genius of a Herschel or a Faraday? It is with all these things as with the great music of Mendelssohn, or a lecture upon art—if we had the good fortune to listen to one to-morrow—by my distinguished friend the President of the Royal Academy. However small the audience, however contracted the circle in the water, in the first instance, the people are nearer the wider range outside, and the Sister Arts, while they instruct them, derive a wholesome advantage and improvement from their ready sympathy and cordial response. I may instance the case of my friend Mr. Ward's magnificent picture;[*] and the reception of that picture here is an example that it is not now the province of art in painting to hold itself in monastic seclusion, that it can not hope to rest on a single foundation for its great temple—on the mere classic pose of a figure, or the folds of a drapery—but that it must be imbued with human passions and action, informed with human right and wrong, and, being so informed, it may fearlessly put itself upon its trial, like the criminal of old, to be judged by God and its country.

Gentlemen, to return and conclude, as I shall have occasion to trouble you again. For this time I have only once again to repeat what I have already said. As I begun with literature, I shall end with it. I would simply say that I believe no true man, with any thing to tell, need have the least misgiving, either for himself or his message, before a large number of hear-

ers—always supposing that he be not afflicted with the coxcombical idea of writing down to the popular intelligence, instead of writing the popular intelligence up to himself, if, perchance, he be above it; and, provided always that he deliver himself plainly of what is in him, which seems to be no unreasonable stipulation, it being supposed that he has some dim design of making himself understood. On behalf of that literature to which you have done so much honor, I beg to thank you most cordially, and on my own behalf, for the most flattering reception you have given to one whose claim is, that he has the distinction of making it his profession.

[Later in the evening, Mr. Dickens gave as a toast, "The Educational Institutions of Birmingham," in the following speech:]

I am requested to propose—or, according to the hypothesis of my friend, Mr. Owen, I am in the temporary character of a walking advertisement to advertise to you—the Educational Institutions of Birmingham; an advertisement to which I have the greatest pleasure in calling your attention. Gentlemen, it is right that I should, in so many words, mention the more prominent of these institutions, not because your local memories require any prompting, but because the enumeration implies what has been done here, what you are doing, and what you will yet do. I believe the first is the King Edward's Grammar School, with its various branches; and prominent among them is that most admirable means of training the wives of working-men to be good wives and working wives, the prime ornament of their homes, and the cause of happiness to others—I mean those excellent girls' schools in various parts of the town, which, under the excellent superintendence of the principal, I should most sincerely desire to see in every town in England. Next, I believe, is the Spring Hill College, a learned institution belonging to the body of Independents, foremost among whose professors literature is proud to hail Mr. Henry Rogers as one of the soundest and ablest contributors to the Edinburgh Review. The next is the Queen's College, which, I may say, is only a newly-born child; but in the hands of such an admirable doctor, we may hope to see it arrive at a vigorous maturity. The next is the School of Design, which, as has been well observed by my friend Sir Charles Eastlake, is invaluable in such a place as this; and, lastly, there is the Polytechnic Institution, with regard to which, I had long ago occasion to express my profound conviction that it was of unspeakable importance

---

* "Charlotte Corday going to Execution."

to such a community as this, when I had the honor to be present, under the auspices of your excellent representative, Mr. Scholefield. This is the last of what has been done in an educational way. They are all admirable in their kind; but I am glad to find that more is yet doing. A few days ago I received a Birmingham newspaper, containing a most interesting account of a preliminary meeting for the formation of a Reformatory School for juvenile delinquents. You are not exempt here from the honor of saving these poor, neglected, and wretched outcasts. I read of one infant, six years old, who has been twice as many times in the hands of the police as years have passed over his devoted head. These are the eggs from which jail-birds are hatched; if you wish to check that dreadful brood, you must take the young and innocent, and have them reared by Christian hands.

Lastly, I am rejoiced to find that there is on foot a scheme for a new Literary and Scientific Institution, which would be worthy even of this place, if there was nothing of the kind in it—an institution, as I understand it, where the words "exclusion" and "exclusiveness" shall be quite unknown—where all classes may assemble in common trust, respect, and confidence—where there shall be a great gallery of painting and statuary open to the inspection and admiration of all comers—where there shall be a museum of models in which industry may observe its various sources of manufacture, and the mechanic may work out new combinations, and arrive at new results—where the very mines under the earth and under the sea shall not be forgotten, but presented in little to the inquiring eye—an institution, in short, where many and many of the obstacles which now inevitably stand in the rugged way of the poor inventor shall be smoothed away, and where, if he have any thing in him, he will find encouragement and hope.

I observe with unusual interest and gratification, that a body of gentlemen are going for a time to lay aside their individual prepossessions on other subjects, and, as good citizens, are to be engaged in a design as patriotic as well can be. They have the intention of meeting in a few days to advance this great object, and I call upon you, in drinking this toast, to drink success to their endeavor, and to make it the pledge by all good means to promote it.

If I strictly followed out the list of educational institutions in Birmingham, I should not have done here, but I intend to stop, merely observing that I have seen within a short walk of this place one of the most interesting and practical Institutions for the Deaf and Dumb that has ever come under my observation. I have seen in the factories and workshops of Birmingham such beautiful order and regularity, and such great consideration for the work-people provided, that they might justly be entitled to be considered educational too. I have seen in your splendid Town Hall, when the cheap concerts are going on there, also an admirable educational institution. I have seen their results in the demeanor of your working-people, excellently balanced by a nice instinct, as free from servility on the one hand, as from self-conceit on the other. It is a perfect delight to have need to ask a question, if only from the manner of the reply—a manner I never knew to pass unnoticed by an observant stranger. Gather up those threads, and a great many more I have not touched upon, and, weaving all into one good fabric, remember how much is included under the general head of the Educational Institutions of your town.

XI.

LONDON, APRIL 30, 1853.

[At the annual Dinner of the Royal Academy, the President, Sir Charles Eastlake, proposed as a toast, "The Interests of Literature," and selected for the representatives of the world of letters, the Dean of St. Paul's and Mr. Charles Dickens. Dean Milman having returned thanks.]

MR. DICKENS then addressed the President, who, it should be mentioned, occupied a large and handsome chair, the back covered with crimson velvet, placed just before Stanfield's picture of "The Victory."

Mr. Dickens, after tendering his acknowledgments of the toast, and the honor done him in associating his name with it, said that those acknowledgments were not the less heartfelt because he was unable to recognize in this toast the President's usual disinterestedness; since English literature could scarcely be remembered in any place, and certainly not in a school of art, without a very distinct remembrance of his own tasteful writings, to say nothing of that other and better part of himself which, unfortunately, was not visible upon these occasions.

If, like the noble Lord, the commander-in-chief (Viscount Hardinge), he (Mr. Dickens) might venture to illustrate his brief thanks with one word of reference to the noble picture painted by a very dear friend of his, which was a little eclipsed that evening by the radiant and rubicund chair which the President now so happily toned down, he would beg leave to say that, as literature could nowhere be more appropriately honored than in that place, so he thought she could nowhere feel a higher gratification in the ties that bound her to the sister arts. He ever felt in that place that literature found, through their instrumentality, always a new expression, and in a universal language.

XII.

LONDON, MAY 1, 1853.

[At a dinner given by the Lord Mayor at the Mansion House, on the above date, Mr. Justice Talfourd proposed as a toast " Anglo-Saxon Literature," and alluded to Mr. Dickens as having employed fiction as a means of awakening attention to the condition of the oppressed and suffering classes :]

"MR. DICKENS replied to this toast in a graceful and playful strain. In the former part of the evening, in reply to a toast on the chancery department, Vice-Chancellor Wood, who spoke in the absence of the Lord-Chancellor, made a sort of defense of the Court of Chancery, not distinctly alluding to Bleak House, but evidently not without reference to it. The amount of what he said was, that the Court had received a great many more hard opinions than it merited ; that they had been parsimoniously obliged to perform a great amount of business by a very inadequate number of judges ; but that more recently the number of judges had been increased to seven, and there was reason to hope that all business brought before it would now be performed without unnecessary delay.

" Mr. Dickens alluded playfully to this item of intelligence ; said he was exceedingly happy to hear it, as he trusted now that a suit, in which he was greatly interested, would speedily come to an end. I heard a little by-conversation between Mr. Dickens and a gentleman of the bar, who sat opposite me, in which the latter seemed to be reiterating the same assertions, and I understood him to say, that a case not extraordinarily complicated might be got through with in three months. Mr. Dickens said he was very happy to hear it ; but I fancied there was a little shade of incredulity in his manner ; however, the incident showed one thing, that is, that the Chancery were not insensible to the representations of Dickens ; but the whole tone of the thing was quite good-natured and agreeable."*

XIII.

BIRMINGHAM, DECEMBER 30, 1853.

[The first of the Readings generously given by Mr. Charles Dickens on behalf of the Birmingham and Midland Institute, took place on Tuesday evening,

* The above is extracted from Mrs. Stowe's " Sunny Memories of Foreign Lands."—ED.

December 27, 1853, at the Birmingham Town Hall, where, notwithstanding the inclemency of the weather, nearly two thousand persons had assembled. The work selected was the *Christmas Carol*. The high mimetic powers possessed by Mr. Dickens enabled him to personate with remarkable force the various characters of the story, and with admirable skill to pass rapidly from the hard, unbelieving Scrooge, to trusting and thankful Bob Cratchit, and from the genial fullness of Scrooge's nephew to the hideous mirth of the party assembled in Old Joe the Ragshop-keeper's parlor. The reading occupied more than three hours, but so interested were the audience, that only one or two left the Hall previously to its termination, and the loud and frequent bursts of applause attested the successful discharge of the reader's arduous task. On Thursday evening Mr Dickens read " The Cricket on the Hearth." The Hall was again well filled, and the tale, though deficient in the dramatic interest of the " Carol," was listened to with attention, and rewarded with repeated applause. On Friday evening the " Christmas Carol " was read a second time to a large assemblage of work-people, for whom, at Mr. Dickens's special request, the major part of the vast edifice was reserved. Before commencing the tale, Mr. Dickens delivered the following brief address, almost every sentence of which was received with loudly expressed applause :]

MY GOOD FRIENDS,—When I first imparted to the committee of the projected Institute my particular wish that on one of the evenings of my readings here the main body of my audience should be composed of working-men and their families, I was animated by two desires ; first, by the wish to have the great pleasure of meeting you face to face at this Christmas-time, and accompany you myself through one of my little Christmas books ; and, second, by the wish to have an opportunity of stating publicly in your presence, and in the presence of the committee, my earnest hope that the Institute will, from the beginning, recognize one great principle—strong in reason and justice—which I believe to be essential to the very life of such an Institution. It is, that the working-man shall, from the first unto the last, have a share in the management of an Institution which is designed for his benefit, and which calls itself by his name.

I have no fear here of being misunderstood—of being supposed to mean too much in this. If there ever was a time when any one class could of itself do much for its own good, and for the welfare of society—which I greatly doubt —that time is unquestionably past. It is in the fusion of different classes, without confusion ; in the bringing together of employers and employed ; in the creating of a better common understanding among those whose interests are identical, who depend upon each other, who are vitally essential to each other, and who never can be in unnatural antagonism without deplorable results, that one of the chief principles of a Mechanics' Institution should consist. In this world a great deal of the bitterness among us arises from an imperfect understanding of one another. Erect in Birmingham a great Educational Institution, properly educational; educational of the feelings as well as of the reason; to which all orders of Birmingham men contribute; in which all orders of Birmingham men meet; wherein all orders of Birmingham men are faithfully represented—and you will erect a Temple of Concord here which will be a model edifice to the whole of England.

Contemplating as I do the existence of the Artisans' Committee, which not long ago considered the establishment of the Institute so sensibly, and supported it so heartily, I earnestly entreat the gentlemen—earnest I know in the good work, and who are now among us—by all means to avoid the great shortcoming of similar institutions; and in asking the working-man for his confidence, to set him the great example and give him theirs in return. You will judge for yourselves if I promise too much for the working-man, when I say that he will stand by such an enterprise with the utmost of his patience, his perseverance, sense, and support; that I am sure he will need no charitable aid or condescending patronage; but will readily and cheerfully pay for the advantages which it confers; that he will prepare himself in individual cases where he feels that the adverse circumstances around him have rendered it necessary; in a word, that he will feel his responsibility like an honest man, and will most honestly and manfully discharge it. I now proceed to the pleasant task to which I assure you I have looked forward for a long time.

[At the close of the reading Mr. Dickens received a vote of thanks, and "three cheers, with three times three." As soon as the enthusiasm of the audience would allow him to speak, Mr. Dickens said:]

You have heard so much of my voice since we met to-night, that I will only say, in acknowledgment of this affecting mark of your regard, that I am truly and sincerely interested in you; that any little service I have rendered to you I have freely rendered from my heart; that I hope to become an honorary member of your great Institution, and will meet you often there when it becomes practically useful; that I thank you most affectionately for this new mark of your sympathy and approval; and that I wish you many happy returns of this great birthday-time, and many prosperous years.

XIV.

COMMERCIAL TRAVELLERS.

LONDON, DECEMBER 30, 1854.

[The following speech was made by Mr. Dickens at the Anniversary Dinner in commemoration of the foundation of the Commercial Travellers' Schools, held at the London Tavern on the above date. Mr. Dickens presided on this occasion, and proposed the toasts.]

I THINK it may be assumed that most of us here present know something about travelling. I do not mean in distant regions or foreign countries, although I dare say some of us have had experience in that way, but at home, and within the limits of the United Kingdom. I dare say most us have had experience of the extinct "fast coaches," the "Wonders," "Taglionis," and "Tallyhos," of other days. I dare say most of us remember certain modest post-chaises, dragging us down interminable roads, through slush and mud, to little country towns with no visible population, except half a dozen men in smock-frocks, half a dozen women with umbrellas and pattens, and a washed-out dog or so shivering under the gables, to complete the desolate picture. We can all discourse, I dare say, if so minded, about our recollections of the "Talbot," the "Queen's Head," or the "Lion" of those days. We have all been to that room on the ground-floor on one side of the old inn yard, not quite free from a certain fragrant smell of tobacco, where the cruets on the sideboard were usually absorbed by the skirts of the box-coats that hung from the wall; where awkward servants waylaid us at every turn, like so many human man-traps; where county members, framed and glazed, were eternally presenting that petition which, somehow or other, had made their glory in the county, although nothing else had ever come of it. Where the books in the windows always wanted the first, last, and middle leaves, and where the one man was always arriving at some unusual hour in the night, and requiring his breakfast at a similarly singular period of the day. I have no doubt we could all be very eloquent on the comforts of our favorite hotel, wherever it was—its beds, its stables, its vast amount of posting, its excellent cheese, its head-waiter, its capital dishes, its pigeon-pies, or its 1820 port. Or possibly we could recall our chaste and innocent admiration of its landlady, or our fraternal regard for its handsome chamber-maid. A celebrated domestic critic, once writing of a famous actress renowned for her virtue and beauty, gave her the character of being an "eminently gatherable-to-one's-arms sort of person." Perhaps some one amongst us has borne a somewhat similar tribute to the mental charms of the fair deities who presided at our hotels.

With the travelling characteristics of later times we are all, no doubt, equally familiar. We know all about that station to which we must take our ticket, although we never get there; and the other one at which we arrive after dark, certain to find it half a mile from the town, where the old road is sure to have been abolished, and the new road is going to be made —where the old neighborhood has been tumbled down, and the new one is not half built up. We know all about that party on the platform who, with the best intentions, can do nothing for our luggage except pitch it into all sorts of unattainable places. We know all about that short omnibus, in which one is to be doubled up, to the imminent danger of the crown of one's hat; and about that fly, whose leading peculiarity is never to be there when it is wanted. We know, too, how instantaneously the lights of the station disappear when the train starts, and about that grope to the new Railway Hotel, which will be an excellent house when the customers come, but which at present has nothing to offer but a liberal allowance of damp mortar and new lime.

I record these little incidents of home travel mainly with the object of increasing your interest in the purpose of this night's assemblage. Every traveller has a home of his own, and he learns to appreciate it the more from his wandering. If he has no home, he learns the same lesson unselfishly by turning to the homes of other men. He may have his experiences of cheerful and exciting pleasures abroad; but home is the best, after all, and its pleasures are the most heartily and enduringly prized. Therefore, ladies and gentlemen, every one must be prepared to learn that commercial travellers, as a body, know how to prize those domestic relations from which their pursuits so frequently sever them; for no one could possibly invent a more delightful or more convincing testimony to the fact than they themselves have offered in founding and maintaining a school for the children of deceased or unfortunate members of their own body; those children who now appeal to you in mute but eloquent terms from the gallery.

It is to support that school, founded with such high and friendly objects, so very honorable to your calling, and so useful in its solid and practical results, that we are here to-night. It is to roof that building which is to shelter the children of your deceased friends with one crowning ornament, the best that any building can have, namely, a receipt stamp for the full amount of the cost. It is for this that your active sympathy is appealed to, for the completion of your own good work. You know how to put your hands to the plough in earnest as well as any men in existence, for this little book informs me that you raised last year no less a sum than £8000, and while fully half of that sum consisted of new donations to the building fund, I find that the regular revenue of the charity has only suffered to the extent of £30. After this, I most earnestly and sincerely say that, were we all authors together, I might boast, if in my profession were exhibited the same unity and steadfastness I find in yours.

I will not urge on you the casualties of a life of travel, or the vicissitudes of business, or the claims fostered by that bond of brotherhood which ought always to exist amongst men who are united in a common pursuit. You have already recognized those claims so nobly, that I will not presume to lay them before you in any further detail. Suffice it to say that I do not think it is in your nature to do things by halves. I do not think you could do so if you tried, and I have a moral certainty that you never will try. To those gentlemen present who are not members of the travellers' body, I will say, in the words of the French proverb, "Heaven helps those who help themselves." The Commercial Travellers having helped themselves so gallantly, it is clear that the visitors who come as a sort of celestial representatives ought to bring that aid in their pockets which the precept teaches us to expect from them. With these few remarks, I beg to give you as a toast, "Success to the Commercial Travellers' School."

[In proposing the health of the Army in the Crimea, Mr. Dickens said:]

It does not require any extraordinary sagacity in a commercial assembly to appreciate the dire evils of war. The great interests of trade enfeebled by it, the enterprise of better times paralyzed by it, all the peaceful arts bent down before it, too palpably indicate its character and results, so that far less practical intelligence than that by which I am surrounded would be sufficient to appreciate the horrors of war. But there are seasons when the evils of peace, though not so acutely felt, are immeasurably greater, and when a powerful nation, by admitting the right of any autocrat to do wrong, sows by such complicity the seeds of its own ruin, and overshadows itself in time to come with that fatal influence which great and ambitious powers are sure to exercise over their weaker neighbors.

Therefore it is, ladies and gentlemen, that the tree has not its root in English ground from which the yard wand can be made that will measure—the mine has not its place in English soil that will supply the material of a pair of scales to weigh the influence that may be at stake in the war in which we are now straining all our energies. That war is, at any time and in any shape, a most dreadful and deplorable calamity, we need no proverb to tell us; but it is just because it is such a calamity, and because that calamity must not forever be impending over us at the fancy of one man against all mankind, that we must not allow that man to darken from our view the figures of peace and justice between whom and us he now interposes.

Ladies and gentlemen, if ever there were a time when the true spirits of two countries were really fighting in the cause of human advancement and freedom—no matter what diplomatic notes or other nameless botherations, from number one to one hundred thousand and one, may have preceded their taking the field—if ever there were a time when noble hearts were deserving well of mankind by exposing themselves to the obedient bayonets of a rash and barbarian tyrant, it is now, when the faithful children of England and France are fighting so bravely in the Crimea. Those faithful children are the admiration and wonder of the world, so gallantly are they discharging their duty; and therefore I propose to an assembly emphatically representing the interests and arts of peace to drink the health of the Allied Armies of England and France, with all possible honors.

[In proposing the health of the Treasurer, Mr. Dickens said]

If the President of this Institution had been here, I should possibly have made one of the best speeches you ever heard; but as he is not here, I shall turn to the next toast on my list: "The health of your worthy Treasurer, Mr. George Moore," a name which is a synonym for integrity, enterprise, public spirit, and benevolence. He is one of the most zealous officers I ever saw in my life; he appears to me to have been doing nothing during the last week but rushing into and out of railway-carriages, and making eloquent speeches at all sorts of public dinners in favor of this charity. Last evening he was at Manchester, and this evening he comes here, sacrificing his time and convenience, and exhausting in the mean time the contents of two vast leaden inkstands and no end of pens, with the energy of fifty bankers' clerks rolled into one. But I clearly foresee that the Treasurer will have so much to do to-night, such gratifying sums to acknowledge, and such large lines of figures to write in his books, that I feel the greatest consideration I can show him is to propose his health without further observation, leaving him to address you in his own behalf. I propose to you, therefore, the health of Mr. George Moore, the Treasurer of this charity, and I need hardly add that it is one which is to be drunk with all the honors.

[Later in the evening, Mr. Dickens rose and said:]

So many travellers have been going up Mont Blanc lately, both in fact and in fiction, that I have heard recently of a proposal for the establishment of a Company to employ Sir Joseph Paxton to take it down. Only one of those travellers, however, has been enabled to bring Mont Blanc to Piccadilly, and, by his own ability and good-humor, so to thaw its eternal ice and snow, as that the most timid lady may ascend it twice a day, "during the holidays," without the smallest danger or fatigue. Mr. Albert Smith, who is present among us to-night, is undoubtedly "a traveller." I do not know whether he takes many orders, but this I can testify, on behalf of the children of his friends, that he gives them in the most liberal manner.

We have also among us my friend, Mr. Peter Cunningham, who is also a traveller, not only by right of his able edition of Goldsmith's "Traveller," but in right of his admirable Handbook, which proves him to be a traveller in the right spirit through all the labyrinths of London. We have also among us my friend Horace Mayhew, very well known also for his books, but especially for his genuine admiration of the company at that end of the room [*Mr. Dickens here pointed to the ladies' gallery*], and who, whenever the fair sex is mentioned, will be found to have the liveliest personal interest in the conversation.

Ladies and gentlemen, I am about to propose to you the health of these three distinguished visitors. They are all admirable speakers; but Mr. Albert Smith has confessed to me that, on fairly balancing his own merits as a speaker and a singer, he rather thinks he excels in the latter art. I have, therefore, yielded to his estimate of himself, and I have now the pleasure of informing you that he will lead off the speeches of the other two gentlemen with a song. Mr. Albert Smith has just said to me in an earnest tone of voice, "What song would you recommend?" and I replied, "Galignani's Messenger." Ladies and gentlemen, I therefore beg to propose the health of Messrs. Albert Smith, Peter Cunningham, and Horace Mayhew, and call on the first-named gentleman for a song.

XV.

ADMINISTRATIVE REFORM.

THEATRE ROYAL, DRURY LANE, WEDNES-
DAY, JUNE 27, 1855.

I CAN not, I am sure, better express my sense
of the kind reception accorded to me by this
great assembly, than by promising to compress
what I shall address to it within the closest possible limits. It is more than eighteen hundred
years ago since there was a set of men who
"thought they should be heard for their much
speaking." As they have propagated exceedingly since that time, and as I observe that they
flourish just now to a surprising extent about
Westminster, I will do my best to avoid adding
to the numbers of that prolific race. The noble lord at the head of the Government, when
he wondered in Parliament, about a week ago,
that my friend, Mr. Layard, did not blush for
having stated in this place what the whole
country knows perfectly well to be true, and
what no man in it can by possibility better
know to be true than those disinterested supporters of that noble lord who had the advantage of hearing him and cheering him night
after night, when he first became premier—I
mean that he did officially and habitually joke,
at a time when this country was plunged in
deep disgrace and distress—I say, that noble
lord, when he wondered so much that the man
of this age, who has, by his earnest and adventurous spirit, done the most to distinguish
himself and it, did not blush for the tremendous audacity of having so come between the
wind and his nobility, turned an airy period
with reference to the private theatricals at
Drury Lane Theatre. Now I have some slight
acquaintance with theatricals, private and public, and I will accept that figure of the noble
lord. 1 will not say that if I wanted to form
a company of Her Majesty's servants, I think I
should know where to put my hand on "the
comic old gentleman;" nor, that if I wanted to
get up a pantomime, I fancy I should know
what establishment to go to for the tricks and
changes; also, for a very considerable host of
supernumeraries, to trip one another up in that
contention with which many of us are familiar,
both on these and on other boards, in which the
principal objects thrown about are loaves and
fishes. But I will try to give the noble lord the
reason for these private theatricals, and the
reason why, however ardently he may desire
to ring the curtain down upon them, there is
not the faintest present hope of their coming to
a conclusion. It is this: The public theatricals
which the noble lord is so condescending as to
manage are so intolerably bad, the machinery
is so cumbrous, the parts so ill-distributed, the
company so full of "walking gentlemen," the
managers have such large families, and are so
bent upon putting those families into what is
theatrically called "first business"—not because of their aptitude for it, but because they
are their families, that we find ourselves obliged
to organize an opposition. We have seen the
"Comedy of Errors" played so dismally like a
tragedy that we really can not bear it. We
are, therefore, making bold to get up the "School
of Reform," and we hope, before the play is out,
to improve that noble Lord by our performance
very considerably. If he object that we have
no right to improve him without his license, we
venture to claim that right in virtue of his or-
chestra, consisting of a very powerful piper whom
we always pay.

Sir, as this is the first political meeting I
have ever attended, and as my trade and calling is not associated with politics, perhaps it
may be useful for me to show how I came to
be here, because reasons similar to those which
have influenced me may still be trembling in
the balance in the minds of others. I want at
all times, in full sincerity, to do my duty by my
countrymen. If I feel an attachment towards
them, there is nothing disinterested or meritorious in that, for I can never too affectionately
remember the confidence and friendship that
they have long reposed in me. My sphere of
action—which I shall never change—I shall
never overstep, further than this, or for a longer
period than I do to-night. By literature I have
lived, and through literature I have been content to serve my country; and I am perfectly
well aware that I can not serve two masters.
In my sphere of action I have tried to understand the heavier social grievances, and to help
to set them right. When the "Times" newspaper proved its then almost incredible case, in
reference to the ghastly absurdity of that vast
labyrinth of misplaced men and misdirected
things, which had made England unable to
find on the face of the earth an enemy one-
twentieth part so potent to effect the misery and
ruin of her noble defenders as she has been
herself, I believe that the gloomy silence into
which the country fell was by far the darkest
aspect in which a great people had been exhibited for many years. With shame and indignation lowering among all classes of society,
and this new element of discord piled on the
heaving basis of ignorance, poverty, and crime,
which is always below us—with little adequate
expression of the general mind, or apparent understanding of the general mind, in Parliament

—with the machinery of Government and the Legislature going round and round, and the people fallen from it and standing aloof, as if they left it to its last remaining function of destroying itself, when it had achieved the destruction of so much that was dear to them—I did and do believe that the only wholesome turn affairs so menacing could possibly take, was the awaking of the people, the outspeaking of the people, the uniting of the people in all patriotism and loyalty to effect a great peaceful constitutional change in the administration of their own affairs. At such a crisis this association arose; at such a crisis I joined it: considering its further case to be—if further case could possibly be needed—that what is every body's business is nobody's business, that men must be gregarious in good citizenship as well as in other things, and that it is a law in nature that there must be a centre of attraction for particles to fly to, befoıe any serviceable body with recognized functions can come into existence. This association has arisen, and we belong to it. What are the objections to it? I have heard in the main but three, which I will now briefly notice. It is said that it is proposed by this Association to exercise an influence, through the constituencies, on the House of Commons. I have not the least hesitation in saying that I have the smallest amount of faith in the House of Commons at present existing, and that I consider the exercise of such influence highly necessary to the welfare and honor of this country. I was reading no later than yesterday the book of Mr. Pepys, which is rather a favorite of mine, in which he, two hundred years ago, writing of the House of Commons, says:

"My cousin Roger Pepys tells me that it is matter of the greatest grief to him in the world that he should be put upon this trust of being a Parliament man; because he says nothing is done, that he can see, out of any truth and sincerity, but mere envy and design."

Now, how it comes to pass that after two hundred years, and many years after a Reform Bill, the House of Commons is so little changed, I will not stop to inquire. I will not ask how it happens that bills which cramp and worry the people, and restrict their scant enjoyments, are so easily passed, and how it happens that measures for their real interests are so very difficult to be got through Parliament. I will not analyze the confined air of the lobby, or reduce to their primitive gases its deadening influences on the memory of that Honorable Member who was once a candidate for the honor of your—and my—independent vote and interest. I will not ask what is that Secretarian figure, full of blandishments, standing on the threshold, with its finger on its lips. I will not ask how it comes that those personal altercations, involving all the removes and definitions of Shakspeare's Touchstone—the retort courteous—the quip modest—the reply churlish—the reproof valiant—the counter-check quarrelsome—the lie circumstantial and the lie direct—are of immeasurably greater interest in the House of Commons than the health, the taxation, and the education, of a whole people. I will not penetrate into the mysteries of that secret chamber in which the Bluebeard of Party keeps his strangled public questions, and with regard to which, when he gives the key to his wife, the new-comer, he strictly charges her on no account to open the door. I will merely put it to the experience of every body here, whether the House of Commons is not occasionally a little hard of hearing, a little dim of sight, a little slow of understanding, and whether, in short, it is not in a sufficiently invalided state to require close watching, and the occasional application of sharp stimulants; and whether it is not capable of considerable improvement? I believe that, in order to preserve it in a state of real usefulness and independence, the people must be very watchful and very jealous of it; and it must have its memory jogged, and be kept awake when it happens to have taken too much Ministerial narcotic; it must be trotted about, and must be hustled and pinched in a friendly way, as is the usage in such cases. I hold that no power can deprive us of the right to administer our functions as a body comprising electors from all parts of the country, associated together because their country is dearer to them than drowsy twaddle, unmeaning routine, or worn-out conventionalities.

This brings me to objection number two. It is stated that this Association sets class against class. Is this so? [Cries of "No."] No, it finds class set against class, and seeks to reconcile them. I wish to avoid placing in opposition those two words—Aristocracy and People. I am one who can believe in the virtues and uses of both, and would not on any account deprive either of a single just right belonging to it. I will use, instead of these words, the terms, the governors and the governed. These two bodies the Association finds with a gulf between them, in which are lying, newly-buried, thousands on thousands of the bravest and most devoted men that even England ever bred. It is to prevent the recurrence of innumerable smaller evils, of which, unchecked, that great calamity was the crowning height and the necessary consummation, and to bring together those two fronts looking now so strangely at each other, that this Association seeks to help to bridge over that abyss with a structure founded on common justice and supported by common sense. Setting class against class! That is the very parrot prattle that we have so long heard! Try its justice by the following example: A respectable gentleman had a large establishment, and a great number of servants who were good for nothing, who, when he asked them to give his children bread, gave them stones; who, when they were told to give those children fish, gave them serpents. When they were ordered to send to the East, they sent to the West; when they ought to have been serving dinner in the North, they were consulting exploded cookery-books in the South; who wasted, destroyed, tumbled over one another when required to do any thing, and were bringing every thing to ruin. At last the respectable gentleman calls his house-steward, and says, even then more in sorrow than in anger, "This is a terrible business; no fortune can stand it—no mortal equanimity can bear it! I must change my system; I must obtain servants who will do their duty." The house-steward throws up his eyes in pious horror, ejaculates " Good God, master, you are setting class against class !" and then rushes off into the servants' hall, and delivers a long and melting oration on that wicked feeling.

I now come to the third objection, which is common among young gentlemen who are not particularly fit for any thing but spending money which they have not got. It is usually comprised in the observation, "How very extraordinary it is that these Administrative Reform fellows can't mind their own business." I think it will occur to all that a very sufficient mode of disposing of this objection is to say, that it is our own business we mind when we come forward in this way, and it is to prevent it from being mismanaged by them. I observe from the Parliamentary debates—which have of late, by-the-by, frequently suggested to me that there is this difference between the bull of Spain and the bull of Nineveh, that, whereas, in the Spanish case, the bull rushes at the scarlet, in the Ninevite case the scarlet rushes at the bull—I have observed from the Parliamentary debates that, by a curious fatality, there has been a great deal of the reproof valiant and the counter-check quarrelsome, in reference to every case showing the necessity of Administrative Reform, by whomsoever produced, whensoever, and wheresoever. I dare say I should have no difficulty in adding two or three cases to the list which I know to be true, and which I have no doubt would be contradicted, but I

consider it a work of supererogation ; for, if the people at large be not already convinced that a sufficient general case has been made out for Administrative Reform, I think they never can be, and they never will be. There is, however, an old indisputable, very-well-known story, which has so pointed a moral at the end of it that I will substitute it for a new case : by doing of which I may avoid, I hope, the sacred wrath of St. Stephen's. Ages ago a savage mode of keeping accounts on notched sticks was introduced into the Court of Exchequer, and the accounts were kept, much as Robinson Crusoe kept his calendar on the desert island. In the course of considerable revolutions of time, the celebrated Cocker was born, and died; Walkinghame, of the Tutor's Assistant, and well versed in figures, was also born, and died; a multitude of accountants, book-keepers, and actuaries, were born, and died. Still official routine inclined to these notched sticks, as if they were pillars of the constitution, and still the Exchequer accounts continued to be kept on certain splints of elm-wood called "tallies." In the reign of George III. an inquiry was made by some revolutionary spirit, whether pens, ink, and paper, slates and pencils, being in existence, this obstinate adherence to an obsolete custom ought to be continued, and whether a change ought not to be effected.

All the red tape in the country grew redder at the bare mention of this bold and original conception, and it took till 1826 to get these sticks abolished. In 1834 it was found that there was a considerable accumulation of them ; and the question then arose, what was to be done with such worn-out, worm-eaten, rotten old bits of wood? I dare say there was a vast amount of minuting, memoranduming, and dispatch-boxing on this mighty subject. The sticks were housed at Westminster, and it would naturally occur to any intelligent person that nothing could be easier than to allow them to be carried away for fire-wood by the miserable people who live in that neighborhood. However, they never had been useful, and official routine required that they never should be, and so the order went forth that they were to be privately and confidentially burnt. It came to pass that they were burnt in a stove in the House of Lords. The stove, overgorged with these preposterous sticks, set fire to the panelling; the panelling set fire to the House of Lords; the House of Lords set fire to the House of Commons; the two houses were reduced to ashes; architects were called in to build others; we are now in the second million of the cost thereof; the national pig is not nearly over the stile yet; and the little old woman, Britannia, hasn't got home to-night.

Now, I think we may reasonably remark, in conclusion, that all obstinate adherence to rubbish which the time has long outlived is certain to have in the soul of it more or less that is pernicious and destructive; and that will some day set fire to something or other: which, if given boldly to the winds would have been harmless; but which, obstinately retained, is ruinous. I believe myself that when Administrative Reform goes up it will be idle to hope to put it down, on this or that particular instance. The great, broad, and true cause that our public progress is far behind our private progress, and that we are not more remarkable for our private wisdom and success in matters of business than we are for our public folly and failure, I take to be as clearly established as the sun, moon, and stars. To set this right, and to clear the way in the country for merit everywhere; accepting it equally whether it be aristocratic or democratic, only asking whether it be honest or true, is, I take it, the true object of this Association. This object it seeks to promote by uniting together large numbers of the people, I hope, of all conditions, to the end that they may better comprehend, bear in mind, understand themselves, and impress upon others, the common public duty. Also, of which there is great need, that by keeping a vigilant eye on the skirmishers thrown out from time to time by the Party of Generals, they may see that their feints and manœuvres do not oppress the small defaulters and release the great, and that they do not gull the public with a mere field-day Review of Reform, instead of an earnest, hard-fought Battle. I have had no consultation with any one upon the subject, but I particularly wish that the directors may devise some means of enabling intelligent working-men to join this body on easier terms than subscribers who have larger resources. I could wish to see great numbers of them belong to us, because I sincerely believe that it would be good for the common weal.

Said the noble Lord at the head of the Government, when Mr. Layard asked him for a day for his motion, "Let the hon. gentleman find a day for himself."

> "Now, in the names of all the gods at once,
> Upon what meat doth this our Cæsar feed,
> That he is grown so great?"

If our Cæsar will excuse me, I would take the liberty of reversing that cool and lofty sentiment, and I would say, "First Lord, your duty it is to see that no man is left to find a day for himself. See you, who take the responsibility of government, who aspire to it, live for it, intrigue for it, scramble for it, who hold to it tooth-and-nail when you can get it, see you that no man is left to find a day for himself. In this old country, with its seething hard-worked millions, its heavy taxes, its swarms of ignorant, its crowds of poor, and its crowds of wicked, woe the day when the dangerous man shall find a day for himself, because the head of the Government failed in his duty in not anticipating it by a brighter and a better one! Name you the day, First Lord; make a day; work for a day beyond your little time, Lord Palmerston, and History, in return, may then—not otherwise—find a day for you; a day equally associated with the contentment of the loyal, patient, willing-hearted English people, and with the happiness of your Royal Mistress and her fair line of children."

XVI.

SHEFFIELD, DECEMBER 22, 1855.

[On Saturday evening Mr. Charles Dickens read his Christmas Carol in the Mechanics' Hall in behalf of the funds of the Institute.

After the reading, the Mayor said he had been charged by a few gentlemen in Sheffield to present to Mr. Dickens for his acceptance a very handsome service of table cutlery, a pair of razors, and a pair of fish carvers, as some substantial manifestation of their gratitude to Mr. Dickens for his kindness in coming to Sheffield. Henceforth the Christmas of 1855 would be associated in his mind with the name of that gentleman.]

MR. CHARLES DICKENS, in receiving the presentation, said, he accepted with heartfelt delight and cordial gratitude such beautiful specimens of Sheffield workmanship; and he begged to assure them that the kind observations which had been made by the Mayor, and the way in which they had been responded to by that assembly, would never be obliterated from his remembrance. The present testified not only to the work of Sheffield hands, but to the warmth and generosity of Sheffield hearts. It was his earnest desire to do right by his readers, and to leave imaginative and popular literature associated with the private homes and public rights of the people of England. The case of cutlery with which he had been so kindly presented should be retained as an heirloom in his family; and he assured then that he should ever be faithful to his death to the principles which had earned for him their approval. In taking his reluctant leave of them, he wished them many merry Christmases, and many happy New-years.

XVII.

LONDON, FEBRUARY 9, 1858.

[At the Anniversary Festival of the Hospital for Sick Children, on Tuesday, February 9, 1858, about one hundred and fifty gentlemen sat down to dinner in the Freemasons' Hall. Later in the evening all the seats in the gallery were filled with ladies interested in the success of the Hospital. After the usual loyal and other toasts, the Chairman, Mr. Dickens, proposed "Prosperity to the Hospital for Sick Children," and said:]

LADIES AND GENTLEMEN,—It is one of my rules in life not to believe a man who may happen to tell me that he feels no interest in children. I hold myself bound to this principle by all kind consideration, because I know, as we all must, that any heart which could really toughen its affections and sympathies against those dear little people must be wanting in so many humanizing experiences of innocence and tenderness as to be quite an unsafe monstrosity among men. Therefore I set the assertion down, whenever I happen to meet with it—which is sometimes, though not often—as an idle word, originating possibly in the genteel languor of the hour, and meaning about as much as that knowing social lassitude, which has used up the cardinal virtues and quite found out things in general, usually does mean. I suppose it may be taken for granted that we, who come together in the name of children and for the sake of children, acknowledge that we have an interest in them; indeed, I have observed, since I sat down here, that we are quite in a childlike state altogether, representing an infant institution, and not even yet a grown-up company. A few years are necessary to the increase of our strength and the expansion of our figure; and then these tables, which now have a few tucks in them, will be let out, and then this hall, which now sits so easily upon us, will be too tight and small for us. Nevertheless, it is likely that even we are not without our experience now and then of spoiled children. I do not mean of our own spoiled children, because nobody's own children ever were spoiled, but I mean the disagreeable children of our particular friends. We know by experience what it is to have them down after dinner, and, across the rich perspective of a miscellaneous dessert to see, as in a black dose darkly, the family doctor looming in the distance. We know, I have no doubt we all know, what it is to assist at those little maternal anecdotes and table entertainments illustrated with imitations and descriptive dialogue, which might not be inaptly called, after the manner of my friend Mr. Albert Smith, the toilsome ascent of Miss Mary and the eruption (cutaneous) of Master Alexander. We know what it is when those children won't go to bed; we know how they prop their eyelids open with their forefingers when they will sit up; how, when they become fractious, they say aloud that they don't like us, and our nose is too long, and why don't we go? And we are perfectly acquainted with those kicking bundles which are carried off at last protesting. An eminent eye-witness told me that he was one of a company of learned pundits who assembled at the house of a very distinguished philosopher of the last generation to hear him expound his stringent views concerning infant education and early mental development, and he told me that while the philosopher did this in very beautiful and lucid language, the philosopher's little boy, for his part, edified the assembled sages by dabbling up to the elbows in an apple-pie which had been provided for their entertainment, having previously anointed his hair with the syrup, combed it with his fork, and brushed it with his spoon. It is probable that we also have our similar experiences sometimes of principles that are not quite practice, and that we know people claiming to be very wise and profound about nations of men who show themselves to be rather weak and shallow about units of babies.

But, ladies and gentlemen, the spoiled children whom I have to present to you after this dinner of to-day are not of this class. I have glanced at these for the easier and lighter introduction of another, a very different, a far more numerous, and a far more serious class. The spoiled children whom I must show you are the spoiled children of the poor in this great city, the children who are, every year, for ever and ever irrevocably spoiled out of this breathing life of ours by tens of thousands, but who may in vast numbers be preserved if you, assisting and not contravening the ways of Providence, will help to save them. The two grim nurses, Poverty and Sickness, who bring these children before you, preside over their births, rock their wretched cradles, nail down their little coffins, pile up the earth above their graves. Of the annual deaths in this great town, their unnatural deaths form more than one-third. I shall not ask you, according to the custom, as to the other class—I shall not ask you on behalf of these children to observe how good they are, how pretty they are, how clever they are, how promising they are, whose beauty they most resemble—I shall only ask you to observe how weak they are, and how like death they are! And I shall ask you, by the remembrance of every thing that lies between your own infancy and that so miscalled second childhood when the child's graces are gone, and nothing but its helplessness remains; I shall ask you to turn your thoughts to *these* spoiled children, in the sacred names of Pity and Compassion.

Some years ago, being in Scotland, I went with one of the most humane members of the humane medical profession, on a morning tour among some of the worst-lodged inhabitants of the old town of Edinburgh. In the closes and wynds of that picturesque place—I am sorry to remind you what fast friends picturesqueness and typhus often are—we saw more poverty and sickness in an hour than many people would believe in a life. Our way lay from one to another of the most wretched dwellings, reeking with horrible odors; shut out from the sky, shut out from the air—mere pits and dens. In a room in one of these places, where there was an empty porridge-pot on the cold hearth, with a ragged woman and some ragged children crouching on the bare ground near it—where, I remember as I speak, that the very light, refracted from a high, damp-stained and time-stained house-wall, came trembling in, as if the fever which had shaken every thing else there had shaken even it—there lay, in an old egg-box which the mother had begged from a shop, a little, feeble, wasted, wan, sick child. With his little wasted face, and his little hot, worn hands folded over his breast, and his little bright, attentive eyes, I can see him now, as I have seen him for several years, looking steadily at us. There he lay in his little frail box, which was not at all a bad emblem of the little body from which he was slowly parting—there he lay, quite quiet, quite patient, saying never a word. He seldom cried, the mother said; he seldom complained; "he lay there, seemin' to woonder what it was a' aboot." God knows, I thought, as I stood looking at him, he had his reasons for wondering—reasons for wondering how it could possibly come to be that he lay there, left alone, feeble and full of pain, when he ought to have been as bright and as brisk as the birds that never got near him— reasons for wondering how he came to be left there, a little decrepit old man pining to death, quite a thing, of course, as if there were no crowds of healthy and happy children playing on the grass under the summer's sun within a stone's throw of him; as if there were no bright, moving sea on the other side of the great hill overhanging the city; as if there were no great clouds rushing over it; as if there were no life, and movement, and vigor anywhere in the world—nothing but stoppage and decay. There he lay looking at us, saying, in his silence, more pathetically than I have ever heard any thing said by any orator in my life, "Will you please to tell me what this means, strange man? and if you can give me any good reason why I should be so soon so far advanced on my way to Him who said that children were to come into His presence, and were not to be forbidden, but who scarcely meant, I think, that they should come by this hard road by which I am travelling; pray give that reason to me, for I seek it very earnestly, and wonder about it very much;" and to my mind he has been wondering about it ever since. Many a poor child, sick and neglected, I have seen since that time in this London; many a poor sick child I have seen most affectionately and kindly tended by poor people, in an unwholesome house and under untoward circumstances, wherein its recovery was quite impossible; but at all such times I have seen my poor little drooping friend in his egg-box, and he has always addressed his dumb speech to me, and I have always found him wondering what it meant, and why, in the name of a gracious God, such things should be!

Now, ladies and gentlemen, such things need not be, and will not be, if this company, which is a drop of the life-blood of the great compassionate public heart, will only accept the means of rescue and prevention which it is mine to offer. Within a quarter of a mile of this place where I speak, stands a courtly old house, where once, no doubt, blooming children were born, and grew up to be men and women, and married, and brought their own blooming children back to patter up the old oak staircase which stood but the other day, and to wonder at the old oak carvings on the chimney-pieces. In the airy wards into which the old state drawing-rooms and family bed-chambers of that house are now converted are such little patients that the attendant nurses look like reclaimed giantesses, and the kind medical practitioner like an amiable Christian ogre. Grouped about the little low tables in the centre of the rooms are such tiny convalescents that they seem to be playing at having been ill. On the doll's beds are such diminutive creatures that each poor sufferer is supplied with its tray of toys; and, looking round, you may see how the little tired, flushed cheek has toppled over half the brute creation on its way into the ark; or how one little dimpled arm has mowed down (as I saw myself) the whole tin soldiery of Europe. On the walls of these rooms are graceful, pleasant, bright, childish pictures. At the beds' heads are pictures of the figure which is the universal embodiment of all mercy and compassion—the figure of Him who was once a child himself, and a poor one. Besides these little creatures on the beds, you may learn in that place that the number of small out-patients brought to that house for relief is no fewer than ten thousand in the compass of one single year. In the room in which these are received you may see against the wall a box, on which it is written, that it has been calculated, that if every grateful mother who brings a child there will drop a penny into it, the Hospital funds may possibly be increased in a year by so large a sum as forty pounds. And you may read in the Hospital Report, with a glow of pleasure, that these poor women are so respondent as to have made, even in a toiling year of difficulty and high prices, this estimated forty, fifty pounds. In the printed papers of this same Hospital you may read with what a generous earnestness the highest and wisest members of the medical profession testify to the great need of it; to the immense difficulty of treating children in the same hospital with grown-up people, by reason of their different ailments and requirements, to the vast amount of pain that will be assuaged, and of life that will be saved, through this Hospital; not only among the poor, observe, but among the prosperous too, by reason of the increased knowledge of children's illnesses, which can not fail to arise from a more systematic mode of studying them. Lastly, gentlemen, and I am sorry to say, worst of all—(for I must present no rose-colored picture of this place to you—I must not deceive you); lastly, the visitor to this Children's Hospital, reckoning up the number of its beds, will find himself perforce obliged to stop at very little over thirty; and will learn, with sorrow and surprise, that even that small number, so forlornly, so miserably diminutive, compared with this vast London, can not possibly be maintained, unless the Hospital be made better known; I limit myself to saying better known, because I will not believe that in a Christian community of fathers and mothers, and brothers and sisters, it can fail, being better known, to be well and richly endowed.

Now, ladies and gentlemen, this, without a word of adornment—which I resolved when I got up not to allow myself—this is the simple case. This is the pathetic case which I have to put to you; not only on behalf of the thousands of children who annually die in this great city, but also on behalf of the thousands of children who live half developed, racked with preventible pain, shorn of their natural capacity for health and enjoyment. If these innocent creatures can not move you for themselves, how can I possibly hope to move you in their name? The most delightful paper, the most charming essay, which the tender imagination of Charles Lamb conceived, represents him as sitting by his fireside on a winter night telling stories to his own dear children, and delighting in their society, until he suddenly comes to his old, solitary, bachelor self, and finds that they were but dream-children who might have been, but never were. "We are nothing," they say to him; "less than nothing, and dreams. We are only what might have been, and we must wait upon the tedious shore of Lethe, millions of ages, before we have existence and a name." "And immediately awaking," he says, "I found myself in my arm-chair." The dream-children whom I would now raise, if I could, before every one of you, according to your various circumstances, should be the dear child you love, the dearer child you have lost, the child you might have had, the child you certainly have been. Each of these dream-children should hold in its powerful hand one of the little children now lying in the Child's Hospital, or now shut out of it to perish. Each of these dream-children should say to you, "Oh, help this little suppliant in my name; oh, help it for my sake!" Well!—And immediately awaking, you should find yourselves in the Freemasons' Hall, happily arrived at the end of a rather long speech, drinking "Prosperity to the Hospital for Sick Children," and thoroughly resolved that it shall flourish.

XVIII.

EDINBURGH, MARCH 26, 1858.

[On the above date Mr. Dickens gave a reading of his "Christmas Carol" in the Music Hall, before the members and subscribers of the Philosophical Institution. At the conclusion of the reading the Lord Provost of Edinburgh presented him with a massive silver wassail cup. Mr. Dickens acknowledged the tribute as follows:]

MY LORD PROVOST, LADIES AND GENTLEMEN,—I beg to assure you I am deeply sensible of your kind welcome, and of this beautiful and great surprise; and that I thank you cordially with all my heart. I never have forgotten, and I never can forget, that I have the honor to be a burgess and guild-brother of the Corporation of Edinburgh. As long as sixteen or seventeen years ago, the first great public recognition and encouragement I ever received was bestowed on me in this generous and magnificent city—in this city so distinguished in literature, and so distinguished in the arts. You will readily believe that I have carried into the various countries I have since traversed, and through all my subsequent career, the proud and affectionate remembrance of that eventful epoch in my life; and that coming back to Edinburgh is to me like coming home.

Ladies and gentlemen, you have heard so much of my voice to-night, that I will not inflict on you the additional task of hearing any more. I am better reconciled to limiting myself to these very few words, because I know and feel full well that no amount of speech to which I could give utterance could possibly express my sense of the honor and distinction you have conferred on me, or the heartfelt gratification I derive from this reception.

XIX.

LONDON, MARCH 29, 1858.

[At the thirteenth Anniversary Festival of the General Theatrical Fund, held at the Freemasons' Tavern, at which Thackeray presided, Mr. Dickens made the following speech.]

IN our theatrical experience as playgoers we are all equally accustomed to predict, by certain little signs and portents on the stage, what is going to happen there. When the young lady, an admiral's daughter, is left alone to indulge in a short soliloquy, and certain smart spirit-rappings are heard to proceed immediately from beneath her feet, we foretell that a song is impending. When two gentlemen enter, for whom, by a happy coincidence, two chairs, and no more, are in waiting, we augur a conversation, and that it will assume a retrospective biographical character. When any of the performers who belong to the sea-faring or marauding professions are observed to arm themselves with very small swords to which are attached very large hilts, we predict that the affair will end in a combat. Carrying out the association of ideas, it may have occurred to some that when I asked my old friend in the chair to allow me to propose a toast, I had him in my eye; and I have him now on my lips.

The duties of a trustee of a Theatrical Fund, an office which I hold, are not so frequent or so great as its privileges. He is in fact a mere walking gentleman, with the melancholy difference that he has no one to love. If this advantage could be added to his character, it would be one of a more agreeable nature than it is, and his forlorn position would be greatly improved. His duty is to call every half-year at the banker's, when he signs his name in a large greasy, inconvenient book, to certain documents of which he knows nothing, and then he delivers it to the property man and exits anywhere.

He, however has many privileges. It is one of his privileges to watch the steady growth of an institution in which he takes great interest; it is one of his privileges to bear his testimony to the prudence, the goodness, the self-denial, and the excellence of a class of persons who have been too long depreciated, and whose virtues are too much denied, out of the depths of an ignorant and stupid superstition. And lastly, it is one of his privileges sometimes to be called on to propose the health of the chairman at the annual dinners of the institution, when that chairman is one for whose genius he entertains the warmest admiration, and whom he respects as a friend, and as one who does honor to literature, and in whom literature is honored. I say when that is the case, he feels that this last privilege is a great and high one. From the earliest days of this institution I have ventured to impress on its managers that they would consult its credit and success by choosing its chairman as often as possible within the circle of literature and the arts; and I will venture to say that no similar institution has been presided over by so many remarkable and distinguished men. I am sure, however, that it never has had, and that it never will have, simply because it can not have, a greater lustre cast upon it than by the presence of the noble English writer who fills the chair to-night.

It is not for me at this time, and in this place, to take on myself to flutter before you the well-thumbed pages of Mr. Thackeray's books, and to tell you to observe how full they are of wit and wisdom, how outspeaking, and how devoid of fear or favor; but I will take leave to remark, in paying my due homage and respect to them, that it is fitting that such a writer and such an institution should be brought together. Every writer of fiction, although he may not adopt the dramatic form, writes in effect for the stage. He may never write plays; but the truth and passion which are in him must be more or less reflected in the great mirror which he holds up to nature. Actors, managers, and authors are all represented in this company, and it may be supposed that they all have studied the deep wants of the human heart in many theatres; but none of them could have studied its mysterious workings in any theatre to greater advantage than in the bright and airy pages of "Vanity Fair." To this skillful showman, who has so often delighted us, and who has charmed us again to-night, we have now to wish God speed, and that he may continue for many years* to exercise his potent art. To him fill a bumper toast, and fervently utter, God bless him!

---

* Alas! the "many years" were to be barely six, when the speaker was himself destined to write some memorial pages commemorative of his illustrious friend ("Cornhill Magazine," February, 1864).—ED.

XX.

LONDON, APRIL 29, 1858.

[The reader will already have observed that in the Christmas week of 1853, and on several subsequent occasions, Mr. Dickens had read the "Christmas Carol" and the "Chimes" before public audiences, but always in aid of the funds of some institution, or for other benevolent purposes. The first reading he ever gave for his own benefit took place on the above date in St. Martin's Hall (now converted into the Queen's Theatre). This reading Mr. Dickens prefaced with the following speech :]

LADIES AND GENTLEMEN,—It may perhaps be known to you that, for a few years past, I have been accustomed occasionally to read some of my shorter books to various audiences, in aid of a variety of good objects, and at some charge to myself, both in time and money. It having at length become impossible in any reason to comply with these always accumulating demands, I have had definitively to choose between now and then reading on my own account, as one of my recognized occupations, or not reading at all. I have had little or no difficulty in deciding on the former course. The reasons that have led me to it—besides the consideration that it necessitates no departure whatever from the chosen pursuits of my life—are threefold : firstly, I have satisfied myself that it can involve no possible compromise of the credit and independence of literature; secondly, I have long held the opinion, and have long acted on the opinion, that in these times whatever brings a public man and his public face to face, on terms of mutual confidence and respect, is a good thing; thirdly, I have had a pretty large experience of the interest my hearers are so generous as to take in these occasions, and of the delight they give to me, as a tried means of strengthening those relations—I may almost say of personal friendship—which it is my great privilege and pride, as it is my great responsibility, to hold with a multitude of persons who will never hear my voice nor see my face. Thus it is that I come, quite naturally, to be here among you at this time; and thus it is that I proceed to read this little book, quite as composedly as I might proceed to write it, or to publish it in any other way.

XXI.

LONDON, MAY 1, 1858.

[The following short speech was made at the Banquet of the Royal Academy, after the health of Mr. Dickens and Mr. Thackeray had been proposed by the President, Sir Charles Eastlake :]

FOLLOWING the order of your toast, I have to take the first part in the duet to be performed in acknowledgment of the compliment you have paid to literature. In this home of art I feel it to be too much an interchange of compliments, as it were, between near relations, to enter into any lengthened expression of our thanks for the honor you have done us. I feel that it would be changing this splendid assembly into a sort of family party. I may, however, take leave to say that your sister, whom I represent, is strong and healthy; that she has a very great affection for, and an undying interest in you, and that it is always a very great gratification to her to see herself so well remembered within these walls, and to know that she is an honored guest at your hospitable board.

XXII.

LONDON, JULY 21, 1858.

[On the above date, a public meeting was held at the Princess's Theatre, for the purpose of establishing the now famous Royal Dramatic College. Mr. Charles Kean was the Chairman, and Mr. Dickens delivered the following speech :]

LADIES AND GENTLEMEN,—I think I may venture to congratulate you beforehand on the pleasant circumstance that the movers and seconders of the resolutions which will be submitted to you will, probably, have very little to say. Through the Report which you have heard read, and through the comprehensive address of the chairman, the cause which brings us together has been so very clearly stated to you, that it can stand in need of very little, if of any further exposition. But, as I have the honor to move the first resolution which this handsome gift, and the vigorous action that must be taken upon it, necessitate, I think I shall only give expression to what is uppermost in the general mind here, if I venture to remark that, many as the parts are in which Mr. Kean has distinguished himself on these boards, he has never appeared in one in which the large spirit of an artist, the feeling of a man, and the grace of a gentleman, have been more admirably blended than in this day's faithful adherence to the calling of which he is a prosperous ornament, and in this day's manly advocacy of its cause.

Ladies and gentlemen, the resolution intrusted to me is :

"That the report of the provisional committee be adopted, and that this meeting joyfully accepts, and gratefully acknowledges, the gift of five acres of land referred to in the said Report."*

---

* Mr. Henry Dodd had proposed to give five acres of land in Berkshire, but in consequence of his desiring to attach certain restrictions, after a long and unsatisfactory correspondence, the Committee, on 13th January following, rejected the offer.—*Communicated.*

It is manifest, I take it, that we are all agreed upon this acceptance and acknowledgment, and that we all know very well that this generous gift can inspire but one sentiment in the breast of every lover of the dramatic art. As it is far too often forgotten, by those who are indebted to it for many a restorative flight out of this working-day world, that the silks, and velvets, and elegant costumes of its professors must be every night exchanged for the hideous coats and waistcoats of the present day, in which we have now the honor and the misfortune of appearing before you, so when we do meet with a nature so considerably generous as this donor's, and do find an interest in the real life and struggles of the people who have delighted it, so very spontaneous and so very liberal, we have nothing to do but to accept and to admire, we have no duty left but to " take the goods the gods provide us," and to make the best and the most of them. Ladies and gentlemen, allow me to remark, that in this mode of turning a good gift to the highest account, lies the truest gratitude.

In reference to this, I could not but reflect, whilst Mr. Kean was speaking, that in an hour or two from this time, the spot upon which we are now assembled will be transformed into the scene of a crafty and a cruel bond. I know that, a few hours hence, the Grand Canal of Venice will flow, with picturesque fidelity, on the very spot where I now stand dryshod, and that " the quality of mercy " will be beautifully stated to the Venetian Council by a learned young doctor from Padua, on these very boards on which we now enlarge upon the quality of charity and sympathy. Knowing this, it came into my mind to consider how different the real bond of to-day from the ideal bond of to-night. Now, all generosity, all forbearance, all forgetfulness of little jealousies and unworthy divisions, all united action for the general good. Then, all selfishness, all malignity, all cruelty, all revenge, and all evil—now all good. Then, a bond to be broken within the compass of a few—three or four—swiftly passing hours—now, a bond to be valid and of good effect generations hence.

Ladies and gentlemen, of the execution and delivery of this bond, between this generous gentleman on the one hand, and the united members of a too often and too long disunited art upon the other, be you the witnesses. Do you attest of every thing that is liberal and free in spirit, that is " so nominated in the bond;" and of every thing that is grudging, self-seeking, unjust, or unfair, that it is by no sophistry ever to be found there. I beg to move the resolution which I have already had the pleasure of reading.

XXIII.

MANCHESTER. DECEMBER 3, 1858.

[The following speech was delivered at the annual meeting of the Institutional Association of Lancashire and Cheshire, held in the Free-trade Hall on the evening of the above day, at which Mr. Dickens presided:]

IT has of late years become noticeable in England that the autumn season produces an immense amount of public speaking. I notice that no sooner do the leaves begin to fall from the trees, than pearls of great price begin to fall from the lips of the wise men of the east, and north, and west, and south; and any body 'may have them by the bushel, for the picking up. Now, whether the comet has this year had a quickening influence on this crop, as it is by some supposed to have had upon the corn-harvest and the vintage, I do not know; but I do know that I have never observed the columns of the newspapers to groan so heavily under a pressure of orations, each vying with the other in the two qualities of having little or nothing to do with the matter in hand, and of being always addressed to any audience in the wide world rather than the audience to which it was delivered.

The autumn having gone, and the winter come, I am so sanguine as to hope that we in our proceedings may break through this enchanted circle and deviate from this precedent; the rather as we have something real to do, and are come together, I am sure, in all plain fellowship and straightforwardness, to do it. We have no little straws of our own to throw up to show us which way any wind blows, and we have no oblique biddings of our own to make for any thing outside this hall.

At the top of the public announcement of this meeting are the words, " Institutional Association of Lancashire and Cheshire." Will you allow me, in reference to the meaning of those words, to present myself before you as the embodied spirit of ignorance recently enlightened, and to put myself through a short voluntary examination as to the results of my studies. To begin with: the title did not suggest to me any thing in the least like the truth. I have been for some years pretty familiar with the terms, " Mechanics' Institutions," and " Literary Societies," but they have, unfortunately, become too often associated in my mind with a body of great pretensions, lame as to some important member or other, which generally inhabits a new house much too large for it, which is seldom paid for, and which takes the name of the mechanics most grievously in vain, for I have usually seen a mechanic and a dodo in that place together.

I, therefore, began my education, in respect of the meaning of this title, very coldly indeed, saying to myself, "Here's the old story." But the perusal of a very few lines of my book soon gave me to understand that it was not by any means the old story; in short, that this association is expressly designed to correct the old story, and to prevent its defects from becoming perpetuated. I learnt that this Institutional Association is the union, in one central head, of one hundred and fourteen local Mechanics' Institutions and Mutual Improvement Societies, at an expense of no more than five shillings to each society; suggesting to all how they can best communicate with and profit by the fountain-head and one another; keeping their best aims steadily before them; advising them how those aims can be best attained; giving a direct end and object to what might otherwise easily become waste forces; and sending among them not only oral teachers, but, better still, boxes of excellent books, called "Free Itinerating Libraries." I learned that these books are constantly making the circuit of hundreds upon hundreds of miles, and are constantly being read with inexpressible relish by thousands upon thousands of toiling people, but that they are never damaged or defaced by one rude hand. These and other like facts lead me to consider the immense importance of the fact, that no little cluster of working-men's cottages can arise in any Lancashire or Cheshire valley, at the foot of any running stream which enterprise hunts out for water-power, but it has its educational friend and companion ready for it, willing for it, acquainted with its thoughts and ways and turns of speech even before it has come into existence.

Now, ladies and gentlemen, this is the main consideration that has brought me here. No central association at a distance could possibly do for those working-men what this local association does. No central association at a distance could possibly understand them as this local association does. No central association at a distance could possibly put them in that familiar and easy communication one with another, as that I, man or boy, eager for knowledge, in that valley seven miles off, should know of you, man or boy, eager for knowledge, in that valley twelve miles off, and should occasionally trudge to meet you, that you may impart your learning in one branch of acquisition to me, whilst I impart mine in another to you. Yet this is distinctly a feature, and a most important feature, of this society.

On the other hand, it is not to be supposed that these honest men, however zealous, could, as a rule, succeed in establishing and maintaining their own institutions of themselves. It is obvious that combination must materially diminish their cost, which is in time a vital consideration; and it is equally obvious that experience, essential to the success of all combination, is especially so when its object is to diffuse the results of experience and of reflection.

Well, ladies and gentlemen, the student of the present profitable history of this society does not stop here in his learning; when he has got so far, he finds with interest and pleasure that the parent society at certain stated periods invites the more eager and enterprising members of the local society to submit themselves to voluntary examination in various branches of useful knowledge, of which examination it takes the charge and arranges the details, and invites the successful candidates to come to Manchester to receive the prizes and certificates of merit which it impartially awards. The most successful of the competitors in the list of these examinations are now among us, and these little marks of recognition and encouragement I shall have the honor presently of giving them, as they come before you, one by one, for that purpose.

I have looked over a few of those examination-papers, which have comprised history, geography, grammar, arithmetic, book - keeping, decimal coinage, mensuration, mathematics, social economy, the French language—in fact, they comprise all the keys that open all the locks of knowledge. I felt most devoutly gratified, as to many of them, that they had not been submitted to me to answer, for I am perfectly sure that if they had been, I should have had mighty little to bestow upon myself to - night. And yet it is always to be observed and seriously remembered that these examinations are undergone by people whose lives have been passed in a continual fight for bread, and whose whole existence has been a constant wrestle with

"Those twin jailers of the daring heart—
Low birth and iron fortune."[*]

I could not but consider, with extraordinary admiration, that these questions have been replied to, not by men like myself, the business of whose life is with writing and with books, but by men, the business of whose life is with tools and with machinery.

Let me endeavor to recall, as well as my memory will serve me, from among the most interesting cases of prize-holders and certificate-gainers who will appear before you, some two

---

[*] Claude Melnotte, in "The Lady of Lyons," Act iii. scene 2.

or three of the most conspicuous examples. There are two poor brothers from near Chorley, who work from morning to night in a coal-pit, and who, in all weathers, have walked eight miles a night, three nights a week, to attend the classes in which they have gained distinction. There are two poor boys from Bollington, who began life as piecers at one shilling or eighteen pence a week, and the father of one of whom was cut to pieces by the machinery at which he worked, but not before he had himself founded the institution in which this son has since come to be taught. These two poor boys will appear before you to-night, to take the second-class prize in chemistry. There is a plasterer from Bury, sixteen years of age, who took a third-class certificate last year at the hands of Lord Brougham; he is this year again successful in a competition three times as severe. There is a wagon-maker from the same place, who knew little or absolutely nothing until he was a grown man, and who has learned all he knows, which is a great deal, in the local institution. There is a chain-maker, in very humble circumstances, and working hard all day, who walks six miles a night, three nights a week, to attend the classes in which he has won so famous a place. There is a moulder in an iron foundry, who, whilst he was working twelve hours a day before the furnace, got up at four o'clock in the morning to learn drawing. "The thought of my lads," he writes in his modest account of himself, "in their peaceful slumbers above me, gave me fresh courage, and I used to think that if I should never receive any personal benefit, I might instruct them when they came to be of an age to understand the mighty machines and engines which have made our country, England, pre-eminent in the world's history." There is a piecer at mule-frames, who could not read at eighteen, who is now a man of little more than thirty, who is the sole support of an aged mother, who is arithmetical teacher in the institution in which he himself was taught, who writes of himself that he made the resolution never to take up a subject without keeping to it, and who has kept to it with such an astonishing will, that he is now well versed in Euclid and Algebra, and is the best French scholar in Stockport. The drawing-classes in that same Stockport are taught by a working blacksmith; and the pupils of that working blacksmith will receive the highest honors of to-night. Well may it be said of that good blacksmith, as it was written of another of his trade, by the American poet:

"Toiling, rejoicing, sorrowing,
    Onward through life he goes;

Each morning sees some task begun,
    Each evening sees its close.
Something attempted, something done,
    Has earned a night's repose."

To pass from the successful candidates to the delegates from local societies now before me, and to content myself with one instance from amongst them. There is among their number a most remarkable man, whose history I have read with feelings that I could not adequately express under any circumstances, and least of all when I know he hears me, who worked when he was a mere baby at hand-loom weaving until he dropped from fatigue: who began to teach himself as soon as he could earn five shillings a week: who is now a botanist, acquainted with every production of the Lancashire valley; who is a naturalist, and has made and preserved a collection of the eggs of British birds, and stuffed the birds: who is now a conchologist, with a very curious, and in some respects an original collection of fresh-water shells, and has also preserved and collected the mosses of fresh-water and of the sea: who is worthily the president of his own local Literary Institution, and who was at his work this time last night as foreman in a mill.

So stimulating has been the influence of these bright examples, and many more, that I notice among the applications from Blackburn for preliminary test examination papers, one from an applicant who gravely fills up the printed form by describing himself as ten years of age, and who, with equal gravity, describes his occupation as "nursing a little child." Nor are these things confined to the men. The women employed in factories, milliner's work, and domestic service, have begun to show, as it is fitting they should, a most decided determination not to be outdone by the men; and the women of Preston in particular have so honorably distinguished themselves, and shown in their examination-papers such an admirable knowledge of the science of household management and household economy, that if I were a working bachelor of Lancashire or Cheshire, and if I had not cast my eye or set my heart upon any lass in particular, I should positively get up at four o'clock in the morning with the determination of the iron-moulder himself, and should go to Preston in search of a wife.

Now, ladies and gentlemen, these instances, and many more, daily occurring, always accumulating, are surely better testimony to the working of this Association than any number of speakers could possibly present to you. Surely the presence among us of these indefatigable people is the Association's best and most effective triumph in the present and the past, and is its noblest stimulus to effort in the future. As its temporary mouth-piece, I would beg to say to that portion of the company who attend to receive the prizes, that the institution can never hold itself apart from them;—can never set itself above them; that their distinction and success must be its distinction and success; and that there can be but one heart beating between them and it. In particular, I would most especially entreat them to observe that nothing will ever be farther from this Association's mind than the impertinence of patronage. The prizes that it gives, and the certificates that it gives, are mere admiring assurances of sympathy with so many striving brothers and sisters, and are only valuable for the spirit in which they are given, and in which they are received. The prizes are money prizes, simply because the Institution does not presume to doubt that persons who have so well governed themselves, know best how to make a little money serviceable—because it would be a shame to treat them like grown-up babies by laying it out for them, and because it knows it is given, and knows it is taken, in perfect clearness of purpose, perfect trustfulness, and, above all, perfect independence.

Ladies and gentlemen, reverting once more to the whole collective audience before me, I will, in another two minutes, release the hold which your favor has given me on your attention. Of the advantages of knowledge I have said, and I shall say, nothing. Of the certainty with which the man who grasps it under difficulties rises in his own respect and in usefulness to the community, I have said, and I shall say, nothing. In the city of Manchester, in the county of Lancaster, both of them remarkable for self-taught men, that were superfluous indeed. For the same reason I rigidly abstain from putting together any of the shattered fragments of that poor clay image of a parrot, which was once always saying, without knowing why, or what it meant, that knowledge was a dangerous thing. I should as soon think of piecing together the mutilated remains of any wretched Hindoo who has been blown from an English gun. Both, creatures of the past, have been—as my friend Mr. Carlyle vigorously has it—"blasted into space;" and there, as to this world, is an end of them.

So I desire, in conclusion, only to sound two strings. In the first place, let me congratulate you upon the progress which real mutual improvement societies are making at this time in your neighborhood, through the noble agency of individual employers and their families, whom

you can never too much delight to honor. Elsewhere, through the agency of the great railway companies, some of which are bestirring themselves in this matter with a gallantry and generosity deserving of all praise. Secondly and lastly, let me say one word out of my own personal heart, which is always very near to it in this connection. Do not let us, in the midst of the visible objects of nature, whose workings we can tell of in figures, surrounded by machines that can be made to the thousandth part of an inch, acquiring every day knowledge which can be proved upon a slate or demonstrated by a microscope—do not let us, in the laudable pursuit of the facts that surround us, neglect the fancy and the imagination which equally surround us as a part of the great scheme. Let the child have its fables; let the man or woman into which it changes, always remember those fables tenderly. Let numerous graces and ornaments that can not be weighed and measured, and that seem at first sight idle enough, continue to have their places about us, be we never so wise. The hardest head may co-exist with the softest heart. The union and just balance of those two is always a blessing to the possessor, and always a blessing to mankind. The Divine Teacher was as gentle and considerate as he was powerful and wise. You all know how He could still the raging of the sea, and could hush a little child. As the utmost results of the wisdom of men can only be at last to help to raise this earth to that condition to which His doctrine, untainted by the blindnesses and passions of men, would have exalted it long ago; so let us always remember that He set us the example of blending the understanding and the imagination, and that, following it ourselves, we tread in His steps, and help our race on to its better and best days. Knowledge, as all followers of it must know, has a very limited power indeed, when it informs the head alone; but when it informs the head and the heart too, it has a power over life and death, the body and the soul, and dominates the universe.

~~~~~~~~~

XXIV.

COVENTRY, DECEMBER 4, 1858.

[On the above evening, a public dinner was held at the Castle Hotel, on the occasion of the presentation to Mr. Charles Dickens of a gold watch, as a mark of gratitude for the reading of his "Christmas Carol," given in December of the previous year, in aid of the funds of the Coventry Institute. The Chair was taken by C. W. Hoskyns, Esq. Mr. Dickens acknowledged the testimonial in the following words:]

MR. CHAIRMAN, MR. VICE-CHAIRMAN, AND GENTLEMEN,—I hope your minds will be greatly relieved by my assuring you that it is one of the rules of my life never to make a speech about myself. If I knowingly did so, under any circumstances, it would be least of all under such circumstances as these, when its effect on my acknowledgment of your kind regard, and this pleasant proof of it, would be to give me a certain constrained air, which I fear would contrast badly with your greeting, so cordial, so unaffected, so earnest, and so true. Furthermore, your Chairman has decorated the occasion with a little garland of good sense, good feeling, and good taste; so that I am sure that any attempt at additional ornament would be almost an impertinence.

Therefore I will at once say how earnestly, how fervently, and how deeply I feel your kindness. This watch, with which you have presented me, shall be my companion in my hours of sedentary working at home, and in my wanderings abroad. It shall never be absent from my side, and it shall reckon off the labors of my future days; and I can assure you that after this night the object of those labors will not less than before be to uphold the right and to do good. And when I have done with time and its measurement, this watch shall belong to my children; and as I have seven boys, and as they have all begun to serve their country in various ways, or to elect into what distant regions they shall roam, it is not only possible, but probable, that this little voice will be heard scores of years hence—who knows?—in some yet unfounded city in the wilds of Australia, or communicating Greenwich time to Coventry Street, Japan.

Once again, and finally, I thank you; and from my heart of hearts I can assure you that the memory of to-night, and of your picturesque and interesting city, will never be absent from my mind, and I can never more hear the lightest mention of the name of Coventry without having inspired in my breast sentiments of unusual emotion and unusual attachment.

[Later in the evening, in proposing the health of the Chairman, Mr. Dickens said :]

There may be a great variety of conflicting opinions with regard to farming, and especially with reference to the management of a clay farm; but, however various opinions as to the merits of a clay farm may be, there can be but one opinion as to the merits of a clay farmer—and it is the health of that distinguished agriculturist which I have to propose.

In my ignorance of the subject, I am bound to say that it may be, for any thing I know, indeed I am ready to admit that it is, exceedingly important that a clay farm should go for a number of years to waste; but I claim some knowl-

edge as to the management of a clay farmer, and I positively object to his ever lying fallow. In the hope that this very rich and teeming individual may speedily be ploughed up, and that we shall gather into our barns and store-houses the admirable crop of wisdom which must spring up whenever he is sown, I take leave to propose his health, begging to assure him that the kind manner in which he offered to me your very valuable present I can never forget.

XXV.

LONDON, MARCH 29, 1862.

[At a dinner of the Artists' General Benevolent Institution, the following Address was delivered by Mr. Charles Dickens from the Chair :]

SEVEN or eight years ago, without the smallest expectation of ever being called upon to fill the chair at an anniversary festival of the Artists' General Benevolent Institution, and without the remotest reference to such an occasion, I selected the administration of that Charity as the model on which I desired that another should be reformed, both as regarded the mode in which the relief was afforded, and the singular economy with which its funds were administered. As a proof of the latter quality during the past year, the cost of distributing £1126 among the recipients of the bounty of the Charity amounted to little more than £100, inclusive of all office charges and expenses. The experience and knowledge of those intrusted with the management of the funds are a guaranty that the last available farthing of the funds will be distributed among proper and deserving recipients. Claiming, on my part, to be related in some degree to the profession of an artist, I disdain to stoop to ask for charity, in the ordinary acceptation of the term, on behalf of the Artists. In its broader and higher signification of generous confidence, lasting trustfulness, love and confiding belief, I very readily associate that cardinal virtue with art. I decline to present the Artist to the notice of the public as a grown-up child, or as a strange, unaccountable, moonstricken person, waiting helplessly in the street of life to be helped over the road by the crossing-sweeper; on the contrary, I present the Artist as a reasonable creature, a sensible gentleman, and as one well acquainted with the value of his time, and that of other people, as if he were in the habit of going on high 'Change every day. The artist whom I wish to present to the notice of the meeting is one to whom the perfect enjoyment of the five senses is essential to every achievement of his life. He can gain no wealth nor fame by buying something which he never touched, and selling it to another who would also never touch or see it, but was compelled to strike out for himself every spark of fire which lighted, burned, and perhaps consumed him. He must win the battle of life with his own hand, and with his own eyes, and was obliged to act as general, captain, ensign, non-commissioned officer, private, drummer, great arms, small arms, infantry, cavalry, all in his own unaided self. When, therefore, I ask help for the Artist, I do not make my appeal for one who was a cripple from his birth, but I ask it as part payment of a great debt which all sensible and civilized creatures owe to art, as a mark of respect to art, as a decoration—not as a badge—as a remembrance of what this land, or any land, would be without art, and as the token of an appreciation of the works of the most successful artists of this country. With respect to the society of which I am the advocate, I am gratified that it is so liberally supported by the most distinguished artists, and that it has the confidence of men who occupy the highest rank as artists, above the reach of reverses, and the most distinguished in success and fame, and whose support is above all price. Artists who have obtained wide-world reputation know well that many deserving and persevering men, or their widows and orphans, have received help from this fund, and some of the artists who have received this help are now enrolled among the subscribers to the Institution.

~~~~~~~~~~~

XXVI.

LONDON, MAY 20, 1862.

[The following speech was made by Mr. Dickens, in his capacity as Chairman, at the annual Festival of the News-venders' and Provident Institution, held at the Freemasons' Tavern on the above date.]

When I had the honor of being asked to preside last year, I was prevented by indisposition, and I besought my friend, Mr. Wilkie Collins, to reign in my stead. He very kindly complied, and made an excellent speech. Now I tell you the truth, that I read that speech with considerable uneasiness, for it inspired me with a strong misgiving that I had better have presided last year with neuralgia in my face and my subject in my head, rather than preside this year with my neuralgia all gone and my subject anticipated. Therefore, I wish to preface the toast this evening by making the managers of this Institution one very solemn and repentant promise, and it is, if ever I find myself obliged to provide a substitute again, they may rely upon my sending the most speechless man of my acquaintance.

The Chairman last year presented you with an amiable view of the universality of the newsman's calling. Nothing, I think, is left for me but to imagine the newsman's burden itself, to unfold one of those wonderful sheets which he every day disseminates, and to take a bird's-eye view of its general character and contents. So, if you please, choosing my own time—though the newsman can not choose his time, for he must be equally active in winter or summer, in sunshine or sleet, in light or darkness, early or late—but, choosing my own time, I shall for two or three moments start off with the newsman on a fine May morning, and take a view of the wonderful broadsheets which every day he scatters broadcast over the country. Well, the first thing that occurs to me following the newsman is, that every day we are born, that every day we are married—some of us—and that every day we are dead; consequently, the first thing the newsvender's column informs me is, that Atkins has been born, that Catkins has been married, and that Datkins is dead. But the most remarkable thing I immediately discover in the next column is, that Atkins has grown to be seventeen years old, and that he has run away; for, at last, my eye lights on the fact that William A., who is seventeen years old, is adjured immediately to return to his disconsolate parents, and every thing will be arranged to the satisfaction of every one. I am afraid he will never return, simply because, if he had meant to come back, he would never have gone away. Immediately below, I find a mysterious character in such a mysterious difficulty that it is only to be expressed by several disjointed letters, by several figures, and several stars; and then I find the explanation in the intimation that the writer has given his property over to his uncle, and that the elephant is on the wing. Then, still glancing over the shoulder of my industrious friend, the newsman, I find there are great fleets of ships bound to all parts of the earth, that they all want a little more stowage, a little more cargo, that they have a few more berths to let, that they have all the most spacious decks, that they are all built of teak, and copper-bottomed, that they all carry surgeons of experience, and that they are all A 1 at Lloyds', and anywhere else. Still glancing over the shoulder of my friend the newsman, I find I am offered all kinds of house-lodging, clerks, servants, and situations, which I can possibly or impossibly want. I learn, to my intense gratification, that I need never grow old, that I may always preserve the juvenile bloom of my complexion; that if ever I turn ill it is entirely my own fault; that if I have any complaint, and want brown cod-liver oil or Turkish baths, I am told where to get them, and that, if I want an income of seven pounds a week, I may have it by sending half a crown in postage-stamps. Then I look to the police intelligence, and I can discover that I may bite off a human living nose cheaply, but if I take off the dead nose of a pig or a calf from a shop-window, it will cost me exceedingly dear. I also find that if I allow myself to be betrayed into the folly of killing an inoffensive tradesman on his own door-step, that little incident will not affect the testimonials to my character, but that I shall be described as a most amiable young man, and as, above all things, remarkable for the singular inoffensiveness of my character and disposition. Then I turn my eye to the Fine Arts, and, under that head, I see that a certain "J. O." has most triumphantly exposed a certain "J. O. B.," which "J. O. B." was remarkable for this particular ugly feature, that I was requested to deprive myself of the best of my pictures for six months; that for that time it was to be hung on a wet wall, and that I was to be requited for my courtesy in having my picture most impertinently covered with a wet blanket. To sum up the results of a glance over my newsman's shoulder, it gives a comprehensive knowledge of what is going on over the continent of Europe, and also of what is going on over the continent of America, to say nothing of such little geographical regions as India and China.

Now, my friends, this is the glance over the newsman's shoulders from the whimsical point of view, which is the point, I believe, that most promotes digestion. The newsman is to be met with on steamboats, railway stations, and at every turn. His profits are small, he has a great amount of anxiety and care, and no little amount of personal wear and tear. He is indispensable to civilization and freedom, and he is looked for with pleasurable excitement every day, except when he lends the paper for an hour, and when he is punctual in calling for it, which is sometimes very painful. I think the lesson we can learn from our newsman is some new illustrations of the uncertainty of life, some illustration of its vicissitudes and fluctuations. Mindful of this permanent lesson, some members of the trade originated this society, which affords them assistance in time of sickness and indigence. The subscription is infinitesimal. It amounts annually to five shillings. Looking at the returns before me, the progress of the society would seem to be slow, but it has only been slow for the best of all reasons, that it has been sure. The pensions granted are all obtained from the interest on the funded capital, and, therefore, the Institution is literally as safe as the Bank. It is stated that there are several news-venders who are not members of this society; but that is true in all institutions which have come under my experience. The persons who are most likely to stand in need of the benefits which an institution confers, are usually the persons to keep away until bitter experience comes to them too late.

XXVII.

LONDON, MAY 11, 1864.

[On the above date Mr. Dickens presided at the Adelphi Theatre, at a public meeting for the purpose of founding the Shakspeare Schools, in connection with the Royal Dramatic College, and delivered the following address :]

LADIES AND GENTLEMEN,—Fortunately for me, and fortunately for you, it is the duty of the chairman, on an occasion of this nature, to be very careful that he does not anticipate those speakers who come after him. Like Falstaff, with a considerable difference, he has to be the cause of speaking in others. It is rather his duty to sit and hear speeches with exemplary attention than to stand up to make them ; so I shall confine myself, in opening these proceedings as your business official, to as plain and as short an exposition as I can possibly give you of the reasons why we come together.

First of all I will take leave to remark that we do not come together in commemoration of Shakspeare. We have nothing to do with any commemoration, except that we are of course humble worshippers of that mighty genius, and that we propose by-and-by to take his name, but by no means to take it in vain. If, however, the Tercentenary celebration were a hundred years hence, or a hundred years past, we should still be pursuing precisely the same object, though we should not pursue it under precisely the same circumstances. The facts are these: There is, as you know, in existence an admirable institution called the Royal Dramatic College, which is a place of honorable rest and repose for veterans in the dramatic art. The charter of this college, which dates some five or six years back, expressly provides for the establishment of schools in connection with it ; and I may venture to add that this feature of the scheme, when it was explained to him, was specially interesting to his Royal Highness the late Prince Consort, who hailed it as evidence of the desire of the promoters to look forward as well as to look back ; to found educational institutions for the rising generation, as well as to establish a harbor of refuge for the generation going out, or at least having their faces turned towards the setting sun. The leading members of the dramatic art, applying themselves first to the more pressing necessity of the two, set themselves to work on the construction of their harbor of refuge, and this they did with the zeal, energy, good-will, and good faith that always honorably distinguish them in their efforts to help one another. Those efforts were very powerfully aided by the respected gentleman* under whose roof we are assembled, and who, I hope, may be only half as glad of seeing me on these boards as I always am to see him here. With such energy and determination did Mr. Webster and his brothers and sisters in art proceed with their work, that at this present time all the dwelling-houses of the Royal Dramatic College are built, completely furnished, fitted with every appliance, and many of them inhabited. The central hall of the College is built, the grounds are beautifully planned and laid out, and the estate has become the nucleus of a prosperous neighborhood. This much achieved, Mr. Webster was revolving in his mind how he should next proceed towards the establishment of the schools, when, this tercentenary celebration being in hand, it occurred to him to represent to the National Shakspeare Committee their just and reasonable claim to participate in the results of any subscription for a monument to Shakspeare. He represented to the committee that the social recognition and elevation of the followers of Shakspeare's own art, through the education of their children, was surely a monument worthy even of that great name. He urged upon the committee that it was certainly a sensible, tangible project, which the public good sense would immediately appreciate and approve. This claim the committee at once acknowledged; but I wish you distinctly to understand that if the committee had never been in existence, if the tercentenary celebration had never been attempted, those schools, as a design anterior to both, would still have solicited public support.

Now, ladies and gentlemen, what it is proposed to do is, in fact, to found a new self-supporting public school; with this additional feature, that it is to be available for both sexes. This, of course, presupposes two separate distinct schools. As these schools are to be built on land belonging to the Dramatic College, there will be from the first no charge, no debt, no incumbrance of any kind under that important head. It is, in short, proposed simply to

establish a new self-supporting public school, in a rapidly increasing neighborhood, where there is a large and fast accumulating middle-class population, and where property in land is fast rising in value. But, inasmuch as the project is a project of the Royal Dramatic College, and inasmuch as the schools are to be built on their estate, it is proposed evermore to give their school the great name of Shakspeare, and evermore to give the followers of Shakspeare's art a prominent place in them. With this view, it is confidently believed that the public will endow a foundation, say, for forty foundation scholars —say, twenty girls and twenty boys—who shall always receive their education gratuitously, and who shall always be the children of actors, actresses, or dramatic writers. This school, you will understand, is to be equal to the best existing public school. It is to be made to impart a sound, liberal, comprehensive education, and it is to address the whole great middle class at least as freely, as widely, and as cheaply as any existing public school.

Broadly, ladies and gentleman, this is the whole design. There are foundation scholars at Eton, foundation scholars at nearly all our old schools, and if the public, in remembrance of a noble part of our standard national literature, and in remembrance of a great humanizing art, will do this thing for these children, it will at the same time be doing a wise and good thing for itself, and will unquestionably find its account in it. Taking this view of the case—and I can not be satisfied to take any lower one—I can not make a sorry face about "the poor player." I think it is a term very much misused and very little understood—being, I venture to say, appropriated in a wrong sense by players themselves. Therefore, ladies and gentlemen, I can only present the player to you exceptionally in this wise—that he follows a peculiar and precarious vocation, a vocation very rarely affording the means of accumulating money—that that vocation must, from the nature of things, have in it many undistinguished men and women to one distinguished one—that it is not a vocation the exerciser of which can profit by the labors of others, but in which he must earn every loaf of his bread in his own person, with the aid of his own face, his own limbs, his own voice, his own memory, and his own life and spirits; and these failing, he fails. Surely this is reason enough to render him some little help in opening for his children their paths through life. I say their paths advisedly, because it is not often found, except under the pressure of necessity, or where there is strong hereditary talent—which is always an exceptional case—that the children of actors and actresses take to the stage. Persons, therefore, need not in the least fear that by helping to endow these schools they would help to overstock the dramatic market. They would do directly the reverse, for they would divert into channels of public distinction and usefulness those good qualities which would otherwise languish in that market's over-rich superabundance.

This project has received the support of the head of the most popular of our English public schools. On the committee stands the name of that eminent scholar and gentleman, the Provost of Eton. You justly admire this liberal spirit, and your admiration—which I cordially share—brings me naturally to what I wish to say, that I believe there is not in England any institution so socially liberal as a public school. It has been called a little cosmos of life outside, and I think it is so, with the exception of one of life's worst foibles—for, as far as I know, nowhere in this country is there so complete an absence of servility to mere rank, to mere position, to mere riches, as in a public school. A boy there is always what his abilities or his personal qualities make him. We may differ about the curriculum and other matters, but of the frank, free, manly, independent spirit preserved in our public schools, I apprehend there can be no kind of question. It has happened in these later times that objection has been made to children of dramatic artists in certain little snivelling private schools—but in public schools never. Therefore, I hold that the actors are wise, and gratefully wise, in recognizing the capacious liberality of a public school, in seeking not a little hole-and-corner place of education for their children exclusively, but in addressing the whole of the great middle class, and proposing to them to come and join them, the actors, on their own property, in a public school, in a part of the country where no such advantage is now to be found.

I have now done. The attempt has been a very timid one. I have endeavored to confine myself within my means, or, rather like the possessor of an extended estate, to hand it down in an unembarrassed condition. I have laid a trifle of timber here and there, and grubbed up a little brushwood, but merely to open the view, and I think I can descry in the eye of the gentleman who is to move the first resolution that he distinctly sees his way. Thanking you for the courtesy with which you have heard me, and not at all doubting that we shall lay a strong foundation of these schools to-day, I will call, as the mover of the first resolution, on Mr. Robert Bell.

XXVIII.

LONDON, MAY 9, 1865.

[On the above date Mr. Dickens presided at the Annual Festival of the News-venders' Benevolent Association, and, in proposing the toast of the evening, delivered the following speech :]

LADIES AND GENTLEMEN,—Dr. Johnson's experience of that club, the members of which have travelled over one another's minds in every direction, is not to be compared with the experience of the perpetual president of a society like this. Having on the previous occasion said every thing about it that he could possibly find to say, he is again produced, with the same awful formalities, to say every thing about it that he can not possibly find to say. It struck me, when Dr. F. Jones was referring just now to Easter Monday, that the case of such an ill-starred president is very like that of the stag at Epping Forest on Easter Monday. That unfortunate animal, when he is uncarted at the spot where the meet takes place, generally makes a point, I am told, of making away at a cool trot, venturesomely followed by the whole field, to the yard where he lives, and there subsides into a quiet and inoffensive existence, until he is again brought out to be again followed by exactly the same field, under exactly the same circumstances, next Easter Monday.

The difficulties of the situation—and here I mean the president, and not the stag—are greatly increased in such an instance as this by the peculiar nature of the institution. In its unpretending solidity, reality, and usefulness, believe me—for I have carefully considered the point—it presents no opening whatever of an oratorical nature. If it were one of those costly charities, so-called, whose yield of wool bears no sort of proportion to their cry for cash, I very likely might have a word or two to say on the subject. If its funds were lavished in patronage and show, instead of being honestly expended in providing small annuities for hard-working people who have themselves contributed to its funds—if its management were intrusted to people who could by no possibility know any thing about it, instead of being invested in plain, business, practical hands—if it hoarded when it ought to spend—if it got by cringing and fawning what it never deserved, I might possibly impress you very much by my indignation. If its managers could tell me that it was insolvent, that it was in a hopeless condition, that its accounts had been kept by Mr. Edmunds—or by "Tom,"—if its treasurer had run away with the money-box, then I might have made a pathetic appeal to your feelings. But I have no such chance. Just as a nation is happy whose records are barren, so is a society fortunate that has no history—and its president unfortunate. I can only assure you that this society continues its plain, unobtrusive, useful career. I can only assure you that it does a great deal of good at a very small cost, and that the objects of its care and the bulk of its members are faithful working servants of the public—sole ministers of their wants at untimely hours, in all seasons, and in all weathers; at their own doors, at the street corners, at every railway train, at every steamboat; through the agency of every establishment and the tiniest little shops; and that, whether regarded as master or as man, their profits are very modest and their risks numerous, while their trouble and responsibility are very great.

The news-venders and newsmen are a very subordinate part of that wonderful engine—the newspaper press. Still I think we all know very well that they are to the fountain-head what a good service of water-pipes is to a good water supply. Just as a goodly store of water at Watford would be a tantalization to thirsty London if it were not brought into town for its use, so any amount of news accumulated at Printing-house Square, or Fleet Street, or the Strand, would be if there were no skill and enterprise engaged in its dissemination.

We are all of us in the habit of saying in our every-day life, that "We never know the value of any thing until we lose it." Let us try the news-venders by the test. A few days ago we discovered one morning that there was a strike among the cab-drivers. Now, let us imagine a strike of newsmen. Imagine the trains waiting in vain for the newspapers. Imagine all sorts and conditions of men dying to know the shipping news, the commercial news, the foreign news, the legal news, the criminal news, the dramatic news. Imagine the paralysis on all the provincial exchanges; the silence and desertion of all the newsmen's exchanges in London. Imagine the circulation of the blood of the nation and of the country standing still—the clock of the world. Why, even Mr. Reuter, the great Reuter — whom I am always glad to imagine slumbering at night by the side of Mrs. Reuter, with a galvanic battery under his bolster, bell and wires to the head of his bed, and bells at each ear—think how even he would click and flash those wondrous dispatches of his, and how they would become mere nothing without the activity and honesty which catch up the threads and stitches of the electric needle, and scatter them over the land.

It is curious to consider—and the thought occurred to me this day, when I was out for a stroll pondering over the duties of this evening, which even then were looming in the distance, but not quite so far off as I could wish — I found it very curious to consider that though the newsman must be allowed to be a very unpicturesque rendering of Mercury, or Fame, or what-not conventional messenger from the clouds, and although we must allow that he is of this earth, and has a good deal of it on his boots, still that he has two very remarkable characteristics, to which none of his celestial predecessors can lay the slightest claim. One is that he is always the messenger of civilization; the other that he is at least equally so, not only in what he brings, but in what he ceases to bring. Thus the time was, and not so many years ago either, when the newsman constantly brought home to our doors—though I am afraid not to our hearts, which were custom-hardened — the most terrific accounts of murders, of our fellow-creatures being publicly put to death for what we now call trivial offenses, in the very heart of London, regularly every Monday morning. At the same time the newsman regularly brought to us the infliction of other punishments, which were demoralizing to the innocent part of the community, while they did not operate as punishments in deterring offenders from the perpetration of crimes. In those same days, also, the newsman brought to us daily accounts of a regularly accepted and received system of loading the unfortunate insane with chains, littering them down on straw, starving them on bread and water, damaging their clothes, and making periodical exhibitions of them at a small charge; and that on a Sunday one of our public resorts was a kind of demoniacal zoological gardens. They brought us accounts at the same time of some damage done to the machinery which was destined to supply the operative classes with employment. In the same time they brought us accounts of riots for bread, which were constantly occurring, and undermining society and the state: of the most terrible explosions of class against class, and of the habitual employment of spies for the discovery—if not for the origination—of plots, in which both sides found in those days some relief. In the same time the same newsmen were apprising us of a state of society all around us in which the grossest sensuality and intemperance were the rule; and not as now, when the ignorant, the wicked, and the wretched are the inexcusably vicious exceptions—a state of society in which the professional bully was rampant, and when deadly duels were daily fought for the most absurd and disgraceful causes. All this the newsman has ceased to tell us of. This state of society has discontinued in England forever; and when we remember the undoubted truth, that the change could never have been effected without the aid of the load which the newsman carries, surely it is not very romantic to express the hope on his behalf that the public will show to him some little token of the sympathetic remembrance which we are all of us glad to bestow on the bearers of happy tidings — the harbingers of good news.

Now, ladies and gentlemen, you will be glad to hear that I am coming to a conclusion; for that conclusion I have a precedent. You all of you know how pleased you are, on your return from a morning's walk, to learn that the collector has called. Well, I am the collector for this district, and I hope you will bear in mind that I have respectfully called. Regarding the institution on whose behalf I have presented myself, I need only say technically two things. First, that its annuities are granted out of its funded capital, and therefore it is safe as the bank; and, secondly, that they are attainable by such a slight exercise of prudence and forethought, that a payment of 25s. extending over a period of five years, entitles a subscriber—if a male—to an annuity of £16 a year, and a female to £12 a year. Now, bear in mind that this is an institution on behalf of which the collector has called, leaving behind his assurance that what you can give to one of the most faithful of your servants shall be well bestowed and faithfully applied to the purposes to which you intend them, and to those purposes alone.

~~~~~~~~~

XXIX.

NEWSPAPER PRESS FUND.

LONDON, MAY 20, 1865.

[At the second annual dinner of the Institution, held at the Freemason's Tavern, on Saturday, the 20th May, 1865, the following speech was delivered by the chairman, Mr. Charles Dickens, in proposing the toast of the evening:]

LADIES AND GENTLEMEN,—When a young child is produced after dinner to be shown to a circle of admiring relations and friends, it may generally be observed that their conversation—I suppose in an instinctive remembrance of the uncertainty of infant life—takes a retrospective turn. As how much the child has grown since the last dinner; what a remarkably fine child it is, to have been born only two or three years ago; how much stronger it looks now than before it had the measles, and so forth. When a young institution is produced after dinner, there

is not the same uncertainty or delicacy as in the case of the child, and it may be confidently predicted of it that if it deserve to live it will surely live, and that if it deserve to die it will surely die. The proof of desert in such a case as this must be mainly sought, I suppose, firstly, in what the society means to do with its money; secondly, in the extent to which it is supported by the class with whom it originated and for whose benefit it is designed; and, lastly, in the power of its hold upon the public. I add this lastly, because no such institution, that ever I heard of, ever yet dreamed of existing apart from the public, or ever yet considered it a degradation to accept the public support.

Now, what the Newspaper Press Fund proposes to do with its money is to grant relief to members in want or distress, and to the widows, families, parents, or other near relatives of deceased members in right of a moderate provident annual subscription—commutable, I observe, for a moderate provident life subscription—and its members comprise the whole paid class of literary contributors to the press of the United Kingdom, and every class of reporters. The number of its members at this time last year was something below 100. At the present time it is somewhat above 170, not including 30 members of the press who are regular subscribers, but have not as yet qualified as regular members. This number is steadily on the increase, not only as regards the metropolitan press, but also as regards the provincial throughout the country. I have observed within these few days that many members of the press at Manchester have lately at a meeting expressed a strong brotherly interest in this Institution, and a great desire to extend its operations and to strengthen its hands, provided that something in the independent nature of life assurance and the purchase of deferred annuities could be introduced into its details, and always assuming that in it the metropolis and the provinces stand on perfectly equal ground. This appears to me to be a demand so very moderate, that I can hardly have a doubt of a response on the part of the managers, or of the beneficial and harmonious results. It only remains to add, on this head of desert, the agreeable circumstance that out of all the money collected in aid of the society during the last year more than one-third came exclusively from the press.

Now, ladies and gentlemen, in regard to the last claim—the last point of desert—the hold upon the public—I think I may say that probably not one single individual in this great company has failed to-day to see a newspaper, or has failed to-day to hear something derived from a newspaper which was quite unknown to him or to her yesterday. Of all those restless crowds that have this day thronged the streets of this enormous city, the same may be said as the general gigantic rule. It may be said almost equally of the brightest and the dullest, the largest and the least provincial town in the empire; and this, observe, not only as to the active, the industrious, and the healthy among the population, but also to the bedridden, the idle, the blind, and the deaf and dumb. Now, if the men who provide this all-pervading presence, this wonderful, ubiquitous newspaper, with every description of intelligence on every subject of human interest, collected with immense pains and immense patience, often by the exercise of a laboriously-acquired faculty united to a natural aptitude, much of the work done in the night, at the sacrifice of rest and sleep, and (quite apart from the mental strain) by the constant overtasking of the two most delicate of the senses, sight and hearing—I say, if the men who, through the newspapers, from day to day, or from night to night, or from week to week, furnish the public with so much to remember, have not a righteous claim to be remembered by the public in return, then I declare before God I know no working class of the community who have.

It would be absurd, it would be impertinent, in such an assembly as this, if I were to attempt to expatiate upon the extraordinary combination of remarkable qualities involved in the production of any newspaper. But assuming the majority of this associated body to be composed of reporters—because reporters, of one kind or other, compose the majority of the literary staff of almost every newspaper that is not a compilation—I would venture to remind you, if I delicately may, in the august presence of members of Parliament, how much we, the public, owe to the reporters, if it were only for their skill in the two great sciences of condensation and rejection. Conceive what our sufferings, under an Imperial Parliament, however popularly constituted, under however glorious a constitution, would be if the reporters could not skip. Dr. Johnson, in one of his violent assertions, declared that "the man who was afraid of any thing must be a scoundrel, sir." By no means binding myself to this opinion—though admitting that the man who is afraid of a newspaper will generally be found to be rather something like it, I must still freely own that I should approach my Parliamentary debate with infinite fear and trembling if it were so unskillfully served up for my breakfast. Ever since the time when the old man and his son took their

donkey home, which were the old Greek days, I believe, and probably ever since the time when the donkey went into the ark—perhaps he did not like his accommodation there—but certainly from that time downwards, he has objected to go in any direction required of him—from the remotest periods it has been found impossible to please every body.

I do not for a moment seek to conceal that I know this institution has been objected to. As an open fact challenging the freest discussion and inquiry, and seeking no sort of shelter or favor but what it can win, it has nothing, I apprehend, but itself, to urge against objection. No institution conceived in perfect honesty and good faith has a right to object to being questioned to any extent, and any institution so based must be in the end the better for it. Moreover, that this society has been questioned in quarters deserving of the most respectful attention I take to be an indisputable fact. Now, I for one have given that respectful attention, and I have come out of the discussion to where you see me. The whole circle of the arts is pervaded by institutions between which and this I can descry no difference. The painters' art has four or five such institutions. The musicians' art, so generously and charmingly represented here, has likewise several such institutions. In my own art there is one, concerning the details of which my noble friend, the president of the society, and myself have torn each other's hair to a considerable extent, and which I would, if I could, assimilate more nearly to this. In the dramatic art there are four, and I never yet heard of any objection to their principle, except, indeed, in the cases of some famous actors of large gains who, having through the whole period of their successes positively refused to establish a right in them, became, in their old age and decline, repentant suppliants for their bounty. Is it urged against this particular institution that it is objectionable because a parliamentary reporter, for instance, might report a subscribing M.P. in large, and a non-subscribing M.P. in little? Apart from the sweeping nature of this charge, which, it is to be observed, lays the unfortunate member and the unfortunate reporter under pretty much the same suspicion —apart from this consideration, I reply that it is notorious in all newspaper offices that every such man is reported according to the position he can gain in the public eye, and according to the force and weight of what he has to say. And if there were ever to be among the members of this society one so very foolish to his brethren, and so very dishonorable to himself, as venally to abuse his trust, I confidently ask those here, the best acquainted with journalism, whether they believe it possible that any newspaper so ill-conducted as to fail instantly to detect him could possibly exist as a thriving enterprise for one single twelvemonth? No, ladies and gentlemen, the blundering stupidity of such an offense would have no chance against the acute sagacity of newspaper editors. But I will go farther, and submit to you that its commission, if it be to be dreaded at all, is far more likely on the part of some recreant camp-follower of a scattered, disunited, and half-recognized profession, than when there is a public opinion established in it, by the union of all classes of its members for the common good: the tendency of which union must, in the nature of things, be to raise the lower members of the press towards the higher, and never to bring the higher members to the lower level.

I hope I may be allowed, in the very few closing words that I feel a desire to say in remembrance of some circumstances, rather special, attending my present occupation of this chair, to give those words something of a personal tone. I am not here advocating the case of a mere ordinary client of whom I have little or no knowledge. I hold a brief to-night for my brothers. I went into the gallery of the House of Commons as a parliamentary reporter when I was a boy not eighteen, and I left it—I can hardly believe the inexorable truth—nigh thirty years ago. I have pursued the calling of a reporter under circumstances of which many of my brethren at home in England here, many of my modern successors, can form no adequate conception. I have often transcribed for the printer, from my short-hand notes, important public speeches in which the strictest accuracy was required, and a mistake in which would have been to a young man severely compromising, writing on the palm of my hand, by the light of a dark lantern, in a post-chaise and four, galloping through a wild country, and through the dead of the night, at the then surprising rate of fifteen miles an hour. The very last time I was at Exeter, I strolled into the castle yard there to identify, for the amusement of a friend, the spot on which I once " took," as we used to call it, an election speech of my noble friend Lord Russell, in the midst of a lively fight maintained by all the vagabonds in that division of the county, and under such a pelting rain, that I remember two good-natured colleagues, who chanced to be at leisure, held a pocket-handkerchief over my note-book, after the manner of a state canopy in an ecclesiastic-al procession. I have worn my knees by writing on them on the old back row of the old gallery of the old House of Commons; and I have worn my feet by standing to write in a preposterous pen in the old House of Lords, where we used to be huddled together like so many sheep—kept in waiting, say, until the woolsack might want re-stuffing. Returning home from excited political meetings in the country to the waiting press in London, I do verily believe I have been upset in almost every description of vehicle known in this country. I have been, in my time, belated on miry by-roads, towards the small hours, forty or fifty miles from London, in a wheelless carriage, with exhausted horses and drunken post-boys, and have got back in time for publication, to be received with never-forgotten compliments by the late Mr. Black, coming in the broadest of Scotch from the broadest of hearts I ever knew.

Ladies and gentlemen, I mention these trivial things as an assurance to you that I never have forgotten the fascination of that old pursuit. The pleasure that I used to feel in the rapidity and dexterity of its exercise has never faded out of my breast. Whatever little cunning of hand or head I took to it, or acquired in it, I have so retained as that I fully believe I could resume it to-morrow, very little the worse from long disuse. To this present year of my life, when I sit in this hall, or where not, hearing a dull speech—the phenomenon does occur—I sometimes beguile the tedium of the moment by mentally following the speaker in the old, old way; and sometimes, if you can believe me, I even find my hand going on the table-cloth, taking an imaginary note of it all. Accept these little truths as a confirmation of what I know; as a confirmation of my undying interest in this old calling. Accept them as a proof that my feeling for the vocation of my youth is not a sentiment taken up to-night to be thrown away to-morrow—but is a faithful sympathy which is a part of myself. I verily believe—I am sure—that if I had never quitted my old calling I should have been foremost and zealous in the interests of this Institution, believing it to be a sound, a wholesome, and a good one. Ladies and gentlemen, I am to propose to you to drink " Prosperity to the Newspaper Press Fund," with which toast I will connect, as to its acknowledgment, a name that has shed new brilliancy on even the foremost newspaper in the world—the illustrious name of Mr. Russell.

XXX.

KNEBWORTH, JULY 29, 1865.

[On the above date the members of the "Guild of Literature and Art" proceeded to the neighborhood of Stevenage, near the magnificent seat of the President, Lord Lytton, to inspect three houses built in the Gothic style, on the ground given him for the purpose. After their survey, the party drove to Knebworth to partake of the hospitality of Lord Lytton. Mr. Dickens, who was one of the guests, proposed the health of the host in the following words:]

LADIES AND GENTLEMEN,—It was said by a very sagacious person, whose authority I am sure my friend of many years will not impugn, seeing that he was named Augustus Tomlinson, the kind friend and philosopher of Paul Clifford —it was said by that remarkable man, "Life is short, and why should speeches be long?" An aphorism so sensible under all circumstances, and particularly in the circumstances in which we are placed, with this delicious weather and such charming gardens near us, I shall practically adopt on the present occasion; and the rather so because the speech of my friend was exhaustive of the subject, as his speeches always are, though not in the least exhaustive of his audience. In thanking him for the toast which he has done us the honor to propose, allow me to correct an error into which he has fallen. Allow me to state that these houses never could have been built but for his zealous and valuable co-operation, and also that the pleasant labor out of which they have arisen would have lost one of its greatest charms and strongest impulses, if it had lost his ever-ready sympathy with that class in which he has risen to the foremost rank, and of which he is the brightest ornament.

Having said this much as simply due to my friend, I can only say, on behalf of my associates, that the ladies and gentlemen whom we shall invite to occupy the houses we have built will never be placed under any social disadvantage. They will be invited to occupy them as artists, receiving them as a mark of the high respect in which they are held by their fellow-workers. As artists I hope they will often exercise their calling within those walls for the general advantage; and they will always claim, on equal terms, the hospitality of their generous neighbor.

Now I am sure I shall be giving utterance to the feelings of my brothers and sisters in literature in proposing "Health, long life, and prosperity to our distinguished host." Ladies and gentlemen, you know very well that when the health, life, and beauty now overflowing these halls shall have fled, crowds of people will come to see the place where he lived and wrote. Setting aside the orator and statesman—for happily we know no party here but this agreeable party—setting aside all, this you know very well, that this is the home of a very great man whose connection with Hertfordshire every other county in England will envy for many long years to come. You know that when this hall is dullest and emptiest, you can make it, when you please, brightest and fullest by peopling it with the creations of his brilliant fancy. Let us all wish together that they may be many more— for the more they are the better it will be, and, as he always excels himself, the better they will be. I ask you to listen to their praises and not to mine, and to let them, not me, propose his health.

XXXI.

LONDON, FEBRUARY 14, 1866.

[On this occasion Mr. Dickens officiated as Chairman at the annual dinner of the Dramatic, Equestrian, and Musical Fund, at Willis's Rooms, where he made the following speech:]

LADIES,—Before I couple you with the gentlemen, which will be at least proper to the inscription over my head (St. Valentine's Day)— before I do so, allow me, on behalf of my grateful sex here represented, to thank you for the great pleasure and interest with which your gracious presence at these festivals never fails to inspire us. There is no English custom which is so manifestly a relic of savage life as that custom which usually excludes you from participation in similar gatherings. And although the crime carries its own heavy punishment along with it, in respect that it divests a public dinner of its most beautiful ornament and of its most fascinating charm, still the offense is none the less to be severely reprehended on every possible occasion, as outraging equally nature and art. I believe that as little is known of the saint whose name is written here as can well be known of any saint or sinner. We, your loyal servants, are deeply thankful to him for having somehow gained possession of one day in the year—for having, as no doubt he has, arranged the almanac for 1866— expressly to delight us with the enchanting fiction that we have some tender proprietorship in you which we should scarcely dare to claim on a less auspicious occasion. Ladies, the utmost devotion sanctioned by the saint we beg to lay at your feet, and any little innocent privileges to which we may be entitled by the same authority we beg respectfully but firmly to claim at your hands.

Now, ladies and gentlemen, you need no

ghost to inform you that I am going to propose "Prosperity to the Dramatic, Musical, and Equestrian Sick Fund Association," and, further, that I should be going to ask you actively to promote that prosperity by liberally contributing to its funds, if that task were not reserved for a much more persuasive speaker. But I rest the strong claim of the society for its useful existence and its truly charitable functions on a very few words, though, as well as I can recollect, upon something like six grounds. First, it relieves the sick; secondly, it buries the dead; thirdly, it enables the poor members of the profession to journey to accept new engagements whenever they find themselves stranded in some remote, inhospitable place, or when, from other circumstances, they find themselves perfectly crippled as to locomotion for want of money; fourthly, it often finds such engagements for them by acting as their honest, disinterested agent; fifthly, it is its principle to act humanely upon the instant, and never, as is too often the case within my experience, to beat about the bush till the bush is withered and dead; lastly, the society is not in the least degree exclusive, but takes under its comprehensive care the whole range of the theatre and the concert-room, from the manager in his room of state, or in his caravan, or at the drum-head—down to the theatrical housekeeper, who is usually to be found amongst the cobwebs and the flies, or down to the hall porter, who passes his life in a thorough draught, and, to the best of my observation, in perpetually interrupted endeavors to eat something with a knife and fork out of a basin, by a dusty fire, in that extraordinary little gritty room, upon which the sun never shines, and on the portals of which are inscribed the magic words, "Stage-door."

Now, ladies and gentlemen, this society administers its benefits sometimes by way of loan; sometimes by way of gift; sometimes by way of assurance at very low premiums; sometimes to members, oftener to non-members; always expressly, remember, through the hands of a secretary or committee well acquainted with the wants of the applicants, and thoroughly versed, if not by hard experience, at least by sympathy, in the calamities and uncertainties incidental to the general calling. One must know something of the general calling to know what those afflictions are. A lady who had been upon the stage from her earliest childhood till she was a blooming woman, and who came from a long line of provincial actors and actresses, once said to me when she was happily married; when she was rich, beloved, courted; when she was mistress of a fine house—once

said to me at the head of her own table, surrounded by distinguished guests of every degree, "Oh, but I have never forgotten the hard time when I was on the stage, and when my baby brother died, and when my poor mother and I brought the little baby from Ireland to England, and acted three nights in England, as we had acted three nights in Ireland, with the pretty creature lying upon the only bed in our lodging before we got the money to pay for its funeral."

Ladies and gentlemen, such things are, every day, to this hour; but, happily, at this day and in this hour this association has arisen to be the timely friend of such great distress.

It is not often the fault of the sufferers that they fall into these straits. Struggling artists must necessarily change from place to place, and thus it frequently happens that they become, as it were, strangers in every place, and very slight circumstances—a passing illness, the sickness of the husband, wife, or child, a serious town, an anathematizing expounder of the gospel of gentleness and forbearance—any one of these causes may often in a few hours wreck them upon a rock in the barren ocean; and then, happily, this society, with the swift alacrity of the life-boat, dashes to the rescue and takes them off. Looking just now over the last report issued by this society, and confining my scrutiny to the head of illness alone, I find that in one year, I think, 672 days of sickness had been assuaged by its means. In nine years, which then formed the term of its existence, as many as 5500 and odd. Well, I thought when I saw 5500 and odd days of sickness, this is a very serious sum, but add the nights! Add the nights—those long, dreary hours in the twenty-four when the shadow of death is darkest, when despondency is strongest, and when hope is weakest, before you gauge the good that is done by this institution, and before you gauge the good that really will be done by every shilling that you bestow here to-night. Add, more than all, that the improvidence, the recklessness of the general multitude of poor members of this profession, I should say, is a cruel, conventional fable. Add that there is no class of society the members of which so well help themselves, or so well help each other. Not in the whole grand chapters of Westminster Abbey and York Minster, not in the whole quadrangle of the Royal Exchange, not in the whole list of members of the Stock Exchange, not in the Inns of Court, not in the College of Physicians, not in the College of Surgeons, can there possibly be found more remarkable instances of uncomplaining poverty, of cheerful, constant self-denial, of the generous remembrance of the claims of kindred and professional brotherhood, than will certainly be found in the dingiest and dirtiest concert-room, in the least lucid theatre —even in the raggedest tent circus that was ever stained by weather.

I have been twitted in print before now with rather flattering actors when I address them as one of their trustees at their General Fund dinner. Believe me, I flatter nobody, unless it be sometimes myself; but in such a company as the present I always feel it my manful duty to bear my testimony to this fact—first, because it is opposed to a stupid, unfeeling libel; secondly, because my doing so may afford some slight encouragement to the persons who are unjustly depreciated; and lastly, and most of all, because I know it is the truth.

Now, ladies and gentlemen, it is time we should what we professionally call "ring down" on these remarks. If you, such members of the general public as are here, will only think the great theatrical curtain has really fallen and been taken up again for the night on that dull, dark vault which many of us know so well; if you will only think of the theatre or other place of entertainment as empty; if you will only think of the "float," or other gas-fittings, as extinguished; if you will only think of the people who have beguiled you of an evening's care, whose little vanities and almost childish foibles are engendered in their competing face to face with you for your favor—surely it may be said their feelings are partly of your making, while their virtues are all their own. If you will only do this, and follow them out of that sham place into the real world, where it rains real rain, snows real snow, and blows real wind; where people sustain themselves by real money, which is much harder to get, much harder to make, and very much harder to give away than the pieces of tobacco-pipe in property-bags—if you will only do this, and do it in a really kind, considerate spirit, this society, then certain of the result of the night's proceedings, can ask no more. I beg to propose to you to drink "Prosperity to the Dramatic, Equestrian, and Musical Sick Fund Association."

[Mr. Dickens, in proposing the next toast, said:]

Gentlemen, as I addressed myself to the ladies last time, so I address you this time, and I give you the delightful assurance that it is positively my last appearance but one on the present occasion. A certain Mr. Pepys, who was Secretary for the Admiralty in the days of Charles II., who kept a diary well in short-hand, which he supposed no one could read, and which consequently remains to this day the most honest diary known to print—Mr. Pepys had two special and very strong likings, the ladies and the theatres. But Mr. Pepys, whenever he committed any slight act of remissness, or any little peccadillo which was utterly and wholly untheatrical, used to comfort his conscience by recording a vow that he would abstain from the theatres for a certain time. In the first part of Mr. Pepys's character I have no doubt we fully agree with him; in the second I have no doubt we do not.

I learn this experience of Mr. Pepys from remembrance of a passage in his diary that I was reading the other night, from which it appears that he was not only curious in plays, but curious in sermons; and that one night when he happened to be walking past St. Dunstan's Church, he turned, went in, and heard what he calls "a very edifying discourse;" during the delivery of which discourse, he notes in his diary —"I stood by a pretty young maid, whom I did attempt to take by the hand." But he adds— "She would not; and I did perceive that she had pins in her pocket with which to prick me if I should touch her again, and was glad that I spied her design." Afterwards, about the close of the same edifying discourse, Mr. Pepys found himself near another pretty, fair young maid, who would seem, upon the whole, to have had no pins, and to have been more impressible.

Now the moral of this story which I wish to suggest to you is, that we have been this evening in St. James's much more timid than Mr. Pepys was in St. Dunstan's, and that we have conducted ourselves very much better. As a slight recompense to us for our highly meritorious conduct, and as a little relief to our overcharged hearts, I beg to propose that we devote this bumper to invoking a blessing on the ladies. It is the privilege of this society annually to hear a lady speak for her own sex. Who so competent to do this as Mrs. Stirling? Surely one who has so gracefully and captivatingly, with such an exquisite mixture of art, and fancy, and fidelity, represented her own sex in innumerable charities, under an infinite variety of phases, can not fail to represent them well in her own character, especially when it is, amidst her many triumphs, the most agreeable of all. I beg to propose to you "The Ladies," and I will couple with that toast the name of Mrs. Stirling.

XXXII.

LONDON, MARCH 28, 1866.

[The following speech was made by Mr. Dickens at the Annual Festival of the Royal General Theatrical Fund, held at the Freemasons' Tavern, in proposing the health of the Lord Mayor (Sir Benjamin Phillips), who occupied the Chair:]

GENTLEMEN,—In my childish days I remember to have had a vague but profound admiration for a certain legendary person called the Lord Mayor's fool. I had the highest opinion of the intellectual capacity of that supposititious retainer of the Mansion House, and I really regarded him with feelings approaching to absolute veneration, because my nurse informed me on every gastronomic occasion that the Lord Mayor's fool liked every thing that was good. You will agree with me, I have no doubt, that if this discriminating jester had existed at the present time he could not fail to have liked his master very much, seeing that so good a Lord Mayor is very rarely to be found, and that a better Lord Mayor could not possibly be.

You have already divined, gentlemen, that I am about to propose to you to drink the health of the right honorable gentleman in the chair. As one of the Trustees of the General Theatrical Fund, I beg officially to tender him my best thanks for lending the very powerful aid of his presence, his influence, and his personal character to this very deserving institution. As his private friends, we ventured to urge upon him to do us this gracious act, and I beg to assure you that the perfect simplicity, modesty, cordiality, and frankness with which he assented, enhanced the gift one thousand fold. I think it must also be very agreeable to a company like this to know that the President of the night is not ceremoniously pretending, "positively for this night only," to have an interest in the drama, but that he has an unusual and thorough acquaintance with it, and that he has a living and discerning knowledge of the merits of the great old actors. It is very pleasant to me to remember that the Lord Mayor and I once beguiled the tedium of a journey by exchanging our experiences upon this subject. I rather prided myself on being something of an old stager, but I found the Lord Mayor so thoroughly up in all the stock pieces, and so knowing and yet so fresh about the merits of those who are most and best identified with them, that I readily recognized in him what would be called in fistic language a very ugly customer—one, I assure you, by no means to be settled by any novice not in thorough good theatrical training.

liest infancy that when the giants in Guildhall hear the clock strike one, they come down to dinner. Similarly, when the City of London shall hear but one single word in just disparagement of its present Lord Mayor, whether as its enlightened chief magistrate, or as one of its merchants, or as one of its true gentlemen, he will then descend from the high personal place which he holds in the general honor and esteem. Until then he will remain upon his pedestal, and my private opinion, between ourselves, is, that the giants will come down long before him.

Gentlemen, in conclusion, I would remark that when the Lord Mayor made his truly remarkable, and truly manly and unaffected speech, I could not but be struck by the odd reversal of the usual circumstances at the Mansion House, which he presented to our view; for whereas it is a very common thing for persons to be brought tremblingly before the Lord Mayor, the Lord Mayor presented himself as being brought tremblingly before us. I hope that the result may hold still further; for whereas it is a common thing for the Lord Mayor to say to a repentant criminal who does not seem to have much harm in him, "Let me never see you here again," so I would propose that we all with one accord say to the Lord Mayor, "Let us by all means see you here again on the first opportunity." Gentlemen, I beg to propose to you to drink, with all the honors, "The health of the right honorable the Lord Mayor."

~~~~~~~

XXXIII.

LONDON, MAY 7, 1866.

[The Members of the Metropolitan Rowing-clubs dining together at the London Tavern, on the above date, Mr. Dickens, as President of the Nautilus Rowing-club, occupied the Chair. The Speech that follows was made in proposing "Prosperity to the Rowing-clubs of London." Mr. Dickens said that:]

HE could not avoid the remembrance of what very poor things the amateur rowing-clubs on the Thames were in the early days of his noviate; not to mention the difference in the build of the boats. He could not get on in the beginning without being a pupil under an anomalous creature called a "fireman waterman," who wore an eminently tall hat, and a perfectly unaccountable uniform, of which it might be said that if it was less adapted for one thing than another, that thing was fire. He recollected that this gentleman had on some former day won a King's prize wherry,

wherry, he and a partner doing all the hard work, while the fireman drank all the beer. The river was very much clearer, freer, and cleaner in those days than these; but he was persuaded that this philosophical old boatman could no more have dreamt of seeing the spectacle which had taken place on Saturday (the procession of the boats of the Metropolitan Amateur Rowing-clubs), or of seeing these clubs matched for skill and speed, than he (the Chairman) should dare to announce through the usual authentic channels that he was to be heard of at the bar below, and that he was perfectly prepared to accommodate Mr. James Mace if he meant business. Nevertheless, he could recollect that he had turned out for a spurt a few years ago on the River Thames with an occasional Secretary, who should be nameless, and some other Eton boys, and that he could hold his own against them. More recently still, the last time that he rowed down from Oxford he was supposed to cover himself with honor, though he must admit that he found the "locks" so picturesque as to require much examination for the discovery of their beauty. But what he wanted to say was this, that though his "fireman waterman" was one of the greatest humbugs that ever existed, he yet taught him what an honest, healthy, manly sport this was. Their waterman would bid them pull away, and assure them that they were certain of winning in some race. And here he would remark that aquatic sports never entailed a moment's cruelty, or a moment's pain, upon any living creature. Rowing men pursued recreation under circumstances which braced their muscles, and cleared the cobwebs from their minds. He assured them that he regarded such clubs as these as a "national blessing." They owed, it was true, a vast deal to steam power—as was sometimes proved at matches on the Thames—but, at the same time, they were greatly indebted to all that tended to keep up a healthy, manly tone. He understood that there had been a committee selected for the purpose of arranging a great amateur regatta, which was to take place off Putney in the course of the season that was just begun. He could not abstain from availing himself of this occasion to express a hope that the committee would successfully carry on its labors to a triumphant result, and that they should see upon the Thames, in the course of this summer, such a brilliant sight as had never been seen there before. To secure this there must be some hard work, skillful combinations, and rather large subscriptions. But although the aggregate result must be great, it by no means followed that it need be at all large in its individual details.

[In conclusion, Mr. Dickens made a laughable comparison between the paying off or purification of the national debt and the purification of the River Thames.]

<hr />

XXXIV.

LONDON, JUNE 5, 1867.

[On the above date Mr. Dickens presided at the ninth Anniversary Festival of the Railway Benevolent Society, at Willis's Rooms, and in proposing the toast of the evening, made the following speech:]

ALTHOUGH we have not yet left behind us by the distance of nearly fifty years the time when one of the first literary authorities of this country insisted upon the speed of the fastest railway train that the Legislature might disastrously sanction being limited by Act of Parliament to ten miles an hour, yet it does somehow happen that this evening, and every evening, there are railway trains running pretty smoothly to Ireland and to Scotland at the rate of fifty miles an hour; much as it was objected in its time to vaccination, that it must have a tendency to impart to human children something of the nature of the cow, whereas I believe to this very time vaccinated children are found to be as easily defined from calves as they ever were, and certainly they have no cheapening influence on the price of veal; much as it was objected that chloroform was a contravention of the will of Providence, because it lessened providentially-inflicted pain, which would be a reason for your not rubbing your face if you had the toothache, or not rubbing your nose if it itched; so it was evidently predicted that the railway system, even if any thing so absurd could be productive of any result, would infallibly throw half the nation out of employment; whereas, you observe that the very cause and occasion of our coming here together to-night is, apart from the various tributary channels of occupation which it has opened out, that it has called into existence a specially and directly employed population of upward of 200,000 persons.

Now, gentlemen, it is pretty clear and obvious that upward of 200,000 persons engaged upon the various railways of the United Kingdom can not be rich; and although their duties require great care and great exactness, and although our lives are every day, humanly speaking, in the hands of many of them, still, for the most of these places there will be always great competition, because they are not posts which require skilled workmen to hold. Wages, as you know very well, can not be high where competition is great, and you also know very well that railway directors, in the bargains they make, and the salaries which they pay, have to deal with the money of the shareholders, to whom they are accountable. Thus it necessarily happens that railway officers and servants are not remunerated, on the whole, by any means splendidly, and that they can not hope in the ordinary course of things to do more than meet the ordinary wants and hazards of life. But it is to be observed that the general hazards are in their case, by reason of the dangerous nature of their avocations, exceptionally great, so very great, I find, as to be statable, on the authority of a parliamentary paper, by the very startling round of figures, that whereas one railway traveller in 8,000,000 of passengers is killed, one railway servant in every 2000 is killed.

Hence, from general, special, as well, no doubt, for the usual prudential and benevolent considerations, there came to be established among railway officers and servants, nine years ago, the Railway Benevolent Association. I may suppose, therefore, as it was established nine years ago, that this is the ninth occasion of publishing from this chair the banns between this institution and the public. Nevertheless, I feel bound individually to do my duty the same as if it had never been done before, and to ask whether there is any just cause or impediment why these two parties—the institution and the public—should not be joined together in holy charity. As I understand the society, its objects are fivefold—first, to guarantee annuities which, it is always to be observed, are paid out of the interest of invested capital, so that those annuities may be secure and safe—annual pensions, varying from £10 to £25, to distressed railway officers and servants incapacitated by age, sickness, or accident; secondly, to guarantee small pensions to distressed widows; thirdly, to educate and maintain orphan· children; fourthly, to provide temporary relief for all those classes till lasting relief can be guaranteed out of funds sufficiently large for the purpose; lastly, to induce railway officers and servants to assure their lives in some well-established office by subdividing the payment of the premiums into small periodical sums, and also by granting a reversionary bonus of £10 per cent. on the amount assured from the funds of the institution.

This is the society we are met to assist—simple, sympathetic, practical, easy, sensible, unpretending. The number of its members is large, and rapidly on the increase: they number twelve thousand; the amount of invested capital is very nearly £15,000; it has done a world of good and a world of work in these first nine years of its life; and yet I am proud to say that the annual cost of the maintenance of the institution is no more than £250. And now if you do not know all about it in a small compass, either I do not know all about it myself, or the fault must be in my "packing."

One naturally passes from what the institution is and has done, to what it wants. Well, it wants to do more good, and it can not possibly do more good until it has more money. It can not safely, and therefore it can not honorably, grant more pensions to deserving applicants until it grows richer, and it can not grow rich enough for its laudable purpose by its own unaided self. The thing is absolutely impossible. The means of these railway officers and servants are far too limited. Even if they were helped to the utmost by the great railway companies, their means would still be too limited; even if they were helped—and I hope they shortly will be—by some of the great corporations of this country whom railways have done so much to enrich. These railway officers and servants, on their road to a very humble and modest superannuation, can no more do without the help of the great public, than the great public, on their road from Torquay to Aberdeen, can do without them. Therefore I desire to ask the public whether the servants of the great railways—who, in fact, are their servants, their ready, zealous, faithful, hard-working servants—whether they have not established, whether they do not every day establish, a reasonable claim to liberal remembrance.

Now, gentlemen, on this point of the case there is a story, once told me by a friend of mine, which seems to my mind to have a certain application. My friend was an American sea-captain, and therefore it is quite unnecessary to say his story was quite true. He was captain and part owner of a large American merchant liner. On a certain voyage out, in exquisite summer weather, he had for cabin passengers one beautiful young lady, and ten more or less beautiful young gentlemen. Light winds or dead calms prevailing, the voyage was slow. They had made half their distance when the ten young gentlemen were all madly in love with the beautiful young lady. They had all proposed to her, and bloodshed among the rivals seemed imminent pending the young lady's decision. On this extremity the beautiful young lady confided in my friend the captain, who gave her discreet advice. He said: "If your affections are disengaged, take that one of the young gentlemen whom you like the best, and settle the question." To this the beautiful young lady made reply, "I can not do that, because I like them all equally well." My friend, who was a man of resource, hit upon this ingenious expedient: said he, "To-morrow morning at midday, when lunch is announced, do you plunge bodily overboard, head foremost. I will be alongside in a boat to rescue you, and take the one of the ten who rushes to your rescue, and then you can afterwards have him." The beautiful young lady highly approved, and did accordingly. But after she plunged in, nine out of the ten more or less beautiful young gentlemen plunged in after her; and the tenth remained and shed tears, looking over the side of the vessel. They were all picked up, and restored dripping to the deck. The beautiful young lady, upon seeing them, said, "What am I to do? See what a plight they are in. How can I possibly choose, because every one of them is equally wet?" Then said my friend the captain, acting upon a sudden inspiration, "Take the dry one." I am sorry to say that she did so, and they lived happy ever afterwards.

Now, gentlemen, in my application of this story, I exactly reverse my friend the captain's anecdote, and I entreat the public in looking about to consider who are fit subjects for their bounty, to give each his hand with something in it, and not to award a dry hand to the industrious railway servant who is always at his back. And I would ask any one with a doubt upon this subject to consider what his experience of the railway servant is from the time of his departure to his arrival at his destination. I know what mine is. Here he is, in velveteen or in a policeman's dress, scaling cabs, storming carriages, finding lost articles by a sort of instinct, binding up lost umbrellas and walking-sticks, wheeling trucks, counselling old ladies, with a wonderful interest in their affairs—mostly very complicated—and sticking labels upon all sorts of articles. I look around—there he is, in a station-master's uniform, directing and overseeing, with the head of a general and with the courteous manners of a gentleman; and then there is the handsome figure of the guard, who inspires confidence in timid passengers. I glide out of the station, and there he is again with his flags in his hand at his post in the open country, at the level crossing, at the cutting, at the tunnel mouth, and at every station on the road, until our destination is reached. In regard, therefore, to the railway servants with whom we do come into contact, we may surely have some natural sympathy, and it is on their behalf that I this night appeal to you. I beg now to propose "Success to the Railway Benevolent Society."

XXXV.

LONDON, SEPTEMBER 17, 1867.

[On presiding at a public Meeting of the Printers' Readers, held at the Salisbury Hotel, on the above date, Mr. Dickens said :]

THAT as the meeting was convened, not to hear him, but to hear a statement of facts and figures very nearly affecting the personal interests of the great majority of those present, his preface to the proceedings need be very brief. Of the details of the question he knew, of his own knowledge, absolutely nothing; but he had consented to occupy the chair on that occasion at the request of the London Association of Correctors of the Press for two reasons—first, because he thought that openness and publicity in such cases were a very wholesome example very much needed at this time, and were highly becoming to a body of men associated with that great public safeguard — the Press ; secondly, because he knew from some slight practical experience, what the duties of correctors of the press were, and how their duties were usually discharged; and he could testify, and did testify, that they were not mechanical, that they were not mere matters of manipulation and routine ; but that they required from those who performed them much natural intelligence, much superadded cultivation, readiness of reference, quickness of resource, an excellent memory, and a clear understanding. He most gratefully acknowledged that he had never gone through the sheets of any book that he had written without having presented to him by the correctors of the press something that he had overlooked, some slight inconsistency into which he had fallen, some little lapse he had made—in short, without having set down in black and white some unquestionable indication that he had been closely followed through the work by a patient and trained mind, and not merely by a skillful eye. And in this declaration he had not the slightest doubt that the great body of his brother and sister writers would, as a plain act of justice, readily concur. For these plain reasons he was there ; and being there, he begged to assure them that every one present—that every speaker—would have a patient hearing, whatever his opinions might be.

[The proceedings concluded with a very cordial and hearty vote of thanks to Mr. Dickens for taking the Chair on the occasion.]

Mr. Dickens briefly returned thanks, and expressed the belief that their very calm and temperate proceedings would finally result in the establishment of relations of perfect amity between the employers and the employed, and consequently conduce to the general welfare of both.

~~~~~~~~

XXXVI.

LONDON, NOVEMBER 2, 1867.

[On Saturday evening, November 2, 1867, a grand complimentary farewell dinner was given to Mr. Dickens at the Freemasons' Tavern on the occasion of his revisiting the United States of America. Lord Lytton officiated as Chairman, and proposed as a toast—"A Prosperous Voyage, Health, and Long Life to our Illustrious Guest and Countryman, Charles Dickens." The toast was drunk with all the honors, and one cheer more. Mr. Dickens then rose, and spoke as follows:]

No thanks that I can offer you ·can express my sense of my reception by this great assemblage, or can in the least suggest to you how deep the glowing words of my friend, the chairman, and your acceptance of them, have sunk into my heart. But both combined have so greatly shaken the composure which I am used to command before an audience, that I hope you may observe in me some traces of an eloquence more expressive than the richest words. To say that I am fervently grateful to you is to say nothing; to say that I can never forget this beautiful sight, is to say nothing; to say that it brings upon me a rush of emotion not only in the present, but in the thought of its remembrance in the future by those who are dearest to me, is to say nothing; but to feel all this for the moment, even almost to pain, is very much indeed. Mercutio says of the wound in his breast, dealt him by the hand of a foe, that— " 'Tis not so deep as a well, nor so wide as a church door; but 'tis enough, 'twill serve."* I may say of the wound in my breast, newly dealt to me by the hands of my friends, that it is deeper than the soundless sea, and wider than the whole Catholic Church. I may safely add that it has for the moment almost stricken me dumb. I should be more than human, and I assure you I am very human indeed, if I could look around upon this brilliant representative company and not feel greatly thrilled and stirred by the presence of so many brother artists, not only in literature, but also in the sister arts, especially painting, among whose professors, living and unhappily dead, are many of my oldest and best friends. I hope that I may, without presumption, regard this thronging of my brothers around me as a testimony on their part that they believe that the cause of art generally has been safe in my keeping, and that it has never been falsely dealt with by me. Your resounding cheers just now would have been

but so many cruel reproaches to me if I could not here declare that, from the earliest days of my career down to this proud night, I have always tried to be true to my calling. Never unduly to assert it, on the one hand, and never, on any pretense or consideration, to permit it to be patronized in my person, has been the steady endeavor of my life; and I have occasionally been vain enough to hope that I may leave its social position in England better than I found it. Similarly, and equally I hope without presumption, I trust that I may take this general representation of the public here, through so many orders, pursuits, and degrees, as a token that the public believe that, with a host of imperfections and shortcomings on my head, I have as a writer, in my soul and conscience, tried to be as true to them as they have ever been true to me. And here, in reference to the inner circle of the arts and the outer circle of the public, I feel it a duty to-night to offer two remarks. I have in my duty at odd times heard a great deal about literary sets and cliques, and coteries and barriers; about keeping this man up, and keeping that man down; about sworn disciples and sworn unbelievers, and mutual admiration societies, and I know not what other dragons in the upward path. I began to tread it when I was very young, without influence, without money, without companion, introducer, or adviser, and I am bound to put in evidence in this place that I never lighted on these dragons yet. So have I heard in my day, at divers other odd times, much generally to the effect that the English people have little or no love of art for its own sake, and that they do not greatly care to acknowledge or do honor to the artist. My own experience has uniformly been exactly the reverse. I can say that of my countrymen, though I can not say that of my country.

And now passing to the immediate occasion of your doing me this great honor, the story of my going again to America is very easily and briefly told. Since I was there before, a vast and entirely new generation has arisen in the United States. Since I was there before, most of the best known of my books have been written and published; the new generation and the books have come together and have kept together, until at length numbers of those who have so widely and constantly read me, naturally desiring a little variety in the relationship between us, have expressed a strong wish that I should read myself. This wish, at first conveyed to me through public channels and business channels, has gradually become enforced by an immense accumulation of letters from individuals

---

* "Romeo and Juliet." Act iii. scene i.

and associations of individuals, all expressing in the same hearty, homely, cordial, unaffected way, a kind of personal interest in me—I had almost said a kind of personal affection for me, which I am sure you would agree with me it would be dull insensibility on my part not to prize. Little by little this pressure has become so great, that, although, as Charles Lamb says, my household gods strike a terribly deep root, I have torn them from their places, and this day week, at this hour, shall be upon the sea. You will readily conceive that I am inspired besides by a natural desire to see for myself the astonishing change and progress of a quarter of a century over there, to grasp the hands of many faithful friends whom I left there, to see the faces of the multitude of new friends upon whom I have never looked, and last, not least, to use my best endeavor to lay down a third cable of intercommunication and alliance between the Old World and the New. Twelve years ago, when, Heaven knows, I little thought I should ever be bound upon the voyage which now lies before me, I wrote in that form of my writings which obtains by far the most extensive circulation, these words of the American nation: "I know full well, whatever little motes my beamy eyes may have descried in theirs, that they are a kind, large-hearted, generous, and great people." In that faith I am going to see them again; in that faith I shall, please God, return from them in the spring; in that same faith to live and to die. I told you in the beginning that I could not thank you enough, and Heaven knows I have most thoroughly kept my word. If I may quote one other short sentence from myself, let it imply all that I have left unsaid, and yet most deeply feel. Let it, putting a girdle round the earth, comprehend both sides of the Atlantic at once in this moment, and say, as Tiny Tim observes, "God bless us every one."

XXXVII.

BOSTON, APRIL 8, 1868.

[Mr. Dickens gave his last Reading at Boston on the above date. On his entrance a surprise awaited him. His reading-stand had been decorated with flowers and palm-leaves by some of the ladies of the city. He acknowledged this graceful tribute in the following words: "Before allowing Dr. Marigold to tell his story in his own peculiar way, I kiss the kind, fair hands unknown, which have so beautifully decorated my table this evening." After the Reading, Mr. Dickens attempted in vain to retire. Persistent hands demanded "one word more." Returning to his desk, pale, with a tear in his eye that found its way to his voice, he spoke as follows:]

LADIES AND GENTLEMEN,—My gracious and generous welcome in America, which can never be obliterated from my remembrance, began here. My departure begins here, too; for I assure you that I have never until this moment really felt that I am going away. In this brief life of ours, it is sad to do almost any thing for the last time, and I can not conceal from you, although my face will so soon be turned towards my native land, and to all that makes it dear, that it is a sad consideration with me that in a very few moments from this time this brilliant hall and all that it contains will fade from my view—for evermore. But it is my consolation that the spirit of the bright faces, the quick perception, the ready response, the generous and the cheering sounds that have made this place delightful to me, will remain; and you may rely upon it that that spirit will abide with me as long as I have sense and sentiment left.

I do not say this with any limited reference to private friendships that have for years upon years made Boston a memorable and beloved spot to me, for such private references have no business in this public place. I say it purely in remembrance of, and in homage to, the great public heart before me.

Ladies and gentlemen, I beg most earnestly, most gratefully, and most affectionately to bid you, each and all, farewell.

XXXVIII.

NEW YORK, APRIL 18, 1868.

[On the above date Mr. Dickens was entertained at a farewell dinner at Delmonico's Hotel, previous to his return to England. Two hundred gentlemen sat down to it, Mr. Horace Greeley presiding. In acknowledgment of the toast of his health, proposed by the Chairman, Mr. Dickens rose and said:]

GENTLEMEN,—I can not do better than take my cue from your distinguished president, and refer in my first remarks to his remarks in connection with the old natural association between you and me. When I received an invitation from a private association of working members of the press of New York to dine with them to-day, I accepted that compliment in grateful remembrance of a calling that was once my own, and in loyal sympathy towards a brotherhood which, in the spirit, I have never quitted. To the wholesome training of severe newspaper work, when I was a very young man, I constantly refer my first successes; and my sons will hereafter testify of their father that he was always steadily proud of that ladder by which he rose. If it were otherwise, I should have but a very poor opinion of their father, which, perhaps, upon the whole, I have not. Hence, gentlemen, under any circumstances, this company would have been exceptionally interesting and gratifying to me. But whereas I supposed that, like the fairies' pavilion in the "Arabian Nights," it would be but a mere handful, and I find it turn out, like the same elastic pavilion, capable of comprehending a multitude, so much the more proud am I of the honor of being your guest; for you will readily believe that the more widely representative of the press in America my entertainers are, the more I must feel the good-will and the kindly sentiments towards me of that vast institution.

Gentlemen, so much of my voice has lately been heard in the land, and I have for upward of four hard winter months so contended against what I have been sometimes quite admiringly assured was "a true American catarrh"—a possession which I have throughout highly appreciated, though I might have preferred to be naturalized by any other outward and visible signs—I say, gentlemen, so much of my voice has lately been heard, that I might have been contented with troubling you no further from my present standing-point, were it not a duty with which I henceforth charge myself, not only here but on every suitable occasion whatsoever and wheresoever, to express my high and grateful sense of my second reception in America, and to bear my honest testimony to the national generosity and magnanimity. Also, to declare how astounded I have been by the amazing changes that I have seen around me on every side—changes moral, changes physical, changes in the amount of land subdued and peopled, changes in the rise of vast new cities, changes in the growth of older cities almost out of recognition, changes in the graces and amenities of life, changes in the press, without whose advancement no advancement can be made anywhere. Nor am I, believe me, so arrogant as to suppose that in five-and-twenty years there have been no changes in me, and that I had nothing to learn and no extreme impressions to correct when I was here first.

And, gentlemen, this brings me to a point on which I have, ever since I landed here last November, observed a strict silence, though tempted sometimes to break it, but in reference to which I will, with your good leave, take you into my confidence now. Even the press, being human, may be sometimes mistaken or misinformed, and I rather think that I have in one or two rare instances known its information to be not perfectly accurate with reference to myself. Indeed, I have now and again been more surprised by printed news that I have read of myself than by any printed news that I have ever read in my present state of existence. Thus, the vigor and perseverance with which I have

for some months past been collecting materials for and hammering away at a new book on America have much astonished me, seeing that all that time it has been perfectly well known to my publishers on both sides of the Atlantic that I positively declared that no consideration on earth should induce me to write one. But what I have intended, what I have resolved upon (and this is the confidence I seek to place in you), is, on my return to England, in my own person, to bear, for the behoof of my countrymen, such testimony to the gigantic changes in this country as I have hinted at to-night. Also, to record that wherever I have been, in the smallest places equally with the largest, I have been received with unsurpassable politeness, delicacy, sweet temper, hospitality, consideration, and with unsurpassable respect for the privacy daily enforced upon me by the nature of my avocation here, and the state of my health. This testimony, so long as I live, and so long as my descendants have any legal right in my books, I shall cause to be republished, as an appendix to every copy of those two books of mine in which I have referred to America. And this I will do and cause to be done, not in mere love and thankfulness, but because I regard it as an act of plain justice and honor.

Gentlemen, the transition from my own feelings towards and interest in America to those of the mass of my countrymen seems to be a natural one; but, whether or no, I make it with an express object. I was asked in this very city, about last Christmas-time, whether an American was not at some disadvantage in England as a foreigner. The notion of an American being regarded in England as a foreigner at all, of his ever being thought of or spoken of in that character, was so uncommonly incongruous and absurd to me, that my gravity was for the moment quite overpowered. As soon as it was restored, I said that for years and years past I hoped I had had as many American friends and had received as many American visitors as almost any Englishman living, and that my unvarying experience, fortified by theirs, was that it was enough in England to be an American to be received with the readiest respect and recognition anywhere. Hereupon, out of half a dozen people, suddenly spoke out two, one an American gentleman, with a cultivated taste for art, who, finding himself on a certain Sunday outside the walls of a certain historical English castle, famous for its pictures, was refused admission there, according to the strict rules of the establishment, on that day, but who, on merely representing that he was an American gentleman on his travels, had, not to say the picture-gallery, but the whole castle, placed at his immediate disposal. The other was a lady, who, being in London, and having a great desire to see the famous reading - room of the British Museum, was assured by the English family with whom she staid that it was unfortunately impossible, because the place was closed for a week, and she had only three days there. Upon that lady's going to the Museum, as she assured me, alone to the gate, self-introduced as an American lady, the gate flew open, as it were, magically. I am unwillingly bound to add that she certainly was young and exceedingly pretty. Still, the porter of that institution is of an obese habit, and, according to the best of my observation of him, not very impressible.

Now, gentlemen, I refer to these trifles as a collateral assurance to you that the Englishman who shall humbly strive, as I hope to do, to be in England as faithful to America as to England herself, has no previous conceptions to contend against. Points of difference there have been, points of difference there are, points of difference there probably always will be between the two great peoples. But broadcast in England is sown the sentiment that those two peoples are essentially one, and that it rests with them jointly to uphold the great Anglo-Saxon race, to which our president has referred, and all its great achievements before the world. And if I know any thing of my countrymen—and they give me credit for knowing something—if I know any thing of my countrymen, gentlemen, the English heart is stirred by the fluttering of those Stars and Stripes, as it is stirred by no other flag that flies except its own. If I know my countrymen, in any and every relation towards America, they begin, not as Sir Anthony Absolute recommended that lovers should begin, with " a little aversion," but with a great liking and a profound respect ; and whatever the little sensitiveness of the moment, or the little official passion, or the little official policy, now or then, or here or there, may be, take my word for it, that the first enduring, great, popular consideration in England is a generous construction of justice.

Finally, gentlemen, and I say this subject to your correction, I do believe that from the great majority of honest minds on both sides, there can not be absent the conviction that it would be better for this globe to be riven by an earthquake, fired by a comet, overrun by an iceberg, and abandoned to the Arctic fox and bear, than that it should present the spectacle of these two great nations, each of which has, in its own way and hour, striven so hard and so successfully for freedom, ever again being arrayed the one against the other. Gentlemen, I can not thank your president enough or you enough for your kind reception of my health, and of my poor remarks, but, believe me, I do thank you with the utmost fervor of which my soul is capable.

XXXIX.

NEW YORK, APRIL 20, 1868.

[Mr. Dickens's last Reading in the United States was given at the Steinway Hall on the above date. The task finished, he was about to retire, but a tremendous burst of applause stopped him. He came forward and spoke thus :]

LADIES AND GENTLEMEN,—The shadow of one word has impended over me this evening, and the time has come at length when the shadow must fall. It is but a very short one, but the weight of such things is not measured by their length, and two much shorter words express the round of our human existence. When I was reading " David Copperfield " a few evenings since, I felt there was more than usual significance in the words of Peggotty, " My future life lies over the sea." And when I closed this book just now, I felt most keenly that I was shortly to establish such an *alibi* as would have satisfied even the elder Mr. Weller. The relations which have been set up between us, while they have involved for me something more than mere devotion to a task, have been by you sustained with the readiest sympathy and the kindest acknowledgment.

Those relations must now be broken forever. Be assured, however, that you will not pass from my mind. I shall often realize you as I see you now, equally by my winter fire and in the green English summer weather. I shall never recall you as a mere public audience, but rather as a host of personal friends, and ever with the greatest gratitude, tenderness, and consideration. Ladies and gentlemen, I beg to bid you farewell. God bless you, and God bless the land in which I leave you.

XL.

LIVERPOOL, APRIL 10, 1869.

[The following speech was delivered by Mr. Dickens at a Banquet held in his honor at St. George's Hall, Liverpool, after his health had been proposed by Lord Dufferin.]

MR. MAYOR, LADIES AND GENTLEMEN,—Although I have been so well accustomed of late to the sound of my own voice in this neighborhood as to hear it with perfect composure, the occasion is, believe me, very, very different in respect of those overwhelming voices of yours.

As Professor Wilson once confided to me in Edinburgh that I had not the least idea, from hearing him in public, what a magnificent speaker he found himself to be when he was quite alone—so you can form no conception, from the specimen before you, of the eloquence with which I shall thank you again and again in some of the innermost moments of my future life. Often and often, then, God willing, my memory will recall this brilliant scene, and will re-illuminate this banquet-hall. I, faithful to this place in its present aspect, will observe it exactly as it stands—not one man's seat empty, not one woman's fair face absent, while life and memory abide by me.

Mr. Mayor, Lord Dufferin, in his speech so affecting to me, so eloquently uttered, and so rapturously received, made a graceful and gracious allusion to the immediate occasion of my present visit to your noble city. It is no homage to Liverpool, based upon a moment's untrustworthy enthusiasm, but it is the solid fact built upon the rock of experience, that when I first made up my mind, after considerable deliberation, systematically to meet my readers in large numbers, face to face, and to try to express myself to them through the breath of life, Liverpool stood foremost among the great places out of London to which I looked with eager confidence and pleasure. And why was this? Not merely because of the reputation of its citizens for generous estimation of the arts; not merely because I had unworthily filled the chair of its great self-educational institution long ago; not merely because the place had been a home to me since the well-remembered day when its blessed roofs and steeples dipped into the Mersey behind me on the occasion of my first sailing away to see my generous friends across the Atlantic twenty-seven years ago. Not for one of those considerations, but because it had been my happiness to have a public opportunity of testing the spirit of its people. I had asked Liverpool for help towards the worthy preservation of Shakspeare's house. On another occasion I had ventured to address Liverpool in the names of Leigh Hunt and Sheridan Knowles. On still another occasion I had addressed it in the cause of the brotherhood and sisterhood of letters and the kindred arts, and on each and all the response had been unsurpassably spontaneous, open-handed, and munificent.

Mr. Mayor, and ladies and gentlemen, if I may venture to take a small illustration of my present position from my own peculiar craft, I would say that there is this objection, in writing fiction, to giving a story an autobiographical form, that through whatever dangers the narrator may pass, it is clear, unfortunately, to the reader beforehand that he must have come through them somehow, else he could not have lived to tell the tale. Now, in speaking fact, when the fact is associated with such honors as those with which you have enriched me, there is this singular difficulty in the way of returning thanks, that the speaker must infallibly come back to himself through whatever oratorical disasters he may languish on the road. Let me, then, take the plainer and simpler middle course of dividing my subject equally between myself and you. Let me assure you that whatever you have accepted with pleasure, either by word of pen or by word of mouth, from me, you have greatly improved in the acceptance. As the gold is said to be doubly and trebly refined which has seven times passed the furnace, so a fancy may be said to become more and more refined each time it passes through the human heart. You have, and you know you have, brought to the consideration of me that quality in yourselves without which I should but have beaten the air. Your earnestness has stimulated mine, your laughter has made me laugh, and your tears have overflowed my eyes. All that I can claim for myself in establishing the relations which exist between us is constant fidelity to hard work. My literary fellows about me, of whom I am so proud to see so many, know very well how true it is in all art that what seems the easiest done is oftentimes the most difficult to do, and that the smallest truth may come of the greatest pains—much, as it occurred to me at Manchester the other day, as the sensitive touch of Mr. Whitworth's measuring machine comes, at last, of Heaven and Manchester and its mayor only know how much hammering — my companions-in-arms know thoroughly well, and I think it only right the public should know too, that in our careful toil and trouble, and in our steady striving for excellence—not in any little gifts, misused by fits and starts—lies our highest duty at once to our calling, to one another, to ourselves, and to you.

Ladies and gentlemen, before sitting down I find that I have to clear myself of two very unexpected accusations. The first is a most singular charge preferred against me by my old friend Lord Houghton, that I have been somewhat unconscious of the merits of the House of Lords. Now, ladies and gentlemen, seeing that I have had some few not altogether obscure or unknown personal friends in that assembly, seeing that I had some little association with, and knowledge of, a certain obscure peer lately known in England by the name of Lord Brougham; seeing that I regard with some admiration and affection another obscure peer wholly unknown in literary circles, called Lord Lytton; seeing also that I have had for some years some slight admiration of the extraordinary judicial properties and amazingly acute mind of a certain Lord Chief Justice popularly known by the name of Cockburn; and also seeing that there is no man in England whom I respect more in his public capacity, whom I love more in his private capacity, or from whom I have received more remarkable proofs of his honor and love of literature than another obscure nobleman called Lord Russell; taking these circumstances into consideration, I was rather amazed by my noble friend's accusation. When I asked him, on his sitting down, what amazing devil possessed him to make this charge, he replied that he had never forgotten the days of Lord Verisopht. Then, ladies and gentlemen, I understood it all. Because it is a remarkable fact that in the days when that depreciative and profoundly unnatural character was invented there was no Lord Houghton in the House of Lords. And there was in the House of Commons a rather indifferent member called Richard Monckton Milnes.

Ladies and gentlemen, to conclude for the present, I close with the other charge of my noble friend, and here I am more serious, and I may be allowed perhaps to express my seriousness in half a dozen plain words. When I first took literature as my profession in England, I calmly resolved within myself that, whether I succeeded or whether I failed, literature should be my sole profession. It appeared to me at that time that it was not so well understood in England as it was in other countries that literature was a dignified profession, by which any man might stand or fall. I made a compact with myself that in my person literature should stand, and by itself, of itself, and for itself; and there is no consideration on earth which would induce me to break that bargain.

Ladies and gentlemen, finally allow me to thank you for your great kindness, and for the touching earnestness with which you have drunk my health. I should have thanked you with all my heart if it had not so unfortunately happened that, for many sufficient reasons, I lost my heart at between half past six and half past seven to-night.

~~~~~~~~

XLI.

THE OXFORD AND HARVARD BOAT-RACE.

SYDENHAM, AUGUST 30, 1869.

[The International University Boat-race having taken place on August 27, the London Rowing-club invited the Crews to a Dinner at the Crystal Palace on the following Monday. The dinner was followed by a grand display of pyrotechnics. Mr. Dickens, in proposing the health of the Crews, made the following speech:]

GENTLEMEN,—Flushed with fire-works, I can warrant myself to you as about to imitate those gorgeous illusions by making a brief spirt and then dying out. And, first of all, as an invited visitor of the London Rowing-club on this most interesting occasion, I will beg, in the name of the other invited visitors present—always excepting the distinguished guests who are the cause of our meeting—to thank the president for the modesty and the courtesy with which he has deputed to one of us the most agreeable part of his evening's duty. It is the more graceful in him to do this, because he can hardly fail to see that he might very easily do it himself, as this is a case of all others in which it is according to good taste and the very principles of things that the great social vice, speech-making, should hide its diminished head before the great social virtue, action. However, there is an ancient story of a lady who threw her glove into an arena full of wild beasts to tempt her attendant lover to climb down and reclaim it. The lover, rightly inferring from the action the worth of the lady, risked his life for the glove, and then threw it lightly in her face as a token of his eternal adieu.* I take up the president's glove, on the contrary, as a proof of his much higher worth, and of my real interest in the cause in which it was thrown down, and I now profess my readiness to do even injustice to the duty which he has assigned me.

Gentlemen, a very remarkable and affecting volume was published in the United States within a short time before my last visit to that hospitable land, containing ninety-five biographies of young men, for the most part well-born and well nurtured, and trained in various peaceful pursuits of life, who, when the flag of their country waved them from those quiet paths in which they were seeking distinction of various kinds, took arms in the dread civil war which elicited so much bravery on both sides, and died in the defense of their country. These great spirits displayed extraordinary aptitude in the acquisition, even in the invention, of military

---

* Robert Browning, "Bells and Pomegranates."

tactics, in the combining and commanding of great masses of men, in surprising readiness of self-resource for the general good, in humanely treating the sick and the wounded, and in winning to themselves a very rare amount of personal confidence and trust. They had all risen to be distinguished soldiers; they had all done deeds of great heroism; they had all combined with their valor and self-devotion a serene cheerfulness, a quiet modesty, and a truly Christian spirit; and they had all been educated in one school—Harvard University.

Gentlemen, nothing was more remarkable in these fine descendants of our forefathers than the invincible determination with which they fought against odds, and the undauntable spirit with which they resisted defeat. I ask you, who will say after last Friday that Harvard University is less true to herself in peace than she was in war? I ask you, who will not recognize in her boat's crew the leaven of her soldiers, and who does not feel that she has now a greater right than ever to be proud of her sons, and take these sons to her breast when they return with resounding acclamations? It is related of the Duke of Wellington that he once told a lady who foolishly protested that she would like to see a great victory, that there was only one thing worse than a great victory, and that was a great defeat.

But, gentlemen, there is another sense in which to use the term a great defeat. Such is the defeat of a handful of daring fellows who make a preliminary dash of three or four thousand stormy miles to meet great conquerors on their own domain—who do not want the stimulus of friends and home, but who sufficiently hear and feel their own dear land in the shouts and cheers of another—and who strive to the last with a desperate tenacity that makes the beating of them a new feather in the proudest cap. Gentlemen, you agree with me that such a defeat is a great, noble part of a manly, wholesome action; and I say that it is in the essence and life-blood of such a defeat to become at last sure victory.

Now, gentlemen, you know perfectly well the toast I am going to propose, and you know equally well that in thus glancing first towards our friends of the white stripes, I merely anticipate and respond to the instinctive courtesy of Oxford towards our brothers from a distance —a courtesy extending, I hope, and I do not doubt, to any imaginable limits except allowing them to take the first place in last Friday's match, if they could by any human and honorable means be kept in the second. I will not avail myself of the opportunity provided for me by the absence of the greater part of the Oxford crew—indeed, of all but one, and that its most modest and devoted member—I will not avail myself of the golden opportunity considerately provided for me to say a great deal in honor of the Oxford crew. I know that the gentleman who attends here attends under unusual anxieties and difficulties, and that if he were less in earnest his filial affection could not possibly allow him to be here.

It is therefore enough for me, gentlemen, and enough for you, that I should say here and now, that we all unite with one accord in regarding the Oxford crew as the pride and flower of England—and that we should consider it very weak indeed to set any thing short of England's very best in opposition to, or competition with, America; though it certainly must be confessed—I am bound in common justice and honor to admit it—it must be confessed in disparagement of the Oxford men, as I heard a discontented gentleman remark last Friday night, about ten o'clock, when he was baiting a very small horse in the Strand—he was one of eleven with pipes in a chaise cart—I say it must be admitted in disparagement of the Oxford men, on the authority of this gentleman, that they have won so often that they could afford to lose a little now, and that "they ought to do it, but they won't."

Gentlemen, in drinking to both crews, and in offering the poor testimony of our thanks in acknowledgment of the gallant spectacle which they presented to countless thousands last Friday, I am sure I express not only your feeling, and my feeling, and the feeling of the Blue, but also the feeling of the whole people of England, when I cordially give them welcome to our English waters and English ground, and also bid them "God speed" in their voyage home. As the greater includes the less, and the sea holds the river, so I think it is no very bold augury to predict that in the friendly contests yet to come and to take place, I hope, on both sides of the Atlantic—there are great river triumphs for Harvard University yet in store. Gentlemen, I warn the English portion of this audience that these are very dangerous men. Remember that it was an under-graduate of Harvard University who served as a common seaman two years before the mast,[*] and who wrote about the best sea-book in the English tongue. Remember that it was one of those young American gentlemen who sailed his mite of a yacht across the Atlantic in mid-winter, and who sailed in her to sink or swim with the men who believed in him.

---

* R. H. Dana.

And now, gentlemen, in conclusion, animated by your cordial acquiescence, I will take upon myself to assure our brothers from a distance that the utmost enthusiasm with which they can be received on their return home will find a ready echo in every corner of England—and further, that none of their immediate countrymen—I use the qualifying term immediate, for we are, as our president said, fellow-countrymen, thank God—that none of their compatriots who saw, or who will read of, what they did in this great race, can be more thoroughly imbued with a sense of their indomitable courage and their high deserts than are their rivals and their hosts to-night. Gentlemen, I beg to propose to you to drink the crews of Harvard and Oxford University, and I beg to couple with that toast the names of Mr. Simmons and Mr. Willan.

XLII.

BIRMINGHAM, SEPTEMBER 27, 1869.

[Inaugural Address on the opening of the Winter Session of the Birmingham and Midland Institute.

One who was present during the delivery of the following speech, informs the editor that "no note of any kind was referred to by Mr. Dickens—except the quotation from Sydney Smith. The address, evidently carefully prepared, was delivered without a single pause, in Mr. Dickens's best manner, and was a very great success."]

LADIES AND GENTLEMEN,—We often hear of our common country that it is an over-populated one, that it is an over-pauperized one, that it is an over-colonizing one, and that it is an over-taxed one. Now I entertain, especially of late times, the heretical belief that it is an over-talked one, and that there is a deal of public speech-making going about in various directions which might be advantageously dispensed with. If I were free to act upon this conviction, as president for the time being of the great institution so numerously represented here, I should immediately and at once subside into a golden silence, which would be of a highly edifying, because of a very exemplary character. But I happen to be the institution's willing servant, not its imperious master, and it exacts tribute of mere silver or copper speech—not to say brazen—from whomsoever it exalts to my high office. Some African tribes — not to draw the comparison disrespectfully—some savage African tribes, when they make a king, require him perhaps to achieve an exhausting foot-race under the stimulus of considerable popular prodding and goading, or perhaps to be severely and experimentally knocked about the head by his Privy Council, or perhaps to be dipped in a river full of crocodiles, or perhaps to drink immense quantities of something nasty out of a calabash —at all events, to undergo some purifying ordeal in presence of his admiring subjects.

I must confess that I became rather alarmed when I was duly warned by your constituted authorities that whatever I might happen to say here to-night would be termed an inaugural address on the entrance upon a new term of study by the members of your various classes; for, besides that the phrase is something high-sounding for my taste, I avow that I do look forward to that blessed time when every man shall inaugurate his own work for himself, and do it. I believe that we shall then have inaugurated a new era indeed, and one in which the Lord's Prayer will become a fulfilled prophecy upon this earth. Remembering, however, that you may call any thing by any name without in the least changing its nature—bethinking myself that you may, if you be so minded, call a butterfly a buffalo, without advancing a hair's breadth towards making it one—I became composed in my mind, and resolved to stick to the very homely intention I had previously formed. This was merely to tell you, the members, students, and friends of the Birmingham and Midland Institute—firstly, what you can not possibly want to know (this is a very popular oratorical theme); secondly, what your institution has done; and, thirdly, what, in the poor opinion of its president for the time being, remains for it to do and not to do.

Now, first, as to what you can not possibly want to know. You can not need from me any oratorical declamation concerning the abstract advantages of knowledge or the beauties of self-improvement. If you had any such requirement you would not be here. I conceive that you are here because you have become thoroughly penetrated with such principles, either in your own persons or in the persons of some striving fellow-creatures, on whom you have looked with interest and sympathy. I conceive that you are here because you feel the welfare of the great chiefly adult educational establishment, whose doors stand really open to all sorts and conditions of people, to be inseparable from the best welfare of your great town and its neighborhood. Nay, if I take a much wider range than that, and say that we all—every one of us here—perfectly well know that the benefits of such an establishment must extend far beyond the limits of this midland county—its fires and smoke—and must comprehend, in some sort, the whole community, I do not strain the truth. It was suggested by Mr. Babbage, in his ninth "Bridgewater Treatise," that a mere spoken word — a single articulated syllable thrown into the air—may go on reverberating through illimitable space forever and forever, seeing that there is no rim against which it can strike—no boundary at which it can possibly arrive. Similarly it may be said—not as an ingenious speculation, but as a steadfast and absolute fact—that human calculation can not limit the influence of one atom of wholesome knowledge patiently acquired, modestly possessed, and faithfully used.

As the astronomers tell us that it is probable that there are in the universe innumerable solar systems besides ours, to each of which myriads of utterly unknown and unseen stars belong, so it is certain that every man, however obscure, however far removed from the general recognition, is one of a group of men impressible for good and impressible for evil, and that it is in the eternal nature of things that he can not really improve himself without in some degree improving other men. And observe, this is especially the case when he has improved himself in the teeth of adverse circumstances, as in a maturity succeeding to a neglected or an ill-taught youth, in the few daily hours remaining to him after ten or twelve hours' labor, in the few pauses and intervals of a life of toil ; for then his fellows and companions have assurance that he can have known no favoring conditions, and that they can do what he has done, in wresting some enlightenment and self-respect from what Lord Lytton finely calls—

"Those twin jailers of the daring heart,
  Low birth and iron fortune."

As you have proved these truths in your own experience or in your own observation, and as it may be safely assumed that there can be very few persons in Birmingham, of all places under heaven, who would contest the position that the more cultivated the employed the better for the employer, and the more cultivated the employer the better for the employed ; therefore, my references to what you do not want to know shall here cease and determine.

Next, with reference to what your institution has done ; on my summary, which shall be as concise and as correct as my information and my remembrance of it may render possible, I desire to lay emphatic stress. Your institution, sixteen years old, and in which masters and workmen study together, has outgrown the ample edifice in which it receives its 2500 or 2600 members and students. It is a most cheering sign of its vigorous vitality that of its industrial students almost half are artisans in the receipt of weekly wages. I think I am correct in saying that 400 others are clerks, apprentices, trades-

men, or tradesmen's sons. I note with particular pleasure the adherence of a goodly number of the gentler sex, without whom no institution whatever can truly claim to be either a civilizing or a civilized one. The increased attendance at your educational classes is always greatest on the part of the artisans—the class within my experience the least reached in any similar institutions elsewhere, and whose name is the oftenest and the most constantly taken in vain. But it is specially reached here, not improbably because it is, as it should be, specially addressed in the foundation of the industrial department, in the allotment of the direction of the society's affairs, and in the establishment of what are called its penny classes—a bold, and, I am happy to say, a triumphantly successful experiment, which enables the artisan to obtain sound evening instruction in subjects directly bearing upon his daily usefulness or on his daily happiness, as arithmetic (elementary and advanced), chemistry, physical geography, and singing, on payment of the astoundingly low fee of a single penny every time he attends the class. I beg emphatically to say that I look upon this as one of the most remarkable schemes ever devised for the educational behoof of the artisan ; and if your institution had done nothing else in all its life, I would take my stand by it on its having done this.

Apart, however, from its industrial department, it has its general department, offering all the advantages of a first-class literary institution. It has its reading-rooms, its library, its chemical laboratory, its museum, its art department, its lecture hall, and its long list of lectures on subjects of various and comprehensive interest, delivered by lecturers of the highest qualifications. Very well. But it may be asked, what are the practical results of all these appliances ? Now let us suppose a few. Suppose that your institution should have educated those who are now its teachers. That would be a very remarkable fact. Supposing, besides, it should, so to speak, have educated education all around it, by sending forth numerous and efficient teachers into many and divers schools. Suppose the young student, reared exclusively in its laboratory, should be presently snapped up for the laboratory of the great and famous hospitals. Suppose that in nine years its industrial students should have carried off a round dozen of the much-competed-for prizes awarded by the Society of Arts and the Government department, besides two local prizes originating in the generosity of a Birmingham man. Suppose that the Town Council, having it in trust to find an artisan well fit to receive the Whitworth prizes, should find him here. Suppose that one of the industrial students should turn his chemical studies to the practical account of extracting gold from waste color-water, and of taking it into custody, in the very act of running away with hundreds of pounds down the town drains. Suppose another should perceive in his books, in his studious evenings, what was amiss with his master's until then inscrutably defective furnace, and should go straight—to the great annual saving of that master—and put it right. Supposing another should puzzle out the means, until then quite unknown in England, of making a certain description of colored glass. Supposing another should qualify himself to vanquish one by one, as they daily arise, all the little difficulties incidental to his calling as an electro-plater, and should be applied to by his companions in the shop in all emergencies under the name of the "Encyclopædia." Suppose a long procession of such cases, and then consider that these are not suppositions at all, but are plain, unvarnished facts, culminating in the one special and significant fact that, with a single solitary exception, every one of the institution's industrial students who have taken its prizes within ten years have since climbed to higher situations in their way of life.

As to the extent to which the institution encourages the artisan to think, and so, for instance, to rise superior to the little shackling prejudices and observances perchance existing in his trade when they will not bear the test of inquiry, that is only to be equalled by the extent to which it encourages him to feel. There is a certain tone of modest manliness pervading all the little facts which I have looked through which I found remarkably impressive. The decided objection on the part of industrial students to attend classes in their working-clothes breathes this tone, as being a graceful and at the same time perfectly independent recognition of the place and of one another. And this tone is admirably illustrated in a different way, in the case of a poor bricklayer, who, being in temporary reverses through the illness of his family, and having consequently been obliged to part with his best clothes, and being therefore missed from his classes, in which he had been noticed as a very hard worker, was persuaded to attend them in his working-clothes. He replied, " No, it was not possible. It must not be thought of. It must not come into question for a moment. It would be supposed, or it might be thought, that he did it to attract attention." And the same man being offered by one of the officers a loan of money to enable him to rehabilitate his appearance, positively declined it, on the ground that he came to the institution to learn and to know better how to help himself, not otherwise to ask help, or to receive help from any man. Now I am justified in calling this the tone of the institution, because it is no isolated instance, but is a fair and honorable sample of the spirit of the place, and as such I put it at the conclusion—though last, certainly not least—of my references to what your institution has indubitably done.

Well, ladies and gentlemen, I come at length to what, in the humble opinion of the evanescent officer before you, remains for the institution to do, and not to do. As Mr. Carlyle has it, towards the closing pages of his grand history of the French Revolution, "This we are now with due brevity to glance at ; and then courage, oh listener, I see land !"[*] I earnestly hope— and I firmly believe—that your institution will do henceforth as it has done hitherto; it can hardly do better. I hope and believe that it will know among its members no distinction of persons, creed, or party, but that it will conserve its place of assemblage as a high, pure ground, on which all such considerations shall merge into the one universal, Heaven-sent aspiration of the human soul to be wiser and better. I hope and believe that it will always be expansive and elastic ; forever seeking to devise new means of enlarging the circle of its members, of attracting to itself the confidence of still greater and greater numbers, and never evincing any more disposition to stand still than time does, or life does, or the seasons do. And above all things, I hope, and I feel confident from its antecedents, that it will never allow any consideration on the face of the earth to induce it to patronize or to be patronized, for I verily believe that the bestowal and receipt of patronage in such wise has been a curse in England, and that it has done more to prevent really good objects, and to lower really high character, than the utmost efforts of the narrowest antagonism could have effected in twice the time.

I have no fear that the walls of the Birmingham and Midland Institute will ever tremble responsive to the croakings of the timid opponents of intellectual progress; but in this connection generally I can not forbear from offering a remark which is much upon my mind. It is commonly assumed—much too commonly— that this age is a material age, and that a material age is an irreligious age. I have been pained lately to see this assumption repeated in certain influential quarters for which I have a high respect, and desire to have a higher. I

---

* Carlyle's "French Revolution," bk. x., chap. i.

am afraid that by dint of constantly being reiterated, and reiterated without protest, this assumption — which I take leave altogether to deny—may be accepted by the more unthinking part of the public as unquestionably true; just as caricaturists and painters, professedly making a portrait of some public man, which was not in the least like him, to begin with, have gone on repeating and repeating it until the public came to believe that it must be exactly like him, simply because it was like itself, and really have at last, in the fullness of time, grown almost disposed to resent upon him their tardy discovery —really to resent upon him their late discovery —that he was not like it. I confess, standing here in this responsible situation, that I do not understand this much-used and much-abused phrase—the "material age." I can not comprehend—if any body can I very much doubt— its logical signification. For instance, has electricity become more material in the mind of any sane or moderately insane man, woman, or child, because of the discovery that, in the good providence of God, it could be made available for the service and use of man to an immeasurably greater extent than for his destruction? Do I make a more material journey to the bedside of my dying parent or my dying child when I travel there at the rate of sixty miles an hour, than when I travel thither at the rate of six? Rather, in the swiftest case, does not my agonized heart become overfraught with gratitude to that Supreme Beneficence from whom alone could have proceeded the wonderful means of shortening my suspense? What is the materiality of the cable or the wire compared with the materiality of the spark? What is the materiality of certain chemical substances that we can weigh or measure, imprison or release, compared with the materiality of their appointed affinities and repulsions presented to them from the instant of their creation to the day of judgment? When did this so-called material age begin? With the use of clothing? with the discovery of the compass? with the invention of the art of printing? Surely, it has been a long time about; and which is the more material object, the farthing tallow candle that will not give me light, or that flame of gas which will?

No, ladies and gentlemen, do not let us be discouraged or deceived by any fine, vapid, empty words. The true material age is the stupid Chinese age, in which no new or grand revelations of nature are granted, because they are ignorantly and insolently repelled, instead of being diligently and humbly sought. The difference between the ancient fiction of the mad braggart defying the lightning and the modern historical picture of Franklin drawing it towards his kite, in order that he might the more profoundly study that which was set before him to be studied (or it would not have been there), happily expresses, to my mind, the distinction between the much-maligned material sages — material in one sense, I suppose, but in another very immaterial sages—of the Celestial Empire school. Consider whether it is likely or unlikely, natural or unnatural, reasonable or unreasonable, that I, a being capable of thought, and finding myself surrounded by such discovered wonders on every hand, should sometimes ask myself the question—should put to myself the solemn consideration—can these things be among those things which might have been disclosed by divine lips nigh upon two thousand years ago, but that the people of that time could not bear them? And whether this be so or no, if I am so surrounded on every hand, is not my moral responsibility tremendously increased thereby, and with it my intelligence and submission as a child of Adam and of the dust, before that Shining Source which equally of all that is granted and all that is withheld holds in His mighty hands the unapproachable mysteries of life and death.

To the students of your industrial classes generally I have had it in my mind, first, to commend the short motto, in two words, "Courage—Persevere." This is the motto of a friend and worker. Not because the eyes of Europe are upon them, for I don't in the least believe it; nor because the eyes of even England are upon them, for I don't in the least believe it; not because their doings will be proclaimed with blast of trumpet at street corners, for no such musical performances will take place; not because self-improvement is at all certain to lead to worldly success, but simply because it is good and right of itself, and because, being so, it does assuredly bring with it its own resources and its own rewards. I would further commend to them a very wise and witty piece of advice on the conduct of the understanding which was given more than half a century ago by the Rev. Sydney Smith—wisest and wittiest of the friends I have lost. He says— and he is speaking, you will please understand, as I speak, to a school of volunteer students— he says: "There is a piece of foppery which is to be cautiously guarded against, the foppery of universality, of knowing all sciences and excelling in all arts—chemistry, mathematics, algebra, dancing, history, reasoning, riding, fencing, Low Dutch, High Dutch, and natural philosophy. In short, the modern precept of education very often is, 'Take the Admirable Crichton for your model, I would have you ignorant of nothing.' Now," says he, "my advice, on the contrary, is to have the courage to be ignorant of a great number of things, in order that you may avoid the calamity of being ignorant of every thing."

To this I would superadd a little truth which holds equally good of my own life and the life of every eminent man I have ever known. The one serviceable, safe, certain, renumerative, attainable quality in every study and in every pursuit is the quality of attention. My own invention or imagination, such as it is, I can most truthfully assure you, would never have served me as it has, but for the habit of commonplace, humble, patient, daily, toiling, drudging attention. Genius, vivacity, quickness of penetration, brilliancy in association of ideas—such mental qualities, like the qualities of the apparition of the externally armed head in "Macbeth," will not be commanded ; but attention, after due term of submissive service, always will. Like certain plants which the poorest peasant may grow in the poorest soil, it can be cultivated by any one, and it is certain in its own good season to bring forth flowers and fruit. I can most truthfully assure you, by-the-by, that this eulogium on attention is so far quite disinterested on my part, as that it has not the least reference whatever to the attention with which you have honored me.

Well, ladies and gentlemen, I have done. I can not but reflect how often you have probably heard within these walls one of the foremost men, and certainly one of the very best speakers, if not the very best, in England. I could not say to myself when I began just now, in Shakspeare's line—

"I will be BRIGHT and shining gold,"

but I could say to myself, and I did say to myself, "I will be as natural and easy as I possibly can," because my heart has all been in my subject, and I bear an old love towards Birmingham and Birmingham men. I have said that I bear an old love towards Birmingham and Birmingham men ; let me amend a small omission, and add "and Birmingham women." This ring I wear on my finger now is an old Birmingham gift, and if by rubbing it I could raise the spirit that was obedient to Aladdin's ring, I heartily assure you that my first instruction to that genius on the spot should be to place himself at Birmingham's disposal in the best of causes.

[In acknowledging the vote of thanks, Mr. Dickens said :]

Ladies and gentlemen, as I hope it is more than possible that I shall have the pleasure of meeting you again before Christmas is out, and shall have the great interest of seeing the faces and touching the hands of the successful competitors in your lists, I will not cast upon that anticipated meeting the terrible foreshadowing of dread which must inevitably result from a second speech. I thank you most heartily, and I most sincerely and fervently say to you, "Good-night, and God bless you." In reference to the appropriate and excellent remarks of Mr. Dixon, I will now discharge my conscience of my political creed, which is contained in two articles, and has no reference to any party or persons. My faith in the people governing is, on the whole, infinitesimal ; my faith in the People governed is, on the whole, illimitable.

XLIII.

BIRMINGHAM, JANUARY 6, 1870.

[On the evening of the above date, Mr. Dickens, as President of the Birmingham and Midland Institute, distributed the prizes and certificates awarded to the most successful students in the first year. The proceedings took place in the Town Hall. Mr. Dickens entered at eight o'clock, accompanied by the officers of the Institute, and was received with loud applause. After the lapse of a minute or two, he rose and said :]

Ladies and Gentlemen,—When I last had the honor to preside over a meeting of the institution which again brings us together, I took occasion to remark upon a certain superabundance of public speaking which seems to me to distinguish the present time. It will require very little self-denial on my part to practise now what I preached then ; firstly, because I said my little say that night ; and, secondly, because we have definite and highly interesting action before us to night. We have now to bestow the rewards which have been brilliantly won by the most successful competitors in the society's lists. I say the most successful, because to-night we should particularly observe, I think, that there is success in all honest endeavor, and that there is some victory gained in every gallant struggle that is made. To strive at all involves a victory achieved over sloth, inertness, and indifference ; and competition for these prizes involves, besides, in the vast majority of cases, competition with and mastery asserted over circumstances adverse to the effort made. Therefore, every losing competitor among my hearers may be certain that he has still won much—very much—and that he can well afford to swell the triumph of his rivals who have passed him in the race.

I have applied the word "rewards" to these

prizes, and I do so, not because they represent any great intrinsic worth in silver or gold, but precisely because they do not. They represent what is above all price—what can be stated in no arithmetical figures, and what is one of the great needs of the human soul—encouraging sympathy. They are an assurance to every student present or to come in your institution, that he does not work either neglected or unfriended, and that he is watched, felt for, stimulated, and appreciated. Such an assurance, conveyed in the presence of this large assembly, and striking to the breasts of the recipients that thrill which is inseparable from any great united utterance of feeling, is a reward, to my thinking, as purely worthy of the labor as the labor itself is worthy of the reward; and by a sensitive spirit can never be forgotten.

[One of the prize-takers was a Miss Winkle, a name suggestive of "Pickwick," which was received with laughter. Mr. Dickens made some remarks to the lady in an under-tone; and then observed to the audience, "I have recommended Miss Winkle to change her name." The prizes having been distributed, Mr. Dickens made a second brief speech. He said:]

The prizes are now all distributed, and I have discharged myself of the delightful task you have intrusted to me; and if the recipients of these prizes and certificates who have come upon this platform have had the genuine pleasure in receiving their acknowledgments from my hands that I have had in placing them in theirs, they are in a true Christian temper to-night. I have the painful sense upon me, that it is reserved for some one else to enjoy this great satisfaction of mind next time. It would be useless for the few short moments longer to disguise the fact that I happen to have drawn King this Twelfth Night, but that another sovereign will very soon sit upon my inconstant throne. To-night I abdicate, or, what is much the same thing in the modern annals of royalty—I am politely dethroned. This melancholy reflection, ladies and gentlemen, brings me to a very small point, personal to myself, upon which I will beg your permission to say a closing word.

When I was here last autumn I made, in reference to some remarks of your respected member, Mr. Dixon, a short confession of my political faith—or perhaps I should better say want of faith. It imported that I have very little confidence in the people who govern us—please to observe "people" there will be with a small "p"—but that I have great confidence in the People whom they govern; please to observe "people" there with a large "P." This was shortly and elliptically stated, and was with no evil intention, I am absolutely sure, in some

quarters inversely explained. Perhaps as the inventor of a certain extravagant fiction, but one which I do see rather frequently quoted as if there were grains of truth at the bottom of it—a fiction called the "Circumlocution Office"—and perhaps also as the writer of an idle book or two, whose public opinions are not obscurely stated — perhaps in these respects I do not sufficiently bear in mind Hamlet's caution to speak by the card lest equivocation should undo me.

Now I complain of nobody; but simply in order that there may be no mistake as to what I did mean, and as to what I do mean, I will restate my meaning, and I will do so in the words of a great thinker, a great writer, and a great scholar,[*] whose death, unfortunately for mankind, cut short his "History of Civilization in England :"—"They may talk as they will about reforms which Government has introduced and improvements to be expected from legislation, but whoever will take a wider and more commanding view of human affairs will soon discover that such hopes are chimerical. They will learn that lawgivers are nearly always the obstructors of society instead of its helpers, and that in the extremely few cases where their measures have turned out well, their success has been owing to the fact that, contrary to their usual custom, they have implicitly obeyed the spirit of their time, and have been—as they always should be—the mere servants of the people, to whose wishes they are bound to give a public and legal sanction."

～～～～

XLIV.

LONDON, APRIL 6, 1846.[†]

[The first Anniversary Festival of the General Theatrical Fund Association was held on the evening of the above date at the London Tavern. The Chair was taken by Mr. Dickens, who thus proposed the principal toast:]

GENTLEMEN,—In offering to you a toast which has not as yet been publicly drunk in any company, it becomes incumbent on me to offer a few words in explanation : in the first place premising that the toast will be "The General Theatrical Fund."

The Association whose anniversary we celebrate to-night was founded seven years ago, for the purpose of granting permanent pensions to such of the *corps dramatique* as had retired from the stage, either from a decline in their years or a decay of their powers. Collected within the

---

* Henry Thomas Buckle.
† This, and the Speeches which follow, were accidentally omitted in their right places.

scope of its benevolence are all actors and actresses, singers or dancers, of five years' standing in the profession. To relieve their necessities and to protect them from want is the great end of the Society, and it is good to know that for seven years the members of it have steadily, patiently, quietly, and perseveringly pursued this end, advancing by regular contribution moneys which many of them could ill afford, and cheered by no external help or assistance of any kind whatsoever. It has thus served a regular apprenticeship, but I trust that we shall establish to-night that its time is out, and that henceforth the Fund will enter upon a flourishing and brilliant career.

I have no doubt that you are all aware that there are, and were when this institution was founded, two other institutions existing of a similar nature — Covent Garden and Drury Lane—both of long standing, both richly endowed. It can not, however, be too distinctly understood that the present institution is not in any way adverse to those. How can it be when it is only a wide and broad extension of all that is most excellent in the principles on which they are founded? That such an extension was absolutely necessary was sufficiently proved by the fact that the great body of the dramatic corps were excluded from the benefits conferred by a membership of either of these institutions; for it was essential, in order to become a member of the Drury Lane Society, that the applicant, either he or she, should have been engaged for three consecutive seasons as a performer. This was afterwards reduced, in the case of Covent Garden, to a period of two years, but it really is as exclusive one way as the other, for I need not tell you that Covent Garden is now but a vision of the past. You might play the bottle conjuror with its dramatic company, and put them all into a pint bottle. The human voice is rarely heard within its walls save in connection with corn, or the ambidextrous prestidigitation of the Wizard of the North. In like manner, Drury Lane is conducted now with almost a sole view to the opera and ballet, insomuch that the statue of Shakspeare over the door serves as emphatically to point out his grave, as his bust did in the church of Stratford-upon-Avon. How can the profession generally hope to qualify for the Drury Lane or Covent Garden institution, when the oldest and most distinguished members have been driven from the boards on which they have earned their reputations, to delight the town in theatres to which the General Theatrical Fund alone extended?

I will again repeat that I attach no reproach to those other Funds, with which I have had the honor of being connected at different periods of my life. At the time those Associations were established, an engagement at one of those theatres was almost a matter of course, and a successful engagement would last a whole life; but an engagement of two months' duration at Covent Garden would be a perfect Old Parr of an engagement just now. It should never be forgotten that when those two funds were established, the two great theatres were protected by patent, and that at that time the minor theatres were condemned by law to the representation of the most preposterous nonsense, and some gentlemen whom I see around me could no more belong to the minor theatres of that day than they could now belong to St. Bartholomew fair.

As I honor the two old funds for the great good which they have done, so I honor this for the much greater good it is resolved to do. It is not because I love them less, but because I love this more—because it includes more in its operation.

Let us ever remember that there is no class of actors who stand so much in need of a retiring fund as those who do not win the great prizes, but who are nevertheless an essential part of the theatrical system, and by consequence bear a part in contributing to our pleasures. We owe them a debt which we ought to pay. The beds of such men are not of roses, but of very artificial flowers indeed. Their lives are lives of care and privation, and hard struggles with very stern realities. It is from among the poor actors who drink wine from goblets, in color marvellously like toast and water, and who preside at Barmecide feasts with wonderful appetites for steaks—it is from their ranks that the most triumphant favorites have sprung. And surely, besides this, the greater the instruction and delight we derive from the rich English drama, the more we are bound to succor and protect the humblest of those votaries of the art who add to our instruction and amusement.

Hazlitt has well said that "There is no class of society whom so many persons regard with affection as actors. We greet them on the stage, we like to meet them in the streets; they almost always recall to us pleasant associations."[*] When they have strutted and fretted their hour upon the stage, let them not be heard no more—but let them be heard sometimes to say that they are happy in their old age. When they have passed for the last time from behind that glittering row of lights with which we are all familiar, let them not pass

---

[*] "Hazlitt's Round-Table" (Edinburgh, 1817, vol. ii., p. 242), § On Actors and Acting.

away into gloom and darkness, but let them pass into cheerfulness and light—into a contented and happy home.

This is the object for which we have met; and I am too familiar with the English character not to know that it will be effected. When we come suddenly in a crowded street upon the careworn features of a familiar face—crossing us like the ghost of pleasant hours long forgotten—let us not recall those features with pain, in sad remembrance of what they once were, but let us in joy recognize it, and go back a pace or two to meet it once again, as that of a friend who has beguiled us of a moment of care, who has taught us to sympathize with virtuous grief, cheating us to tears for sorrows not our own—and we all know how pleasant are such tears. Let such a face be ever remembered as that of our benefactor and our friend.

I tried to recollect, in coming here, whether I had ever been in any theatre in my life from which I had not brought away some pleasant association, however poor the theatre, and I protest, out of my varied experience, I could not remember even one from which I had not brought some favorable impression, and that commencing with the period when I believed the clown was a being born into the world with infinite pockets, and ending with that in which I saw the other night, outside one of the "Royal Saloons," a playbill which showed me ships completely rigged, carrying men, and careering over boundless and tempestuous oceans. And now, bespeaking your kindest remembrance of our theatres and actors, I beg to propose that you drink as heartily and freely as ever a toast was drunk in this toast-drinking city, "Prosperity to the General Theatrical Fund."

XLV.

LEEDS, DECEMBER 1, 1847.

[On the above evening a Soirée of the Leeds Mechanics' Institution took place, at which about 1200 persons were present. The Chair was taken by Mr. Dickens, who thus addressed the meeting :]

LADIES AND GENTLEMEN,— Believe me — speaking to you with a most disastrous cold, which makes my own voice sound very strangely in my ears—that if I were not gratified and honored beyond expression by your cordial welcome, I should have considered the invitation to occupy my present position in this brilliant assemblage in itself a distinction not easy to be surpassed. The cause in which we are assembled and the objects we are met to promote, I take, and always have taken to be, *the* cause and *the* objects involving almost all others that are es-

sential to the welfare and happiness of mankind. And in a celebration like the present, commemorating the birth and progress of a great educational establishment, I recognize a something, not limited to the spectacle of the moment, beautiful and radiant though it be—not limited even to the success of the particular establishment in which we are more immediately interested — but extending from this place and through swarms of toiling men elsewhere, cheering and stimulating them in the onward, upward path that lies before us all. Wherever hammers beat or wherever factory chimneys smoke, wherever hands are busy or the clanking of machinery resounds—wherever, in a word, there are masses of industrious human beings whom their wise Creator did not see fit to constitute all body, but into each and every one of whom He breathed a mind—there, I would fain believe, some touch of sympathy and encouragement is felt from our collective pulse now beating in this Hall.

Ladies and gentlemen, glancing with such feelings at the report of your institution for the present year sent to me by your respected president—whom I can not help feeling it, by-the-by, a kind of crime to depose, even thus peacefully and for so short a time—I say, glancing over this report, I found one statement of fact in the very opening which gave me an uncommon satisfaction. It is, that a great number of the members and subscribers are among that class of persons for whose advantage Mechanics' Institutions were originated—namely, persons receiving weekly wages. This circumstance gives me the greatest delight. I am sure that no better testimony could be borne to the merits and usefulness of this institution, and that no better guaranty could be given for its continued prosperity and advancement.

To such Associations as this, in their darker hours, there may yet reappear, now and then, the spectral shadow of a certain dead and buried opposition ; but before the light of a steady trust in them on the part of the general people, bearing testimony to the virtuous influences of such institutions by their own intelligence and conduct, the ghost will melt away like early vapor from the ground. Fear of such institutions as these ! We have heard people sometimes speak with jealousy of them—with distrust of them ! Imagine here, on either hand, two great towns like Leeds, full of busy men, all of them feeling necessarily, and some of them heavily, the burdens and inequalities inseparable from civilized society. In this town there is ignorance, dense and dark ; in that town, education—the best of education ; that which the grown man from day to day and year to year furnishes for himself and maintains for himself, and in right of which his education goes on all his life, instead of leaving off, complacently, just when he begins to live in the social system. Now which of these two towns has a good man or a good cause reason to distrust and dread? "The educated one," does some timid politician, with a marvellously weak sight, say (as I have heard such politicians say), "because knowledge is power, and because it won't do to have too much power abroad." Why, ladies and gentlemen, reflect whether ignorance be not power, and a very dreadful power. Look where we will, do we not find it powerful for every kind of wrong and evil? Powerful to take its enemies to its heart, and strike its best friends down—powerful to fill the prisons, the hospitals, and the graves —powerful for blind violence, prejudice, and error, in all their gloomy and destructive shapes. Whereas the power of knowledge, if I understand it, is to bear and forbear; to learn the path of duty and to tread it; to engender that self-respect which does not stop at self, but cherishes the best respect for the best objects—to turn an always enlarging acquaintance with the joys and sorrows, capabilities and imperfections of our race to daily account in mildness of life and gentleness of construction, and humble efforts for the improvement, stone by stone, of the whole social fabric.

I never heard but one tangible position taken against educational establishments for the people, and that was, that in this or that instance, or in these or those instances, education for the people has failed. And I have never traced even this to its source but I have found that the term education, so employed, meant any thing but education—implied the mere imperfect application of old, ignorant, preposterous spelling-book lessons to the meanest purposes—as if you should teach a child that there is no higher end in electricity, for example, than expressly to strike a mutton-pie out of the hand of a greedy boy— and on which it is as unreasonable to found an objection to education in a comprehensive sense, as it would be to object altogether to the combing of youthful hair, because in a certain charity school they had a practice of combing it into the pupils' eyes.

Now, ladies and gentlemen, I turn to the report of this institution, on whose behalf we are met; and I start with the education given there, and I find that it really is an education that is deserving of the name. I find that there are papers read and lectures delivered, on a variety of subjects of interest and importance. I find that there are evening classes formed for the acqui-

sition of sound, useful English information, and for the study of those two important languages, daily becoming more important in the business of life—the French and German. I find that there is a class for drawing, a chemical class, subdivided into the elementary branch and the manufacturing branch, most important here. I find that there is a day-school at twelve shillings a quarter, which small cost, besides including instruction in all that is useful to the merchant and the man of business, admits to all the advantages of the parent institution. I find that there is a School of Design established in connection with the Government School; and that there was in January this year a library of between six and seven thousand books. Ladies and gentlemen, if any man would tell me that any thing but good could come of such knowledge as this, all I can say is, that I should consider him a new and most lamentable proof of the necessity of such institutions, and should regard him in his own person as a melancholy instance of what a man may come to by never having belonged to one, or sympathized with one.

There is one other paragraph in this report which struck my eye in looking over it, and on which I can not help offering a word of joyful notice. It is the steady increase that appears to have taken place in the number of lady members—among whom I hope I may presume are included some of the bright, fair faces that are clustered around me. Gentlemen, I hold that it is not good for man to be alone—even in Mechanics' Institutions; and I rank it as very far from among the last or least of the merits of such places, that he need not be alone there, and that he is not. I believe that the sympathy and society of those who are our best and dearest friends in infancy, in childhood, in manhood, and in old age, the most devoted and least selfish natures that we know on earth, who turn to us always constant and unchanged, when others turn away, should greet us here, if anywhere, and go on with us side by side.

I know, gentlemen, by the evidence of my own proper senses at this moment, that there are charms and graces in such greetings, such as no other greeting can possess. I know that in every beautiful work of the Almighty hand, which is illustrated in your lectures, and in every real or ideal portraiture of fortitude and goodness that you find in your books, there is something that must bring you home again to them for its brightest and best example. And therefore, gentlemen, I hope that you will never be without them, or without an increasing number of them in your studies and your commemorations; and that an immense number of new marriages, and other domestic festivals naturally consequent upon those marriages, may be traced back from time to time to the Leeds Mechanics' Institution.

There are many gentlemen around me, distinguished by their public position and service, or endeared to you by frequent intercourse, or by their zealous efforts on behalf of the cause which brings us together; and to them I shall beg leave to refer you for further observations on this happy and interesting occasion; begging to congratulate you finally upon the occasion itself; upon the prosperity and thriving prospects of your institution; and upon our common and general good fortune in living in these times, when the means of mental culture and improvement are presented cheaply, socially, and cheerfully, and not in dismal cells or lonely garrets. And lastly, I congratulate myself, I assure you most heartily, upon the part with which I am honored on an occasion so congenial to my warmest feelings and sympathies, and I beg to thank you for such evidences of your good-will as I never can coldly remember and never forget.

[In acknowledging the vote of thanks, Mr. Dickens said:]

Ladies and gentlemen, it is a great satisfaction to me that this question has been put by the Mayor, inasmuch as I hope I may receive it as a token that he has forgiven me those extremely large letters, which I must say, from the glimpse I caught of them when I arrived in the town, looked like a leaf from the first primer of a very promising young giant.

I will only observe, in reference to the proceeding of this evening, that after what I have seen, and the excellent speeches I have heard from gentlemen of so many different callings and persuasions, meeting here as on neutral ground, I do more strongly and sincerely believe than I ever have in my life—and that is saying a great deal—that institutions such as this will be the means of refining and improving that social edifice which has been so often mentioned to-night, until—unlike that Babel tower that would have taken heaven by storm —it shall end in sweet accord and harmony amongst all classes of its builders.

Ladies and gentlemen, most respectfully and heartily I bid you good-night and good-bye, and I trust the next time we meet it will be in even greater numbers and in a larger room, and that we often shall meet again to recall this evening, then of the past, and remember it as one of a series of increasing triumphs of your excellent institution.

XLVI.

GLASGOW, DECEMBER 28, 1847.

[The first Soirée commemorative of the Opening of the Glasgow Athenæum took place on the above evening in the City Hall. Mr. Charles Dickens presided, and made the following speech:]

Ladies and Gentlemen,—Let me begin by endeavoring to convey to you the assurance that not even the warmth of your reception can possibly exceed, in simple earnestness, the cordiality of the feeling with which I come amongst you. This beautiful scene and your generous greeting would naturally awaken, under any circumstances, no common feeling within me; but when I connect them with the high purpose of this brilliant assembly—when I regard it as an educational example and encouragement to the rest of Scotland—when I regard it no less as a recognition on the part of every body here of the right, indisputable and inalienable, of all those who are actively engaged in the work and business of life to elevate and improve themselves so far as in them lies, by all good means—I feel as if I stand here to swear brotherhood to all the young men in Glasgow— and, I may say, to all the young women in Glasgow; being unfortunately in no position to take any tenderer vows upon myself—and as if we were pledged from this time henceforth to make common cause together in one of the most laudable and worthy of human objects.

Ladies and gentlemen, a common cause must be made in such a design as that which brings us together this night; for without it nothing can be done, but with it every thing. It is a common cause of right, God knows; for it is idle to suppose that the advantages of such an institution as the Glasgow Athenæum will stop within its own walls or be confined to its own members. Through all the society of this great and important city, upward to the highest and downward to the lowest, it must, I know, be felt for good. Downward in a clearer perception of, and sympathy with, those social miseries which can be alleviated, and those wide-open doors to vice and crime that can be shut and barred; and upward in a greater intelligence, increased efficiency, and higher knowledge, of all who partake of its benefits themselves, or who communicate, as all must do, in a greater or less degree, some portion to the circle of relatives or friends in which they move.

Nor, ladies and gentlemen, would I say for any man, however high his social position, or however great his attainments, that he might not find something to be learned even from immediate contact with such institutions. If he only saw the goddess Knowledge coming out of her secluded palaces and high places to mingle with the throng, and to give them shining glimpses of the delights which were long kept hoarded up, he might learn something. If he only saw the energy and the courage with which those who earn their daily bread by the labor of their hands or heads come night after night, as to a recreation, to that which was, perhaps, the whole absorbing business of his youth, there might still be something very wholesome for him to learn. But when he could see in such places their genial and reviving influences, their substituting of the contemplation of the beauties of nature and art, and of the wisdom of great men, for mere sensual enjoyment or stupid idleness — at any rate he would learn this—that it is at once the duty and the interest of all good members of society to encourage and protect them.

I took occasion to say at an Athenæum in Yorkshire a few weeks since,[*] and I think it a point most important to be borne in mind on such commemorations as these, that when such societies are objected to, or are decried on the ground that, in the views of the objectors, education among the people has not succeeded, the term education is used with not the least reference to its real meaning, and is wholly misunderstood. Mere reading and writing is not education; it would be quite as reasonable to call bricks and mortar architecture, oils and colors art, reeds and cat-gut music, or the child's spelling-books the works of Shakspeare, Milton, or Bacon, as to call the lowest rudiments of education, education, and to visit on that most abused and slandered word their failure in any instance; and precisely because they were not education; because, generally speaking, the word has been understood in that sense a great deal too long; because education for the business of life, and for the due cultivation of domestic virtues, is at least as important from day to day to the grown person as to the child; because real education, in the strife and contention for a livelihood, and the consequent necessity incumbent on a great number of young persons to go into the world when they are very young, is extremely difficult. It is because of these things that I look upon mechanics' institutions and athenæums as vitally important to the well-being of society. It is because the rudiments of education may there be turned to good account in the acquisition of sound principles, and of the great virtues, hope, faith, and charity, to which all our knowledge tends; it is because of that, I take it, that you have met in education's name to-night.

* Vide supra, p. 89.

It is a great satisfaction to me to occupy the place I do in behalf of an infant institution; a remarkably fine child enough, of a vigorous constitution, but an infant still. I esteem myself singularly fortunate in knowing it before its prime, in the hope that I may have the pleasure of remembering in its prime, and when it has attained to its lusty maturity, that I was a friend of its youth. It has already passed through some of the disorders to which children are liable; it succeeded to an elder brother of a very meritorious character, but of rather a weak constitution, and which expired when about twelve months old, from, it is said, a destructive habit of getting up early in the morning: it succeeded this elder brother, and has fought manfully through a sea of troubles. Its friends have often been much concerned for it; its pulse has been exceedingly low, being only 1250, when it was expected to have been 10,000; several relations and friends have even gone so far as to walk off once or twice in the melancholy belief that it was dead. Through all that, assisted by the indomitable energy of one or two nurses, to whom it can never be sufficiently grateful, it came triumphantly, and now of all the youthful members of its family I ever saw, it has the strongest attitude, the healthiest look, the brightest and most cheerful air. I find the institution nobly lodged; I find it with a reading-room, a coffee-room, and a news-room; I find it with lectures given and in progress, in sound, useful and well-selected subjects; I find it with morning and evening classes for mathematics, logic, grammar, music, French, German, Spanish, and Italian, attended by upwards of five hundred persons; but best and first of all, and what is to me more satisfactory than any thing else in the history of the institution, I find that all this has been mainly achieved by the young men of Glasgow themselves, with very little assistance. And, ladies and gentlemen, as the axiom, "Heaven helps those who help themselves," is truer in no case than it is in this, I look to the young men of Glasgow, from such a past and such a present, to a noble future. Every thing that has been done in any other athenæum, I confidently expect to see done here; and when that shall be the case, and when there shall be great cheap schools in connection with the institution, and when it has bound together forever all its friends, and brought over to itself all those who look upon it as an objectionable institution—then, and not till then, I hope the young men of Glasgow will rest from their labors, and think their study done.

If the young men of Glasgow want any

stimulus or encouragement in this wise, they have one beside them in the presence of their fair townswomen, which is irresistible. It is a most delightful circumstance to me, and one fraught with inestimable benefits to institutions of this kind, that at a meeting of this nature those who in all things are our best examples, encouragers, and friends, are not excluded. The abstract idea of the Graces was in ancient times associated with those arts which refine the human understanding; and it is pleasant to see now, in the rolling of the world, the Graces popularizing the practice of those arts by their example, and adorning it with their presence.

I am happy to know that in the Glasgow Athenæum there is a peculiar bond of union between the institution and the fairest part of creation. I understand that the necessary addition to the small library of books being difficult and expensive to make, the ladies have generally resolved to hold a fancy bazar, and to devote the proceeds to this admirable purpose; and I learn with no less pleasure that her Majesty the Queen, in a graceful and womanly sense of the excellence of this design, has consented that the bazar shall be held under her royal patronage. I can only say, that if you do not find something very noble in your books after this, you are much duller students than I take you to be. The ladies—the single ladies, at least—however disinterested I know they are by sex and nature, will, I hope, resolve to have some of the advantages of these books, by never marrying any but members of the Athenæum. It seems to me it ought to be the pleasantest library in the world.

Hazlitt says, in speaking of some of the graceful fancies of some familiar writer of fiction, " How long since I first became acquainted with these characters; what old-fashioned friends they seem; and yet I am not tired of them like so many other friends, nor they of me." In this case the books will not only possess all the attractions of their own friendships and charms, but also the manifold—I may say womanfold—associations connected with their donors. I can imagine how, in fact, from these fanciful associations, some fair Glasgow widow may be taken for the remoter one whom Sir Roger de Coverley could not forget; I can imagine how Sophia's muff may be seen and loved, but not by Tom Jones, going down the High Street on any winter day; or I can imagine the student finding in every fair form the exact counterpart of the Glasgow Athenæum, and taking into consideration the history of Europe without the consent of Sheriff Alison.

I can imagine, in short, how through all the facts and fictions of this library, these ladies will be always active, and that

" Age will not wither them, nor custom stale
    Their infinite variety."

It seems to me to be a moral, delightful, and happy chance, that this meeting has been held at this genial season of the year, when a new time is, as it were, opening before us, and when we celebrate the birth of that divine and blessed Teacher, who took the highest knowledge into the humblest places, and whose great system comprehended all mankind. I hail it as a most auspicious omen, at this time of the year, when many scattered friends and families are re-assembled, for the members of this institution to be calling men together from all quarters, with a brotherly view to the general good, and a view to the general improvement; as I consider that such designs are practically worthy of the faith we hold, and a practical remembrance of the words, " On earth peace, and good-will toward men." I hope that every year which dawns on your institution will find it richer in its means of usefulness, and grayer-headed in the honor and respect it has gained. It can hardly speak for itself more appropriately than in the words of an English writer, when contemplating the English emblem of this period of the year, the holly-tree :

Mr Dickens concluded by quoting the last three stanzas of Southey's poem, " The Holly-Tree."]

———

[In acknowledging a vote of thanks proposed by Sir Archibald (then Mr.) Alison, Mr. Dickens said ·]

Ladies and gentlemen, I am no stranger—and I say it with the deepest gratitude—to the warmth of Scottish hearts ; but the warmth of your present welcome almost deprives me of any hope of acknowledging it. I will not detain you any longer at this late hour; let it suffice to assure you, that for taking the part with which I have been honored in this festival, I have been repaid a thousand-fold by your abundant kindness, and by the unspeakable gratification it has afforded me. I hope that, before many years are past, we may have another meeting in public, when we shall rejoice at the immense progress your institution will have made in the mean time, and look back upon this night with new pleasure and satisfaction. I shall now, in conclusion, repeat most heartily and fervently the quotation of Dr. Ewing, the late Provost of Glasgow, which Bailie Nicol Jarvie, himself " a Glasgow body," observed was " elegantly putten round the town's arms."

XLVII.

LONDON, APRIL 14, 1851.

[The Sixth Annual Dinner of the General Theatrical Fund was held at the London Tavern on the above date. Mr. Charles Dickens occupied the chair, and in giving the toast of the evening said:]

I HAVE so often had the satisfaction of bearing my testimony, in this place, to the usefulness of the excellent institution in whose behalf we are assembled, that I should be really sensible of the disadvantage of having now nothing to say in proposing the toast you all anticipate, if I were not well assured that there is really nothing which needs be said. I have to appeal to you on the old grounds, and no ingenuity of mine could render those grounds of greater weight than they have hitherto successfully proved to you.

Although the General Theatrical Fund Association, unlike many other public societies and endowments, is represented by no building, whether of stone, or brick, or glass, like that astonishing evidence of the skill and energy of my friend Mr. Paxton, which all the world is now called upon to admire, and the great merit of which, as you learn from the best authorities, is, that it ought to have fallen down long before it was built, and yet that it would by no means consent to doing so—although, I say, this Association possesses no architectural home, it is nevertheless as plain a fact, rests on as solid a foundation, and carries as erect a front, as any building in the world. And the best and the utmost that its exponent and its advocate can do, standing here, is to point it out to those who gather round it, and to say, " Judge for yourselves."

It may not, however, be improper for me to suggest to that portion of the company whose previous acquaintance with it may have been limited, what it is not. It is not a theatrical association whose benefits are confined to a small and exclusive body of actors. It is a society whose claims are always preferred in the name of the whole histrionic art. It is not a theatrical association adapted to a state of theatrical things entirely past and gone, and no more suited to present theatrical requirements than a string of pack-horses would be suited to the conveyance of traffic between London and Birmingham. It is not a rich old gentleman, with the gout in his vitals, brushed and got-up once a year to look as vigorous as possible, and brought out for a public airing by the few survivors of a large family of nephews and nieces, who afterwards double-lock the street-door upon the poor relations. It is not a theatrical association which insists that no actor can share its bounty who has not walked so many years on those boards where the English tongue is never heard—between the little bars of music in an aviary of singing birds, to which the unwieldy Swan of Avon is never admitted—that bounty which was gathered in the name and for the elevation of an all-embracing art.

No; if there be such things, this thing is not of that kind. This is a theatrical association, expressly adapted to the wants and to the means of the whole theatrical profession all over England. It is a society in which the word exclusiveness is wholly unknown. It is a society which includes every actor, whether he be Benedict, or Hamlet, or the Ghost, or the Bandit, or the court-physician, or, in the one person, the whole King's army. He may do the "light business" or the " heavy," or the comic or the eccentric. He may be the captain who courts the young lady, whose uncle still unaccountably persists in dressing himself in a costume one hundred years older than his time. Or he may be the young lady's brother in the white gloves and inexpressibles, whose duty in the family appears to be to listen to the female members of it whenever they sing, and to shake hands with every body between all the verses. Or he may be the baron who gives the fête, and who sits uneasily on the sofa under a canopy with the baroness while the fête is going on. Or he may be the peasant at the fête who comes on the stage to swell the drinking chorus, and who, it may be observed, always turns his glass upside down before he begins to drink out of it. Or he may be the clown who takes away the door-step of the house where the evening party is going on. Or he may be the gentleman who issues out of the house on the false alarm, and is precipitated into the area. Or, to come to the actresses, she may be the fairy who resides forever in a revolving star, with an occasional visit to a bower or a palace. Or the actor may be the armed head of the witch's caldron; or even that extraordinary witch, concerning whom I have observed in country places, that he is much less like the notion formed from the description of Hopkins than the Malcolm or Donalbain of the previous scenes. This society, in short, says, " Be you what you may, be you actor or actress, be your path in your profession never so high or never so low, never so haughty or never so humble, we offer you the means of doing good to yourselves, and of doing good to your brethren."

This society is essentially a provident institution, appealing to a class of men to take care of their own interests, and giving a continuous security only in return for a continuous sacrifice and effort. The actor by the means of this society obtains his own right, to no man's wrong; and when, in old age or in disastrous times, he makes his claim on the institution, he is enabled to say, " I am neither a beggar, nor a suppliant. I am but reaping what I sowed long ago." And therefore it is that I can not hold out to you that in assisting this fund you are doing an act of charity in the common acceptation of that phrase. Of all the abuses of that much abused term, none have more raised my indignation than what I have heard in this room in past times in reference to this institution. I say, if you help this institution you will be helping the wagoner who has resolutely put his own shoulder to the wheel, and who has *not* stuck idle in the mud. In giving this aid you will be doing an act of justice, and you will be performing an act of gratitude; and this is what I solicit from you; but I will not so far wrong those who are struggling manfully for their own independence as to pretend to entreat from you an act of charity.

I have used the word gratitude; and let any man ask his own heart, and confess if he have not some grateful acknowledgments for the actor's art? Not peculiarly because it is a profession often pursued, and, as it were, marked, by poverty and misfortune—for other callings, God knows, have their distresses—not because the actor has sometimes to come from scenes of sickness, of suffering, ay, even of death itself, to play his part before us—for all of us, in our spheres, have as often to do violence to our feelings and to hide our hearts in fighting this great battle of life, and in discharging our duties and responsibilities. But the art of the actor excites reflections, sombre or grotesque, awful or humorous, which we are all familiar with. If any man were to tell me that he denied his acknowledgments to the stage, I would simply put to him one question—whether he remembered his first play?

If you, gentlemen, will but carry back your recollection to that great night, and call to mind the bright and harmless world which then opened to your view, we shall, I think, hear favorably of the effect upon your liberality on this occasion from our Secretary.

This is the sixth year of meetings of this kind —the sixth time we have had this fine child down after dinner. His nurse, a very worthy person of the name of Buckstone, who has an excellent character from several places, will presently report to you that his chest is perfectly sound, and that his general health is in the most thriving condition. Long may it be so; long may it thrive and grow; long may we meet (it is my sincere wish) to exchange our con-

gratulations on its prosperity; and longer than the line of Banquo may be that line of figures which, as its patriotic share in the national debt, a century hence shall be stated by the Governor and Company of the Bank of England.

~~~~~~~~~~

XLVIII.

THE ROYAL LITERARY FUND.

LONDON, MARCH 12, 1856.

[The Corporation of the Royal Literary Fund was established in 1790, its object being to administer assistance to authors of genius and learning who may be reduced to distress by unavoidable calamities, or deprived, by enfeebled faculties or declining life, of the power of literary exertion. At the annual general meeting held at the house of the society on the above date, the following speech was made by Mr. Charles Dickens:]

SIR,—I shall not attempt to follow my friend Mr. Bell, who, in the profession of literature, represents upon this committee a separate and distinct branch of the profession, that, like

"The last rose of summer
Stands blooming alone,
While all its companions
Are faded and gone,"

into the very prickly bramble-bush with which he has ingeniously contrived to beset this question. In the remarks I have to make I shall confine myself to four points:—1. That the committee find themselves in the painful condition of not spending enough money, and will presently apply themselves to the great reform of spending more. 2. That with regard to the house, it is a positive matter of history, that the house for which Mr. Williams was so anxious was to be applied to uses to which it never has been applied, and which the administrators of the fund decline to recognize. 3. That, in Mr. Bell's endeavors to remove the Artists' Fund from the ground of analogy it unquestionably occupies with reference to this fund, by reason of their continuing periodical relief to the same persons, I beg to tell Mr. Bell what every gentleman at that table knows—that it is the business of this fund to relieve over and over again the same people.

MR. BELL. But fresh inquiry is always made first.

MR. C. DICKENS. I can only oppose to that statement my own experience when I sat on that committee, and when I have known persons relieved on many consecutive occasions without further inquiry being made. As to the suggestion that we should select the items of expenditure that we complain of, I think it is according to all experience that we should first affirm the principle that the expenditure is too large. If that be done by the meeting, then I will proceed to the selection of the separate items. Now, in rising to support this resolution, I may state at once that I have scarcely any expectation of its being carried, and I am happy to think it will not. Indeed, I consider it the strongest point of the resolution's case that it should not be carried, because it will show the determination of the fund's managers. Nothing can possibly be stronger in favor of the resolution than that the statement should go forth to the world that twice within twelve months the attention of the committee has been called to this great expenditure, and twice the committee have considered that it was not unreasonable. I can not conceive a stronger case for the resolution than this statement of fact as to the expenditure going forth to the public accompanied by the committee's assertion that it is reasonable. Now, to separate this question from details, let us remember what the committee and their supporters asserted last year, and, I hope, will re-assert this year. It seems to be rather the model kind of thing than otherwise now, that if you get £100 you are to spend £40 in management; and if you get £1000, of course you may spend £400 in giving the rest away. Now, in case there should be any ill-conditioned people here who may ask what occasion there can be for all this expenditure, I will give you my experience. I went last year to a highly respectable place of resort, Willis's Rooms, in St. James's, to a meeting of this fund. My original intention was, to hear all I could, and say as little as possible. Allowing for the absence of the younger and fairer portion of the creation, the general appearance of the place was something like Almack's in the morning. A number of stately old dowagers sat in a row on one side, and old gentlemen on the other. The ball was opened with due solemnity by a real marquis, who walked a minuet with the secretary, at which the audience were much affected. Then another party advanced, who, I am sorry to say, was only a member of the House of Commons, and he took possession of the floor. To him, however, succeeded a lord, then a bishop, then the son of a distinguished lord, then one or two celebrities from the City and Stock Exchange, and at last a gentleman who made a fortune by the success of "Candide" sustained the part of Pangloss, and spoke much of what he evidently believed to be the very best management of this best of all possible funds. Now it is in this fondness for being stupendously genteel, and keeping up fine appearances—this vulgar and common social vice of hanging on to great connections at any price, that the money goes. The last time you got a distinguished writer at a public meeting, and he was called on to address you somewhere amongst the small hours, he told you he felt like the man in plush who was permitted to sweep the stage down after all the other people had gone. If the founder of this society were here, I should think he would feel like a sort of Rip Van Winkle reversed, who had gone to sleep backwards for a hundred years and woke up to find his fund still lying under the feet of people who did nothing for it instead of being emancipated and standing alone long ago. This Bloomsbury house is another part of the same desire for show, and the officer who inhabits it. (I mean, of course, in his official capacity, for, as an individual, I much respect him.) When one enters the house it appears to be haunted by a series of mysterious-looking ghosts, who glide about engaged in some extraordinary occupation, and, after the approved fashion of ghosts, but seldom condescend to disclose their business. What are all these meetings and inquiries wanted for? As for the authors, I say, as a writer by profession, that the long inquiry said to be necessary to ascertain whether an applicant deserves relief, is a preposterous pretense, and that working literary men would have a far better knowledge of the cases coming before the board than can ever be attained by that committee. Further, I say openly and plainly, that this fund is pompously and unnaturally administered at great expense, instead of being quietly administered at small expense; and that the secrecy to which it lays claim as its greatest attribute is not kept; for through those "two respectable householders," to whom reference must be made, the names of the most deserving applicants are to numbers of people perfectly well known. The members have now got before them a plain statement of facts as to these charges; and it is for them to say whether they are justifiable, becoming, or decent. I beg most earnestly and respectfully to put it to those gentlemen who belong to this institution, that must now decide, and can not help deciding, what the Literary Fund is for, and what it is not for. The question raised by the resolution is whether this is a public corporation for the relief of men of genius and learning, or whether it is a snug, traditional, and conventional party, bent upon maintaining its own usages with a vast amount of pride; upon its own annual puffery at costly dinner-tables, and upon a course of expensive toadying to a number of distinguished individuals. This is the question which you can not this day escape.

XLIX.

LONDON, NOVEMBER 5, 1857.

[At the fourth Anniversary Dinner of the Warehouse-men and Clerks' Schools, which took place on Thursday evening, Nov. 5th, 1857, at the London Tavern, and was very numerously attended, Mr. Charles Dickens occupied the Chair. On the subject which had brought the company together Mr. Dickens spoke as follows :]

I MUST now solicit your attention for a few minutes to the cause of your assembling together—the main and real object of this evening's gathering ; for I suppose we are all agreed that the motto of these tables is not "Let us eat and drink, for to-morrow we die;" but, "Let us eat and drink, for to-morrow we live." It is because a great and good work is to live to-morrow, and to-morrow, and to-morrow, and to live a greater and better life with every succeeding to-morrow, that we eat and drink here at all. Conspicuous on the card of admission to this dinner is the word "Schools." This set me thinking this morning what are the sorts of schools that I don't like. I found them, on consideration, to be rather numerous. I don't like—to begin with, and to begin, as charity does, at home—I don't like the sort of school to which I once went myself—the respected proprietor of which was by far the most ignorant man I have ever had the pleasure to know ; one of the worst-tempered men, perhaps, that ever lived, whose business it was to make as much out of us and put as little into us as possible, and who sold us at a figure which I remember we used to delight to estimate, as amounting to exactly £2 4s. 6d. per head. I don't like that sort of school, because I don't see what business the master had to be at the top of it instead of the bottom, and because I never could understand the wholesomeness of the moral preached by the abject appearance and degraded condition of the teachers, who plainly said to us by their looks every day of their lives, "Boys, never be learned ; whatever you are, above all things be warned from that in time by our sunken cheeks, by our poor pimply noses, by our meagre diet, by our acid-beer, and by our extraordinary suits of clothes, of which no human being can say whether they are snuff-colored turned black, or black turned snuff-colored, a point upon which we ourselves are perfectly unable to offer any ray of enlightenment, it is so very long since they were undarned and new." I do not like that sort of school, because I have never yet lost my ancient suspicion touching that curious coincidence that the boy with four brothers to come always got the prizes. In fact and short, I do not like that sort of school, which is a pernicious and abominable humbug altogether.

Again, ladies and gentlemen, I don't like that sort of school—a ladies' school—with which the other school used to dance on Wednesdays, where the young ladies, as I look back upon them now, seem to me always to have been in new stays and disgrace—the latter concerning a place of which I know nothing at this day, that bounds Timbuctoo on the north - east — and where memory always depicts the youthful enthraller of my first affection as forever standing against a wall, in a curious machine of wood, which confined her innocent feet in the first dancing position, while those arms, which should have encircled my jacket, those precious arms, I say, were pinioned behind her by an instrument of torture called a backboard, fixed in the manner of a double direction-post. Again, I don't like that sort of school, of which we have a notable example in Kent, which was established ages ago by worthy scholars and good men long deceased, whose munificent endowments have been monstrously perverted from their original purpose, and which, in their distorted condition, are struggled for and fought over with the most indecent pertinacity. Again, I don't like that sort of school—and I have seen a great many such in these latter times—where the bright childish imagination is utterly discouraged, and where those bright childish faces, which it is so very good for the wisest among us to remember in after life—when the world is too much with us, early and late*—are gloomily and grimly scared out of countenance; where I have never seen among the pupils, whether boys or girls, any thing but little parrots and small calculating machines. Again, I don't by any means like schools in leather breeches, and with mortified straw baskets for bonnets, which file along the streets in long melancholy rows under the escort of that surprising British monster—a beadle, whose system of instruction, I am afraid, too often presents that happy union of sound with sense, of which a very remarkable instance is given in a grave report of a trustworthy school inspector, to the effect that a boy in great repute at school for his learning presented on his slate, as one of the ten commandments, the perplexing prohibition, "Thou shalt not commit doldrum." Ladies and gentlemen, I confess, also, that I don't like those schools, even though the instruction given in them be gratuitous, where those sweet little voices which ought to be heard speaking in very different accents, anathematize by rote any human being who does not hold

* An allusion to a well-known Sonnet of Wordsworth, beginning—

"The world is too much with us—late and soon," etc.—ED.

what is taught there. Lastly, I do not like, and I did not like some years ago, cheap distant schools, where neglected children pine from year to year under an amount of neglect, want, and youthful misery far too sad even to be glanced at in this cheerful assembly.

And now, ladies and gentlemen, perhaps you will permit me to sketch in a few words the sort of school that I do like. It is a school established by the members of an industrious and useful order, which supplies the comforts and graces of life at every familiar turning in the road of our existence; it is a school established by them for the orphan and necessitous children of their own brethren and sisterhood; it is a place giving an education worthy of them —an education by them invented, by them conducted, by them watched over; it is a place of education where, while the beautiful history of the Christian religion is daily taught, and while the life of that Divine Teacher who Himself took little children on His knees is daily studied, no sectarian ill-will nor narrow human dogma is permitted to darken the face of the clear heaven which they disclose. It is a children's school which is at the same time no less a children's home, a home not to be confided to the care of cold or ignorant strangers, nor, by the nature of its foundation, in the course of ages to pass into hands that have as much natural right to deal with it as with the peaks of the highest mountains or with the depths of the sea, but to be from generation to generation administered by men living in precisely such homes as those poor children have lost; by men always bent upon making that replacement, such a home as their own dear children might find a happy refuge in if they themselves were taken early away. And I fearlessly ask you, is this a design which has any claim to your sympathy? Is this a sort of school which is deserving of your support?

This is the design, this is the school, whose strong and simple claim I have to lay before you to-night. I must particularly entreat you not to suppose that my fancy and unfortunate habit of fiction has any thing to do with the picture I have just presented to you. It is sober matter of fact. The Warehousemen and Clerks' Schools, established for the maintaining, clothing, and educating of the orphan and necessitous children of those employed in the wholesale trades and manufactures of the United Kingdom, are, in fact, what I have just described. These schools for both sexes were originated only four years ago. In the first six weeks of the undertaking the young men, of themselves and quite unaided, subscribed the large sum of

£3000. The schools have been opened only three years; they have now on their foundation thirty-nine children, and in a few days they will have six more, making a total of forty-five. They have been most munificently assisted by the heads of great mercantile houses, numerously represented, I am happy to say, around me, and they have a funded capital of almost £14,000. This is wonderful progress, but the aim must still be upward, the motto always "Excelsior." You do not need to be told that five-and-forty children can form but a very small proportion of the orphan and necessitous children of those who have been intrusted with the wholesale trades and manufactures of the United Kingdom: you do not require to be informed that the house at New-cross, rented for a small term of years, in which the schools are at present established, can afford but most imperfect accommodation for such a breadth of design. To carry this good work through the two remaining degrees of better and best, there must be more work, more co-operation, more friends, more money. Then be the friends and give the money. Before I conclude, there is one other feature in these schools which I would commend to your special attention and approval. Their benefits are reserved for the children of subscribers; that is to say, it is an essential principle of the institution that it must help those whose parents have helped them, and that the unfortunate children whose father has been so lax, or so criminal, as to withhold a subscription so exceedingly small that when divided by weeks it amounts to only three-pence weekly, can not, in justice, be allowed to jostle out and shoulder away the happier children whose father has had that little forethought or done that little kindness which was requisite to secure for them the benefits of the institution. I really can not believe that there will long be any such defaulting parents. I can not believe that any of the intelligent young men who are engaged in the wholesale houses will long neglect this obvious, this easy duty. If they suppose that the objects of their love, born or unborn, will never want the benefits of the charity, that may be a fatal and blind mistake—it can never be an excuse; for, supposing them to be right in their anticipation, they should do what is asked for the sake of their friends and comrades around them, assured that they will be the happier and the better for the deed.

Ladies and gentlemen, this little "labor of love" of mine is now done. I most heartily wish that I could charm you now not to see me, not to think of me, not to hear me—I most heartily wish that I could make you see in my

7

stead the multitude of innocent and bereaved children who are looking towards these schools, and entreating with uplifted hands to be let in. A very famous advocate once said, in speaking of his fears of failure when he had first to speak in court, being very poor, that he felt his little children tugging at his skirts, and that recovered him. Will you think of the number of little children who are tugging at my skirts, when I ask you, in their names, on their behalf, and in their little persons, and in no strength of my own, to encourage and assist this work?

At a later period of the evening Mr. Dickens proposed the health of the President of the Institution, Lord John Russell. He said he should do nothing so superfluous and so unnecessary as to descant upon his lordship's many faithful, long, and great public services, upon the honor and integrity with which he had pursued his straightforward public course through every difficulty, or upon the manly, gallant, and courageous character, which rendered him certain, in the eyes alike of friends and opponents, to rise with every rising occasion, and which, like the seal of Solomon, in the old Arabian story, inclosed in a not very large casket the soul of a giant. In answer to loud cheers, he said he had felt perfectly certain that that would be the response, for in no English assembly that he had ever seen was it necessary to do more than mention the name of Lord John Russell to insure a manifestation of personal respect and grateful remembrance.

~~~~~~~~

L.

LONDON, MAY 8, 1858.

[The forty-eighth Anniversary of the establishment of the Artists' Benevolent Fund took place on the above date at the Freemasons' Tavern. The Chair was taken by Mr. Charles Dickens, who, after having disposed of the preliminary toasts with his usual felicity, proceeded to advocate the claims of the Institution in whose interest the company had assembled, in the following terms:]

LADIES AND GENTLEMEN,—There is an absurd theatrical story which was once told to me by a dear and valued friend, who has now passed from this sublunary stage, and which is not without its moral as applied to myself, in my present presidential position. In a certain theatrical company was included a man who, on occasions of emergency, was capable of taking part in the whole round of the British drama, provided he was allowed to use his own language in getting through the dialogue. It happened one night that Reginald, in the *Castle Spectre*, was taken ill, and this veteran of a hundred characters was, of course, called up for the vacant part. He responded with his usual promptitude, although knowing nothing whatever of the character, but while they were getting him into the dress, he expressed a not unreasonable wish to know in some vague way what the part was about. He was not particular as to details, but, in order that he might properly portray his sufferings, he thought he should have some slight inkling as to what really had happened to him. As, for example, what murders he had committed, whose father he was, of what misfortunes he was the victim—in short, in a general way to know why he was in that place at all. They said to him, "Here you are, chained in a dungeon, an unhappy father; you have been here for seventeen years, during which time you have never seen your daughter; you have lived upon bread and water, and in consequence are extremely weak, and suffer from occasional lowness of spirits."—"All right," said the actor of universal capabilities, "ring up." When he was discovered to the audience, he presented an extremely miserable appearance, was very favorably received, and gave every sign of going on well, until, through some mental confusion as to his instructions, he opened the business of the act by stating in pathetic terms that he had been confined in that dungeon seventeen years, during which time he had not tasted a morsel of food, to which circumstance he was inclined to attribute the fact of his being at that moment very much out of condition. The audience, thinking this statement exceedingly improbable, declined to receive it, and the weight of that speech hung round him until the end of his performance.

Now I, too, have received instructions for the part I have the honor of performing before you, and it behooves both you and me to profit by the terrible warning I have detailed, while I endeavor to make the part I have undertaken as plain and intelligible as I possibly can.

As I am going to propose to you that we should now begin to connect the business with the pleasure of the evening, by drinking prosperity to the Artists' Benevolent Fund, it becomes important that we should know what that fund is. It is an association supported by the voluntary gifts of those who entertain a critical and admiring estimation of art, and has for its object the granting of annuities to the widows and children of deceased artists—of artists who have been unable in their lives to make any provision for those dear objects of their love surviving themselves. Now it is extremely important to observe that this institution of an

Artists' Benevolent Fund, which I now call on you to pledge, has connected with it, and has arisen out of, another artists' association, which does not ask you for a health, which never did and never will ask you for a health, which is self-supporting, and which is entirely maintained by the prudence and providence of its three hundred artist members. That fund, which is called the Artists' Annuity Fund, is, so to speak, a joint and mutual Assurance Company against infirmity, sickness, and age. To the benefits it affords every one of its members has an absolute right—a right, be it remembered, produced by timely thrift and self-denial, and not assisted by appeals to the charity or compassion of any human being. On that fund there are, if I remember aright, some seventeen annuitants who are in the receipt of eleven hundred a year, the proceeds of their own self-supporting institution. In recommending to you this benevolent fund, which is not self-supporting, they address you, in effect, in these words : " We ask you to help these widows and orphans, because we show you we have first helped ourselves. These widows and orphans may be ours or they may not be ours; but in any case we will prove to you to a certainty that we are not so many wagoners calling upon Jupiter to do our work, because we do our own work; each has his shoulder to the wheel; each, from year to year, has had his shoulder set to the wheel; and the prayer we make to Jupiter and all the gods is simply this —that this fact may be remembered when the wagon has stopped forever, and the spent and worn-out wagoner lies lifeless by the road-side.

" Ladies and gentlemen, I most particularly wish to impress on you the strength of this appeal. I am a painter, a sculptor, or an engraver, of average success. I study and work here for no immense return, while life and health, while hand and eye are mine. I prudently belong to the Annuity Fund, which in sickness, old age, and infirmity, preserves me from want. I do my duty to those who are depending on me while life remains; but when the grass grows above my grave there is no provision for them any longer.

This is the case with the Artists' Benevolent Fund, and in stating this I am only the mouth-piece of three hundred of the trade, who in truth stand as independent before you as if they were three hundred Cockers all regulated by the gospel according to themselves. There are in existence three artists' funds, which ought never to be mentioned without respect. I am an officer of one of them, and can speak from knowledge; but on this occasion I address myself to a case for which there is no provision. I address you on behalf of those professors of the fine arts who have made provision during life, and in submitting to you their claims I am only advocating principles which I myself have always maintained.

When I add that this Benevolent Fund makes no pretensions to gentility, squanders no treasure in keeping up appearances, that it considers that the money given for the widow and orphan should really be held for the widow and the orphan, I think I have exhausted the case which I desire most strenuously to commend to you.

Perhaps you will allow me to say one last word. I will not consent to present to you the professors of Art as a set of helpless babies, who are to be held up by the chin; I present them as an energetic and persevering class of men, whose incomes depend on their own faculties and personal exertions ; and I also make so bold as to present them as men who in their vocation render good service to the community. I am strongly disposed to believe there are very few debates in Parliament so important to the public welfare as a really good picture. I have also a notion that any number of bundles of the dryest legal chaff that ever was chopped would be cheaply expended for one really meritorious engraving. At a highly interesting annual festival at which I have the honor to assist, and which takes place behind two fountains, I sometimes observe that great ministers of state and other such exalted characters have a strange delight in rather ostentatiously declaring that they have no knowledge whatever of art, and particularly of impressing on the company that they have passed their lives in severe studies. It strikes me, when I hear these things, as if these great men looked upon the arts as a sort of dancing dogs, or Punch's show, to be turned to for amusement when one has nothing else to do. Now I always take the opportunity on these occasions of entertaining my humble opinion that all this is complete " bosh ;" and of asserting to myself my strong belief that the neighborhoods of Trafalgar Square or Suffolk Street, rightly understood, are quite as important to the welfare of the empire as those of Downing Street or Westminster Hall. Ladies and gentlemen, on these grounds, and backed by the recommendation of three hundred artists in favor of the Benevolent Fund, I beg to propose its prosperity as a toast for your adoption.

LI.

THE FAREWELL READING.

ST. JAMES'S HALL, MARCH 15, 1870.

[With the "Christmas Carol" and "The Trial from Pickwick," Mr. Charles Dickens brought to a brilliant close the memorable series of public readings which have for sixteen years proved to audiences unexampled in numbers the source of the highest intellectual enjoyment. Every portion of available space in the building was, of course, last night occupied some time before the appointed hour; but could the St. James's Hall have been specially enlarged for the occasion to the dimensions of Salisbury Plain, it is doubtful whether sufficient room would even then have been provided for all anxious to seize the last chance of hearing the distinguished novelist give his own interpretation of the characters called into existence by his own creative pen. As if determined to convince his auditors that, whatever reason had influenced his determination, physical exhaustion was not amongst them, Mr. Dickens never read with greater spirit and energy. His voice to the last retained its distinctive clearness, and the transitions of tone, as each personage in the story, conjured up by a word, rose vividly before the eye, seemed to be more marvellous than ever. The vast assemblage, hushed into breathless attention, suffered not a syllable to escape the ear, and the rich humor and deep pathos of one of the most delightful books ever written found once again the fullest appreciation. The usual burst of merriment responsive to the blithe description of Bob Cratchit's Christmas day, and the wonted sympathy with the crippled child "Tiny Tim," found prompt expression, and the general delight at hearing of Ebenezer Scrooge's reformation was only checked by the saddening remembrance that with it the last strain of the "carol" was dying away. After the "Trial from Pickwick," in which the speeches of the opposing counsel, and the owlish gravity of the judge, seemed to be delivered and depicted with greater dramatic power than ever, the applause of the audience rang for several minutes through the hall, and when it had subsided, Mr. Dickens with evidently strong emotion, but in his usual distinct and expressive manner, spoke as follows:]

LADIES AND GENTLEMEN,—It would be worse than idle—for it would be hypocritical and unfeeling—if I were to disguise that I close this episode in my life with feelings of very considerable pain. For some fifteen years, in this hall and in many kindred places, I have had the honor of presenting my own cherished ideas before you for your recognition, and, in closely observing your reception of them, have enjoyed an amount of artistic delight and instruction which, perhaps, is given to few men to know. In this task, and in every other I have ever undertaken, as a faithful servant of the public, always imbued with a sense of duty to them, and always striving to do his best, I have been uniformly cheered by the readiest response, the most generous sympathy, and the most stimulating support. Nevertheless, I have thought it well, at the full flood-tide of your favor, to retire upon those older associations between us, which date from much farther back than these,

and henceforth to devote myself exclusively to the art that first brought us together. Ladies and gentlemen, in but two short weeks from this time I hope that you may enter, in your own homes, on a new series of readings, at which my assistance will be indispensable;* but from these garish lights I vanish now for evermore, with a heartfelt, grateful, respectful, and affectionate farewell.

[Amidst repeated acclamations of the most enthusiastic description, whilst hats and handkerchiefs were waving in every part of the hall, Mr. Charles Dickens retired, withdrawing with him one of the greatest intellectual treats the public ever enjoyed.]

～～～～～～

LII.

THE NEWS-VENDERS' INSTITUTION.

LONDON, APRIL 5, 1870.

[The Annual Dinner in aid of the Funds of the News-venders' Benevolent and Provident Institution was held on the above evening, at the Freemasons' Tavern. Mr. Charles Dickens presided, and was supported by the Sheriffs of the City of London and Middlesex.

After the usual toasts had been given and responded to,

The Chairman said that if the approved order of their proceedings had been observed, the Corporation of the City of London would no doubt have considered themselves snubbed if they were not toasted by themselves. He was sure that a distinguished member of the Corporation who was present would tell the company what the corporation were going to do; and he had not the slightest doubt they were going to do something highly creditable to themselves, and something highly serviceable to the whole metropolis; and if the secret were not at present locked up in the blue-chamber, they would be all deeply obliged to the gentleman who would immediately follow him, if he let them into it in the same confidence as he had observed with respect to the Corporation of the City of London being snubbed. He begged to give the toast of "The Corporation of the City of London."

Mr. Alderman Cotton, in replying to the toast, said for once, and once only, had their Chairman said an unkind word about the Corporation of London. He had always reckoned Mr. Dickens to be one of the warmest friends of the Corporation; and remembering that he (Mr. Dickens) did really go through a Lord Mayor's Show in a Lord Mayor's carriage, if he had not felt himself quite a Lord Mayor, he must have at least considered himself next to one.

In proposing the toast of the evening, Mr. Dickens said:]

LADIES AND GENTLEMEN,—You receive me with so much cordiality that I fear you believe that I really did once sit in a Lord's Mayor's state coach. Permit me to assure you, in spite of the information received from Mr. Alderman Cotton, that I never had that honor. Further-

---

* Alluding to the forthcoming serial story of "Edwin Drood."

more, I beg to assure you that I never witnessed a Lord Mayor's show except from the point of view obtained by the other vagabonds upon the pavement. Now, ladies and gentlemen, in spite of this great cordiality of yours, I doubt if you fully know yet what a blessing it is to you that I occupy this chair to-night, because, having filled it on several previous occasions for the society on whose behalf we are assembled, and having said every thing that I could think of to say about it, and being, moreover, the president of the institution itself, I am placed to-night in the modest position of a host who is not so much to display himself as to call out his guests—perhaps even to try to induce some among them to occupy his place on another occasion. And, therefore, you may be safely sure that, like Falstaff, but with a modification almost as large as himself, I shall try rather to be the cause of speaking in others than to speak myself to-night. Much in this manner they exhibit at the door of a snuff-shop the effigy of a Highlander with an empty mull in his hand, who, having apparently taken all the snuff he can carry, and discharged all the sneezes of which he is capable, politely invites his friends and patrons to step in and try what they can do in the same line.

It is an appropriate instance of the universality of the newsman's calling that no toast we have drunk to-night—and no toast we shall drink to-night—and no toast we might, could, should, or would drink to night, is separable for a moment from that great inclusion of all possible subjects of human interest which he delivers at our doors every day. Further, it may be worthy the consideration of every body here who has talked cheerfully to his or her neighbor since we have sat down at the table, what in the name of Heaven should we have talked about, and how on earth could we have possibly got on, if our newsman had only for one single day forgotten us. Now, ladies and gentlemen, as our newsman is not by any means in the habit of forgetting us, let us try to form a little habit of not forgetting our newsman. Let us remember that his work is very arduous; that it occupies him early and late; that the profits he derives from us are at the best very small; that the services he renders to us are very great; that if he be a master, his little capital is exposed to all sorts of mischances, anxieties, and hazards; and if he be a journeyman, he himself is exposed to all manner of weathers, of tempers, and of difficult and unreasonable requirements.

Let me illustrate this. I was once present at a social discussion, which originated by chance. The subject was, What was the most absorbing and longest-lived passion in the human breast? What was the passion so powerful that it would almost induce the generous to be mean, the careless to be cautious, the guileless to be deeply designing, and the dove to emulate the serpent? A daily editor of vast experience and great acuteness, who was one of the company, considerably surprised us by saying with the greatest confidence that the passion in question was the passion of getting orders for the play.

There had recently been a terrible shipwreck, and very few of the surviving sailors had escaped in an open boat. One of these, on making land, came straight to London, and straight to the newspaper office, with his story of how he had seen the ship go down before his eyes. That young man had witnessed the most terrible contention between the powers of fire and water for the destruction of that ship and of every one on board. He had rowed away among the floating, dying, and the sinking dead. He had floated by day, and he had frozen by night, with no shelter and no food, and, as he told his dismal tale, he rolled his haggard eyes about the room. When he had finished, and the tale had been noted down from his lips, he was cheered and refreshed and soothed, and asked if any thing could be done for him. Even within him that masterpassion was so strong that he immediately replied he should like an order for the play. My friend the editor certainly thought that was rather a strong case; but he said that during his many years of experience he had witnessed an incurable amount of self-prostration and abasement having no other object, and that almost invariably on the part of people who could well afford to pay.

This made a great impression on my mind, and I really lived in this faith until some years ago it happened upon a stormy night I was kindly escorted from a bleak railway station to the little out-of-the-way town it represented by a sprightly and vivacious newsman, to whom I propounded, as we went along under my umbrella—he being most excellent company—this old question, what was the one all-absorbing passion of the human soul? He replied, without the slightest hesitation, that it certainly was the passion for getting your newspaper in advance of your fellow-creatures; also, if you only hired it, to get it delivered at your own door at exactly the same time as another man who hired the same copy four miles off; and, finally, the invincible determination on the part of both men not to believe the time was up when the boy called.

Ladies and gentlemen, I have not had an opportunity of verifying this experience with my friends of the managing committee, but I have no doubt, from its reception to-night, that my friend the newsman was perfectly right. Well, as a sort of beacon in a sufficiently dark life, and as an assurance that among a little body of working-men there is a feeling of brotherhood and sympathy—which is worth much to all men, or they would herd with wolves—the news-venders once upon a time established the Benevolent and Provident Institution, and here it is. Under the Provident head, certain small annuities are granted to old and hard-working subscribers. Under the Benevolent head, relief is afforded to temporary and proved distress. Under both heads, I am bound to say, the help rendered is very humble and very sparing, but if you like it to be handsomer you have it in your power to make it so. Such as it is, it is most gratefully received, and does a deal of good. Such as it is, it is most discreetly and feelingly administered ; and it is encumbered with no wasteful charges for management or patronage.

You know, upon an old authority, that you may believe any thing except facts and figures, but you really may believe that during the last year we have granted £100 in pensions, and some £70 in temporary relief, and we have invested in Government securities some £400. But, touching this matter of investments, it was suggested at the anniversary dinner, on the high and kind authority of Sir Benjamin Phillips, that we might grant more pensions and invest less money. We urged, on the other hand, that we wished our pensions to be certain and unchangeable—which of course they must be if they are always paid out of our Government interest and never out of our capital. However, so amiable is our nature, that we profess our desire to grant more pensions and to invest more money too. The more you give us to-night again, so amiable is our nature, the more we promise to do in both departments. That the newsman's work has greatly increased, and that it is far more wearing and tearing than it used to be, you may infer from one fact, not to mention that we live in railway times. It is stated in Mitchell's "Newspaper Press Directory," that during the last quarter of a century the number of newspapers which appeared in London had more than doubled, while the increase in the number of people among whom they were disseminated was probably beyond calculation.

Ladies and gentlemen, I have stated the newsman's simple case. I leave it in your hands. Within the last year the institution has had the good fortune to attract the sympathy and gain the support of the eminent man of letters I am proud to call my friend,* who now represents the great Republic of America at the British Court. Also it has the honor of enrolling upon its list of donors and vice-presidents the great name of Longfellow. I beg to propose to you to drink " Prosperity to the News-venders' Benevolent and Provident Institution."

LIII.

MACREADY.

LONDON, MARCH 1, 1851.

[On the evening of the above day the friends and admirers of Mr. Macready entertained him at a public dinner. Upward of six hundred gentlemen assembled to do honor to the great actor on his retirement from the stage. Sir E. B. Lytton took the Chair. Among the other speakers were Baron Bunsen, Sir Charles Eastlake, Mr. Thackeray, Mr. John Forster, Mr. W. J. Fox, and Mr. Charles Dickens, who proposed " The Health of the Chairman " in the following words :]

GENTLEMEN,—After all you have already heard, and so rapturously received, I assure you that not even the warmth of your kind welcome would embolden me to hope to interest you if I had not full confidence in the subject I have to offer to your notice. But my reliance on the strength of this appeal to you is so strong that I am rather encouraged than daunted by the brightness of the track on which I have to throw my little shadow.

Gentlemen, as it seems to me, there are three great requisites essential to the perfect realization of a scene so unusual and so splendid as that in which we are now assembled. The first, and I must say very difficult requisite, is a man possessing the stronghold in the general remembrance, the indisputable claim on the general regard and esteem, which is possessed by my dear and much valued friend, our guest. The second requisite is the presence of a body of entertainers — a great multitude of hosts so cheerful and good-humored (under, I am sorry to say, some personal inconvenience)—so warm-hearted and so nobly in earnest, as those whom I have the privilege of addressing. The third, and certainly not the least of these requisites, is a president who, less by his social position, which he may claim by inheritance, or by fortune, which may have been adventitiously won, and may be again accidentally lost, than by his comprehensive genius, shall fitly represent the best part of

---

* The Hon. John Lothrop Motley.

him to whom honor is done, and the best part of those who unite in the doing of it. Such a president, I think, we have found in our chairman of to-night, and I need scarcely add that our chairman's health is the toast I have to propose to you.

Many of those who now hear me were present, I dare say, at that memorable scene on Wednesday night last,[*] when the great vision which had been a delight and a lesson—very often, I dare say, a support and a comfort to you—which had for many years improved and charmed us, and to which we had looked for an elevated relief from the labors of our lives, faded from our sight forever. I will not stop to inquire whether our guest may or may not have looked backward, through rather too long a period for us, to some remote and distant time when he might possibly bear some far-off likeness to a certain Spanish archbishop whom Gil Blas once served. Nor will I stop to inquire whether it was a reasonable disposition in the audience of Wednesday to seize upon the words—

"And I have bought
Golden opinions from all sorts of people,
Which would be worn now in their newest gloss,
Not cast aside so soon—"[†]

but I will venture to intimate to those whom I am addressing how in my mind I mainly connect that occasion with the present. When I looked round on the vast assemblage, and observed the huge pit hushed into stillness on the rising of the curtain, and that mighty surging gallery, where men in their shirt-sleeves had been striking out their arms like strong swimmers—when I saw that boisterous human flood become still-water in a moment, and remain so from the opening to the end of the play, it suggested to me something besides the trustworthiness of an English crowd, and the delusion under which those labor who are apt to disparage and malign it: it suggested to me that in meeting here to-night we undertook to represent something of the all-pervading feeling of that crowd, through all its intermediate degrees, from the full-dressed lady, with her diamonds sparkling upon her breast in the proscenium-box, to the half-undressed gentleman, who bides his time to take some refreshment in the back row of the gallery. And I consider, gentlemen, that no one who could possibly be placed in this chair could so well head that comprehensive representation, and could so well give the crowning grace to our festivities, as one whose comprehensive genius has in his various works embraced them

all, and who has, in his dramatic genius, enchanted and enthralled them all at once.

Gentlemen, it is not for me here to recall, after what you have heard this night, what I have seen and known in the by-gone times of Mr. Macready's management, of the strong friendship of Sir Bulwer Lytton for him, of the association of his pen with his earliest successes, or of Mr. Macready's zealous and untiring services; but it may be permitted me to say what, in any public mention of him, I can never repress, that in the path we both tread I have uniformly found him from the first the most generous of men; quick to encourage, slow to disparage, ever anxious to assert the order of which he is so great an ornament; never condescending to shuffle it off, and leave it outside state-rooms, as a Mussulman might leave his slippers outside a mosque.

There is a popular prejudice, a kind of superstition, to the effect that authors are not a particularly united body, that they are not invariably and inseparably attached to each other. I am afraid I must concede half a grain or so of truth to that superstition; but this I know, that there can hardly be—that there hardly can have been—among the followers of literature a man of more high standing farther above these little grudging jealousies, which do sometimes disparage its brightness, than Sir Edward Bulwer Lytton.

And I have the strongest reason just at present to bear my testimony to his great consideration for those evils which are sometimes unfortunately attendant upon it, though not on him. For, in conjunction with some other gentlemen now present, I have just embarked in a design with Sir Bulwer Lytton to smooth the rugged way of young laborers, both in literature and the fine arts, and to soften, but by no eleemosynary means, the declining years of meritorious age. And if that project prosper, as I hope it will, and as I know it ought, it will one day be an honor to England where there is now a reproach; originating in his sympathies, being brought into operation by his activity, and endowed from its very cradle by his generosity. There are many among you who will have each his own favorite reason for drinking our chairman's health, resting his claim probably upon some of his diversified successes. According to the nature of your reading, some of you will connect him with prose, others will connect him with poetry. One will connect him with comedy, and another with the romantic passions of the stage, and his assertion of worthy ambition and earnest struggle against

"Those twin jailers of the human heart,
Low birth and iron fortune."

Again, another's taste will lead him to the contemplation of Rienzi and the streets of Rome; another's to the rebuilt and repeopled streets of Pompeii; another's to the touching history of the fireside where the Caxton family learned how to discipline their natures and tame their wild hopes down. But, however various their feelings and reasons may be, I am sure that with one accord each will help the other, and all will swell the greeting, with which I shall now propose to you "The Health of our Chairman, Sir Edward Bulwer Lytton."

LIV.

SANITARY REFORM.

LONDON, MAY 10, 1851.

[The members and friends of the Metropolitan Sanitary Association dined together on the above evening at Gore House, Kensington. The Earl of Carlisle occupied the Chair. Mr. Charles Dickens was present, and in proposing "The Board of Health," made the following speech:]

THERE are very few words for me to say upon the needfulness of sanitary reform, or the consequent usefulness of the Board of Health. That no man can estimate the amount of mischief grown in dirt—that no man can say the evil stops here or stops there, either in its moral or physical effects, or can deny that it begins in the cradle and is not at rest in the miserable grave, is as certain as it is that the air from Gin Lane will be carried by an easterly wind into Mayfair, or that the furious pestilence raging in St. Giles's no mortal list of lady patronesses can keep out of Almack's. Fifteen years ago some of the valuable reports of Mr. Chadwick and Dr. Southwood Smith, strengthening and much enlarging my knowledge, made me earnest in this cause in my own sphere; and I can honestly declare that the use I have since that time made of my eyes and nose have only strengthened the conviction that certain sanitary reforms must precede all other social remedies, and that neither education nor religion can do any thing useful until the way has been paved for their ministrations by cleanliness and decency.

I do not want authority for this opinion: you have heard the speech of the right reverend prelate* this evening—a speech which no sanitary reformer can have heard without emotion. Of what avail is it to send missionaries to the miserable man condemned to work in a fetid court, with every sense bestowed upon him for

_____
* The Bishop of Ripon (Dr. Longley).

his health and happiness turned into a torment, with every month of his life adding to the heap of evils under which he is condemned to exist? What human sympathy within him is that instructor to address? what natural old chord within him is he to touch? Is it the remembrance of his children?—a memory of destitution, of sickness, of fever, and of scrofula? Is it his hopes, his latent hopes of immortality? He is so surrounded by and imbedded in material filth, that his soul can not rise to the contemplation of the great truths of religion. Or if the case is that of a miserable child bred and nurtured in some noisome, loathsome place, and tempted, in these better days, into the ragged school, what can a few hours' teaching effect against the ever-renewed lesson of a whole existence? But give them a glimpse of heaven through a little of its light and air; give them water; help them to be clean; lighten that heavy atmosphere in which their spirits flag and in which they become the callous things they are; take the body of the dead relative from the close room in which the living live with it, and where death, being familiar, loses its awe; and then they will be brought willingly to hear of Him whose thoughts were so much with the poor, and who had compassion for all human suffering.

The toast which I have to propose, The Board of Health, is entitled to all the honor which can be conferred upon it. We have very near us, in Kensington, a transparent illustration that no very great thing can ever be accomplished without an immense amount of abuse being heaped upon it. In connection with the Board of Health we are always hearing a very large word which is always pronounced with a very great relish—the word centralization. Now I submit that in the time of the cholera we had a pretty good opportunity of judging between this so-called centralization and what I may, I think, call "vestrylization." I dare say the company present have read the reports of the Cholera Board of Health, and I dare say they have also read reports of certain vestries. I have the honor of belonging to a constituency which elected that amazing body, the Marylebone vestry, and I think that if the company present will look to what was done by the Board of Health at Glasgow, and then contrast those proceedings with the wonderful cleverness with which affairs were managed at the same period by my vestry, there will be very little difficulty in judging between them. My vestry even took upon itself to deny the existence of cholera as a weak invention of the enemy, and that denial had little or no effect in staying the progress of the disease. We can now contrast what centralization is as represented by a few noisy and interested gentlemen, and what centralization is when worked out by a body combining business habits, sound medical and social knowledge, and an earnest sympathy with the sufferings of the working-classes.

Another objection to the Board of Health is conveyed in a word not so large as the other— "Delay." I would suggest in respect to this, that it would be very unreasonable to complain that a first-rate chronometer didn't go when its master had not wound it up. The Board of Health may be excellently adapted for going and very willing and anxious to go, and yet may not be permitted to go by reason of its lawful master having fallen into a gentle slumber and forgotten to set it agoing. One of the speakers this evening has referred to Lord Castlereagh's caution " not to halloo until they were out of the wood." As regards the Board of Trade, I would suggest that they ought not to halloo until they are out of the Woods and Forests. In that leafy region the Board of Health suffers all sorts of delays, and this should always be borne in mind. With the toast of the Board of Health I will couple the name of a noble lord (Ashley), of whose earnestness in works of benevolence no man can doubt, and who has the courage on all occasions to face the cant which is the worst and commonest of all— the cant about the cant of philanthropy.

~~~~~~~~~

LV.

GARDENING.

LONDON, JUNE 9, 1851.

[At the Anniversary Dinner of the Gardeners' Benevolent Institution, held under the presidency of Mr., afterwards Sir Joseph Paxton, Mr. Charles Dickens made the following speech:]

I FEEL an unbounded and delightful interest in all the purposes and associations of gardening. Probably there is no feeling in the human mind stronger than the love of gardening. The prisoner will make a garden in his prison, and cultivate his solitary flower in the chink of a wall. The poor mechanic will string his scarlet bean from one side of his window to the other, and watch it and tend it with unceasing interest. It is a holy duty in foreign countries to decorate the graves of the dead with flowers, and here, too, the resting-places of those who have passed away from us will soon be gardens. From that old time when the Lord walked in the garden in the cool of the evening, down to the day when a poet-laureate sang,

" Trust me, Clara Vere de Vere,
    From yon blue heaven above us bent
  The gardener Adam and his wife
    Smile at the claims of long descent,"

at all times and in all ages gardens have been among the objects of the greatest interest to mankind. There may be a few, but I believe they are but a few, who take no interest in the products of gardening, except perhaps in "London Pride," or a certain degenerate kind of " Stock," which is apt to grow hereabouts, cultivated by a species of frozen-out gardeners whom no thaw can ever penetrate : except these, the gardeners' art has contributed to the delight of all men in their time. That there ought to be a Benevolent Provident Institution for gardeners is in the fitness of things, and that such an institution ought to flourish and does flourish is still more so.

I have risen to propose to you the health of a gentleman who is a great gardener, and not only a great gardener but a great man—the growth of a fine Saxon root cultivated up with a power of intellect to a plant that is at this time the talk of the civilized world—I allude, of course, to my friend, the chairman of the day. I took occasion to say at a public assembly hard by, a month or two ago, in speaking of that wonderful building Mr. Paxton has designed for the great Exhibition in Hyde Park, that it ought to have fallen down, but that it refused to do so. We were told that the glass ought to have been all broken, the gutters all choked up, and the building flooded, and that the roof and sides ought to have been blown away ; in short, that every thing ought to have done what every thing obstinately persisted in not doing. Earth, air, fire, and water all appear to have conspired together in Mr. Paxton's favor—all have conspired together to one result, which, when the present generation is dust, will be an enduring temple to his honor, and to the energy, the talent, and the resources of Englishmen.

" But," said a gentleman to me the other day, " no doubt Mr. Paxton is a great man, but there is one objection to him that you can never get over, that is, he is a gardener." Now that is our case to-night, that he is a gardener, and we are extremely proud of it. This is a great age, with all its faults, when a man by the power of his own genius and good sense can scale such a daring height as Mr. Paxton has reached, and composedly place his form on the top. This is a great age, when a man impressed with a useful idea can carry out his project without being imprisoned, or thumb-screwed, or persecuted in any form. I can well understand that you, to whom the genius, the intelligence, the industry, and the achievements of our friend are well known, should be anxious to do him honor by placing him in the position he occupies to-night; and I assure you, you have conferred great gratification on one of his friends, in permitting him to have the opportunity of proposing his health, which that friend now does most cordially and with all the honors.

LVI.

ROYAL ACADEMY DINNER.

LONDON, MAY 2, 1870.

[On the occasion of the Second Exhibition of the Royal Academy in their new galleries in Piccadilly, the president, Sir F. Grant, and the council gave their usual inaugurative banquet, and a very distinguished company was present. The dinner took place in the large central room, and covers were laid for 200 guests. The Prince of Wales acknowledged the toast of his health and that of the Princess, the Duke of Cambridge responded to the toast of the army, Mr. Childers to the navy, Lord Elcho to the volunteers, Mr. Motley to "The Prosperity of the United States," Mr. Gladstone to "Her Majesty's Ministers," the Archbishop of York to "The Guests," and Mr. Dickens to "Literature." The last toast having been proposed in a highly eulogistic speech, Mr. Dickens responded:]

MR. PRESIDENT, YOUR ROYAL HIGHNESSES, MY LORDS AND GENTLEMEN,—I beg to acknowledge the toast with which you have done me the great honor of associating my name. I beg to acknowledge it on behalf of the brotherhood of literature, present and absent, not forgetting an illustrious wanderer from the fold, whose tardy return to it we all hail with delight, and who now sits—or lately did sit—within a few chairs of or on your left hand. I hope I may also claim to acknowledge the toast on behalf of the sisterhood of literature also, although that "better half of human nature," to which Mr. Gladstone rendered his graceful tribute, is unworthily represented here, in the present state of its rights and wrongs, by the devouring monster, man.

All the arts, and many of the sciences, bear witness that women, even in their present oppressed condition, can attain to quite as great distinction, and can win quite as lofty names as men. Their emancipation (as I am given to understand) drawing very near, there is no saying how soon they may "push us from our stools" at these tables, or how soon our better

half of human nature, standing in this place of mine, may eloquently depreciate mankind, addressing another better half of human nature sitting in the president's chair.

The literary visitors of the Royal Academy to-night desire me to congratulate their hosts on a very interesting exhibition, in which risen excellence supremely asserts itself, and from which promise of a brilliant succession in time to come is not wanting. They naturally see with special interest the writings and persons of great men—historians, philosophers, poets, and novelists, vividly illustrated around them here. And they hope that they may modestly claim to have rendered some little assistance towards the production of many of the pictures in this magnificent gallery. For without the patient labors of some amongst them unhistoric history might have long survived in this place, and but for the researches and wanderings of others among them, the most preposterous countries, the most impossible peoples, and the absurdest superstitions, manners, and customs, might have usurped the place of truth upon these walls. Nay, there is no knowing, Sir Francis Grant, what unlike portraits you yourself might have painted if you had been left, with your sitters, to idle pens, unchecked reckless rumors, and undenounced lying malevolence.

I can not forbear, before I resume my seat, adverting to a sad theme (the recent death of Daniel Maclise) to which his Royal Highness the Prince of Wales made allusion, and to which the president referred with the eloquence of genuine feeling. Since I first entered the public lists, a very young man indeed, it has been my constant fortune to number amongst my nearest and dearest friends members of the Royal Academy who have been its grace and pride. They have so dropped from my side one by one that I already begin to feel like the Spanish monk of whom Wilkie tells, who had grown to believe that the only realities around him were the pictures which he loved, and that all the moving life he saw, or ever had seen, was a shadow and a dream.

For many years I was one of the two most intimate friends and most constant companions of the late Mr. Maclise. Of his genius in his chosen art I will venture to say nothing here, but of his prodigious fertility of mind and wonderful wealth of intellect, I may confidently assert that they would have made him, if he had been so minded, at least as great a writer as he was a painter. The gentlest and most modest of men, the freshest as to his generous appreciation of young aspirants, and the frankest and largest-hearted as to his peers, incapable of a sordid or ignoble thought, gallantly sustaining the true dignity of his vocation, without one grain of self-ambition, wholesomely natural at the last as at the first, "in wit a man, simplicity a child," no artist of whatsoever denomination, I make bold to say, ever went to his rest leaving a golden memory more pure from dross, or having devoted himself with a truer chivalry to the art goddess whom he worshipped.

[These were the last public words of Charles Dickens.]

LETTERS OF CHARLES DICKENS.

OF the graceful but difficult art of letter-writing Charles Dickens has shown himself as accomplished a master as he has of public speaking, as the following extracts from his correspondence with three distinguished persons now deceased, the Countess of Blessington, Washington Irving, and Douglas Jerrold, will show. The letters given range over a period of seven years, commencing in 1841, and ending in 1847.

DICKENS AND THE COUNTESS OF BLESSINGTON.

CHARLES DICKENS TO LADY BLESSINGTON.

Devonshire Terrace, June 2, 1841.

DEAR LADY BLESSINGTON,—The year goes round so fast that, when any thing occurs to remind me of its whirling, I lose my breath and am bewildered. So your hand-writing last night had as startling an effect upon me, as though you had sealed your note with one of your own eyes.

I remember my promise, as in cheerful duty bound, and with Heaven's grace will redeem it. At this moment, I have not the faintest idea how; but I am going into Scotland on the 19th to see Jeffrey, and while I am away (I shall return, please God, in about three weeks) will look out for some accident, incident, or subject for small description, to send you when I come home. You will take the will for the deed, I know; and remembering that I have a "Clock," which always wants winding up, will not quarrel with me for being brief.

Have you seen Townshend's magnetic boy? You heard of him, no doubt, from Count D'Orsay. If you get him to Gore House, don't, I entreat you, have more than eight people—four is a better number—to see him. He fails in a crowd, and is marvellous before a few.

I am told that down in Devonshire there are young ladies innumerable, who read crabbed manuscripts with the palms of their hands, and newspapers with their ankles, and so forth; and who are, so to speak, literary all over. I begin to understand what a blue-stocking means; and have not the smallest doubt that Lady —— (for instance) could write quite as entertaining a book with the sole of her foot as ever she did with her head.

I am a believer in earnest, and I am sure you would be if you saw this boy, under moderately favorable circumstances, as I hope you will, before he leaves England. Believe me, dear Lady Blessington, faithfully yours,

CHARLES DICKENS.

Devonshire Terrace, 10th March, 1844.

I have made up my mind to "see the world;" and mean to decamp, bag and baggage, next midsummer, for a twelvemonth. I purpose establishing my family in some convenient place, from whence I can make personal ravages on the neighboring country, and, somehow or other, have got it into my head that Nice would be a favorable spot for head-quarters.

You are so well acquainted with these matters, that I am anxious to have the benefit of your kind advice. I do not doubt that you can tell me whether this same Nice be a healthy place the year through, whether it be reasonably cheap, pleasant to look at and to live in, and the like. If you will tell me when you have ten minutes to spare for such a client, I shall be delighted to come to you, and guide myself by your opinion. I will not ask you to forgive me for troubling you, because I am sure beforehand that you will do so.

I beg to be kindly remembered to Count D'Orsay and to your nieces. I was going to say "the Misses Power," but it looks so like the blue-board at a Ladies' School, that I stopped short. CHARLES DICKENS.

Covent Garden, Sunday, Noon, 1844.

Business for other people (and by no means of a pleasant kind) has held me prisoner during two whole days, and will so detain me to-day, in the very agony of my departure for Italy again, that I shall not even be able to reach Gore House once more: on which I had set my heart. * * * I can not bear the thought of going away without some sort of reference to the happy day you gave me on Monday, and the pleasure and delight I had in your earnest greeting. I shall never forget it, believe me. It would be worth going to China—it would be worth going to America, to come home again for the pleasure of such a meeting with you and Count D'Orsay—to whom my love—and something as near it to Miss Power and her sister as it is lawful to send.

It will be an unspeakable satisfaction to me (though I am not maliciously disposed) to know under your own hand at Genoa that my little book made you cry. I hope to prove a better correspondent on my return to those shores. But better or worse, or anyhow, I am ever, my dear Lady Blessington, in no common degree, and not with an every-day regard, yours,   CHARLES DICKENS.

Milan, Wednesday, November 20, 1844.

Appearances are against me. Don't believe them. I have written you, in intention, fifty letters, and I can claim no credit for any one of them (though they were the best letters you ever read), for they all originated in my desire to live in your memory and regard.

Since I heard from Count D'Orsay, I have been beset in I don't know how many ways. First of all, I went to Marseilles, and came back to Genoa. Then I moved to the Peschiere. Then some people, who had been present at the scientific congress here, made a sudden inroad on that establishment, and overran it. Then they went away, and I shut myself up for one month, close and tight, over my little Christmas book, "The Chimes." All my affections and passions got twined and knotted up in it, and I became as haggard as a murderer long before I wrote "The End." When I had done that, like "The man of Thessaly," who, having scratched his eyes out in a quickset hedge, plunged into a bramble-bush to scratch them in again, I fled to Venice, to recover the composure I had disturbed. From thence I went to Verona and to Mantua. And now I am here —just come up from under-ground, and earthy all over, from seeing that extraordinary tomb in which the Dead Saint lies in an alabaster case, with sparkling jewels all about him to mock his dusty eyes, not to mention the twenty-franc pieces which devout votaries were ringing down upon a sort of skylight in the cathedral pavement above, as if it were the counter of his heavenly shop.

You know Verona? You know every thing in Italy I know. I am not learned in geography, and it was a great blow to me to find that Romeo was only banished five-and-twenty miles. It was a great blow to me to see the old house of the Capulets, with some genealogical memorials, still carved in stone, over the gateway of the court-yard. It is a most miserable little inn, at this time ankle-deep in dirt; and noisy vetturini and muddy market-carts were disputing possession of the yard with a brood of geese, all splashed and bespattered as if they had their yesterday's white trowsers on. There was nothing to connect it with the beautiful story, but a very unsentimental middle-aged lady (the Padrona, I suppose) in the door-way, who resembled old Capulet in the one particular of being very great indeed in the family way.

The Roman amphitheatre there delighted me beyond expression. I never saw any thing so full of solemn, ancient interest. There are the four-and-forty rows of seats, as fresh and perfect as if their occupants had vacated them but yesterday—the entrances, passages, dens, rooms, corridors; the numbers over some of the arches. An equestrian troop had been there some days before, and had scooped out a little ring at one end of the arena, and had their performances in that spot. I should like to have seen it, of all things, for its very dreariness. Fancy a handful of people sprinkled over one corner of the great place (the whole population of Verona wouldn't fill it now); and a spangled cavalier bowing to the echoes and the grass-grown walls! I climbed to the topmost seat, and looked away at the beautiful view for some minutes; when I turned round, and looked down into the theatre again, it had exactly the appearance of an immense straw hat, to which the helmet in the Castle of Otranto was a baby; the rows of seats representing the different plaits of straw, and the arena the inside of the crown.

I had great expectations of Venice, but they fell immeasurably short of the wonderful reality. The short time I passed there went by me in a dream. I hardly think it possible to exaggerate its beauties, its sources of interest, its uncommon novelty and freshness. A thousand and one realizations of the thousand and one nights could scarcely captivate and enchant me more than Venice. * * *

Your old house at Albaro—Il Paradiso—is spoken of as yours to this day. What a gallant place it is! I don't know the present inmate, but I hear that he bought and furnished it not long since, with great splendor, in the French style, and that he wishes to sell it. I wish I were rich, and could buy it. There is a third-rate wine-shop below Byron's house; and the place looks dull, and miserable, and ruinous enough.

Old —— is a trifle uglier than when I first arrived. He has periodical parties, at which there are a great many flower-pots and a few ices—no other refreshments. He goes about constantly charged with extemporaneous poetry; and is always ready, like tavern-dinners, on the shortest notice and the most reasonable terms. He keeps a gigantic harp in his bedroom, together with pen, ink, and paper, for fixing his ideas as they flow—a kind of profane King David, but truly good-natured and very harmless.

Pray say to Count D'Orsay every thing that is cordial and loving from me. The travelling-purse he gave me has been of immense service. It has been constantly opened. All Italy seems to yearn to put its hand in it. I think of hanging it, when I come back to England, on a nail as a trophy, and of gashing the brim like the blade of an old sword, and saying to my son and heir, as they do upon the stage: "You see this notch, boy? Five hundred francs were laid low on that day for post-horses. Where this gap is, a waiter charged your father treble the correct amount—and got it. This end, worn into teeth like the rasped edge of an old file, is sacred to the Custom-houses, boy, the passports, and the shabby soldiers at town-gates, who put an open hand and dirty coat-cuff into the coach windows of all Forestieri. Take it, boy. Thy father has nothing else to give!"

My desk is cooling itself in a mail-coach, somewhere down at the back of the cathedral, and the pens and ink in this house are so detestable, that I have no hope of your ever getting to this portion of my letter. But I have the less misery in this state of mind, from knowing that it has nothing in it to repay you for the trouble of perusal. CHARLES DICKENS.

Genoa, May 9, 1845.

Once more in my old quarters; and with rather a tired sole to my foot, from having found such an immense number of different resting-places for it since I went away. I write you my last Italian letter for this bout, designing to leave here, please God, on the ninth of next month, and to be in London again by the end of June. I am looking forward with great delight to the pleasure of seeing you once more; and mean to come to Gore House with such a swoop as shall astonish the Poodle, if, after being accustomed to his own size and sense, he retain the power of being astonished at any thing in the wide world.

You know where I have been, and every mile of ground I have travelled over, and every object I have seen. It is next to impossible, surely, to exaggerate the interest of Rome; though, I think, it *is* very possible to find the main source of interest in the wrong things. Naples disappointed me greatly. The weather was bad during a great part of my stay there. But if I had not had mud I should have had dust, and though I had had sun, I must still have had the Lazzaroni. And they are so ragged, so dirty, so abject, so full of degradation, so sunken and steeped in the hopelessness of better things, that they would make heaven uncomfortable, if they could ever get there. I didn't expect to see a handsome city, but I expected something better than that long dull line of squalid houses, which stretches from the Chiaja to the quarter of the Porta Capuana; and while I was quite prepared for a miserable populace, I had some dim belief that there were bright rags among them, and dancing legs, and shining sun-browned faces. Whereas the honest truth is, that connected with Naples itself I have not one solitary recollection. The country round it charmed me, I need not say. Who can forget Herculaneum and Pompeii?

As to Vesuvius, it burns away in my thoughts, beside the roaring waters of Niagara; and not a splash of the water extinguishes a spark of the fire; but there they go on, tumbling and flaming night and day, each in its fullest glory.

I have seen so many wonders, and each of them has such a voice of its own, that I sit all day long listening to the roar they make, as if it were in a sea-shell; and have fallen into an idleness so complete, that I can't rouse myself sufficiently to go to Pisa on the twenty-fifth, when the triennial illumination of the Cathedral and Leaning Tower, and bridges, and what not, takes place. But I have already been there; and it can not beat St. Peter's, I suppose. So I don't think I shall pluck myself up by the roots and go aboard a steamer for Leghorn.

Let me thank you heartily for the "Keepsake" and the "Book of Beauty." They reached me a week or two ago. I have been very much struck by two papers in them. One, Landor's "Conversation," among the most charming, profound, and delicate productions I have ever read. The other, your lines on Byron's room at Venice. I am as sure that you wrote them from your heart, as I am that they found their way immediately to mine.

It delights me to receive such accounts of Maclise's fresco. If he will only give his magnificent genius fair play, there is not enough cant and dullness even in the criticism of art from which Sterne prayed kind Heaven to defend him, as the worst of all the cants continually canted in this canting world—to keep the giant down an hour.

Our poor friend, the naval governor, has lost his wife, I am sorry to hear, since you and I spoke of his pleasant face. And L. B.,* what a terrible history that was! F—— did himself enduring honor by his manly and zealous devotion to the interests of that orphan family, in the midst of all his pains and trouble. It was very good of him.

Do not let your nieces forget me, if you can help it; and give my love to Count D'Orsay, with many thanks to him for his charming letter. I was greatly amused by his account of —— There was a "cold shade of aristocracy" about it, and a dampness of cold water, which entertained me beyond measure.

CHARLES DICKENS.

Devonshire Terrace, March 2, 1846.

Many thanks for the letters!† I will take the greatest care of them, though I blush to find how little they deserve it.

It vexes me very much that I am going out on Friday, and can not help it. I have no strength of mind, I am afraid. I am always making engagements, in which there is no prospect of satisfaction.

Vague thoughts of a new book are rife within me just now; and I go wandering about at night into the strangest places, according to my usual propensity at such a time, seeking rest, and finding none. As an addition to my composure, I ran over a little dog in the Regent's Park yesterday (killing him on the spot), and gave his little mistress, a girl of thirteen or fourteen, such exquisite distress as I never saw the like of.

I must have some talk with you about those American singers. They must never go back to their own country without your having heard them sing Hood's "Bridge of Sighs." My God, how sorrowful and pitiful it is!

Best regards to Count D'Orsay and the young ladies.   CHARLES DICKENS.

Devonshire Terrace, May 19, 1846.

If I had not a good reason for delaying to acknowledge the receipt of the book you so kindly sent me, I should be a most unworthy dog. But I have been every day expecting to

be able to send you the inclosed little volume, and could get no copies until last night, in consequence of their running very fine against the subscription and demand. May you like it!

I have been greatly entertained by the femme de chambre, who paints love with a woman's eye (I think that the highest praise), and sometimes like a female Gil Blas. The spirit of our two fair friends M. and S. shines through their representative. I would have identified the former anywhere. With cordial remembrance and regards,   CHARLES DICKENS.

48 Rue de Courcelles, Paris, January 24, 1847.

I feel very wicked in beginning this note, and deeply remorseful for not having begun and ended it long ago. But *you* know how difficult it is to write letters in the midst of a writing life; and as you know too (I hope) how earnestly and affectionately I always think of you, wherever I am, I take heart on a little consideration, and feel comparatively good again.

F—— has been cramming into the space of a fortnight every description of impossible and inconsistent occupation in the way of sight-seeing. He has been now at Versailles, now in the Prisons, now at the Opera, now at the Hospitals, now at the Conservatoire, and now at the Morgue, with a dreadful insatiability. I begin to doubt whether I had any thing to do with a book called "Dombey," or ever sat over number five (not finished a fortnight yet) day after day, until I half began, like the monk in poor Wilkie's story, to think it the only reality in life, and to mistake all the realities for short-lived shadows.

Among the multitude of sights, we saw our pleasant little bud of a friend, Rose Cheri, play Clarissa Harlowe the other night. I believe she did it in London just now, and perhaps you may have seen it. A most charming, intelligent, modest, affecting piece of acting it is: with a death superior to any thing I ever saw on the stage, except Macready's "Lear." The theatres are admirable just now. We saw "Gentil Bernard," at the *Variétés* last night, acted in a manner that was absolutely perfect. It was a little picture of Watteau, animated and talking from beginning to end. At the Cirque there is a new show-piece called the "French Revolution," in which there is a representation of the National Convention, and a series of battles (fought by some five hundred people, who look like five thousand), that are wonderful in their extraordinary vigor and truth. Gun-cotton gives its name to the general annual jocose review at the Palais Royal, which is dull enough, saving for the introduction of Alexandre Dumas,

---

* Laman Blanchard.
† This refers to the two previous letters, dated respectively from Milan and Genoa, and possibly to others not preserved, which Mr. Dickens doubtless desired to consult while writing his "Pictures from Italy," upon which he was then engaged.—ED.

sitting in his study, beside a pile of quarto volumes about five feet high, which he says is the first tableau of the first act of the first piece to be played on the first night of his new theatre. The revival of Molière's "Don Juan," at the Français, has drawn money. It is excellently played, and it is curious to observe how different *their* Don Juan and Valet are, from our English ideas of the master and man. They are playing "Lucretia Borgia" again at the 'Porte St. Martin; but it is poorly performed, and hangs fire drearily, though a very remarkable and striking play. We were at V. H.'s* house last Sunday week, a most extraordinary place, looking like an old curiosity-shop, or the property-room of some gloomy, vast old theatre. I was much struck by H—— himself, who looks like a genius, as he is, every inch of him, and is very interesting and satisfactory from head to foot. His wife is a handsome woman, with flashing black eyes. There is also a charming ditto daughter of fifteen or sixteen, with ditto eyes. Sitting among old armor and old tapestry, and old coffers, and grim old chairs and tables, and old canopies of state from old palaces, and old golden lions going to play at skittles with ponderous old golden balls, they made a most romantic show, and looked like a chapter out of one of his own books.

CHARLES DICKENS.

DICKENS AND WASHINGTON IRVING.

In the spring of 1841, some months before Mr. Dickens had decided upon his first visit to the United States, Washington Irving, who was then personally unknown to him, addressed him a letter, full of warm sympathy and generous acknowledgment of his genius, and of the pleasure Dickens's writings had afforded him. Mr. Dickens's answer to that letter is the first of the three which follow.

In February, 1842, Mr. Dickens had the gratification of making the personal acquaintance of his illustrious correspondent, who was induced to overcome his objection to public speaking, and to take the chair at a banquet given in Dickens's honor by some of the citizens of New York. Irving, however, entirely broke down in his speech, and could do little more than propose the toast of the evening.

There were probably never two men of more congenial mind and common sympathies than the author of the "Sketch Book" and the author of "Pickwick;" and it is pleasant to think that the chances of things should have brought them together for a time in so unexpected a way.

* Victor Hugo.

CHARLES DICKENS TO WASHINGTON IRVING.

1841.

MY DEAR SIR,—There is no man in the world who could have given me the heartfelt pleasure you have, by your kind note of the 13th of last month. There is no living writer—and there are very few among the dead—whose approbation I should feel so proud to earn. And with every thing you have written upon my shelves, and in my thoughts, and in my heart of hearts, I may honestly and truly say so. If you could know how earnestly I write this, you would be glad to read it—as I hope you will be, faintly guessing at the warmth of the hand I autographically hold out to you over the broad Atlantic.

I wish I could find in your welcome letter some hint of an intention to visit England. I can't. I have held it at arm's length, and taken a bird's-eye view of it, after reading it a great many times, but there is no greater encouragement in it this way than on a microscopic inspection. I should love to go with you—as I have gone, God knows how often—into Little Britain, and Eastcheap, and Green Arbor Court, and Westminster Abbey. I should like to travel with you, outside the last of the coaches, down to Bracebridge Hall. It would make my heart glad to compare notes with you about that shabby gentleman in the oil-cloth hat and red nose, who sat in the nine-cornered back parlor of the *Mason's Arms;* and about Robert Preston, and the tallow-chandler's widow, whose sitting-room is second nature to me; and about all those delightful places and people that I used to walk about and dream of in the daytime, when a very small and not over-particularly-taken-care-of boy. I have a good deal to say, too, about that dashing Alonzo de Ojeda, that you can't help being fonder of than you ought to be; and much to hear concerning Moorish legend, and poor, unhappy Boabdil. Diedrich Knickerbocker I have worn to death in my pocket, and yet I should show you his mutilated carcass with a joy past all expression.

I have been so accustomed to associate you with my pleasantest and happiest thoughts, and with my leisure hours, that I rush at once into full confidence with you, and fall, as it were naturally, and by the very laws of gravity, into your open arms. Questions come thronging to my pen as to the lips of people who meet after long hoping to do so. I don't know what to say first, or what to leave unsaid, and am constantly disposed to break off and tell you again how glad I am this moment has arrived.

My dear Washington Irving, I can not thank you enough for your cordial and generous praise, or tell you what deep and lasting gratification it has given me. I hope to have many letters from you, and to exchange a frequent correspondence. I send this to say so. After the first two or three, I shall settle down into a connected style, and become gradually rational.

You know what the feeling is, after having written a letter, sealed it, and sent it off. I shall picture you reading this, and answering it, before it has lain one night in the post-office. Ten to one that before the fastest packet could reach New York I shall be writing again.

Do you suppose the post-office clerks care to receive letters? I have my doubts. They get into a dreadful habit of indifference. A postman, I imagine, is quite callous. Conceive his delivering one to himself, without being startled by a preliminary double knock! Always your faithful friend,　CHARLES DICKENS.

Washington, Monday Afternoon,
March 21, 1842.

MY DEAR IRVING,—We passed through—literally passed through—this place again to-day. I did not come to see you, for I really have not the heart to say "good-bye" again, and felt more than I can tell you when we shook hands last Wednesday.

You will not be at Baltimore, I fear? I thought, at the time, that you only said you might be there, to make our parting the gayer. Wherever you go, God bless you! What pleasure I have had in seeing and talking with you, I will not attempt to say. I shall never forget it as long as I live. What *would* I give if we could have but a quiet week together! Spain is a lazy place, and its climate an indolent one. But if you have ever leisure under its sunny skies to think of a man who loves you, and holds communion with your spirit oftener, perhaps, than any other person alive—leisure from listlessness, I mean—and will write to me in London, you will give me an inexpressible amount of pleasure. Your affectionate friend,　CHARLES DICKENS.

Tavistock House, London, July 5, 1856.

MY DEAR IRVING,—If you knew how often I write to you individually and personally, in my books, you would be no more surprised in seeing this note, than you were in seeing me do my duty by that flowery julep (in what I dreamily apprehend to have been a former state of existence) at Baltimore.

Will you let me present to you a cousin of mine, Mr. B——, who is associated with a merchant's house in New York? Of course, he wants to see you and know you. How can *I* wonder at that? How can any body?

I had a long talk with Leslie at the last Academy dinner (having previously been with him in Paris), and he told me that you were flourishing. I suppose you know that he wears a mustache—so do I, for the matter of that, and a beard too—and that he looks like a portrait of Don Quixote.

Holland House has four-and-twenty youthful pages in it now—twelve for my lord and twelve for my lady; and no clergyman coils his leg up under his chair all dinner-time, and begins to uncurve it when the hostess goes. No wheeled chair runs smoothly in, with that beaming face in it; and ——'s little cotton pocket-handkerchief helped to make (I believe) this very sheet of paper. A half-sad, half-ludicrous story of Rogers, is all I will sully it with. You know, I dare say, that, for a year or so before his death, he wandered and lost himself, like one of the Children in the Wood, grown up there and grown down again. He had Mrs. Procter and Mrs. Carlyle to breakfast with him one morning—only those two. Both excessively talkative, very quick and clever, and bent on entertaining him. When Mrs. Carlyle had flashed and shone before him for about three-quarters of an hour on one subject, he turned his poor old eyes on Mrs. Procter, and, pointing to the brilliant discourser with his poor old finger, said (indignantly), "Who is *she?*" Upon this, Mrs. Procter, cutting in, delivered —(it is her own story)—a neat oration on the life and writings of Carlyle, and enlightened him in her happiest and airiest manner; all of which he heard, staring in the dreariest silence, and then said (indignantly as before), "And who are *you?*"

Ever, my dear Irving, most affectionately and truly yours,　CHARLES DICKENS.

～～～～

DICKENS AND DOUGLAS JERROLD.

WITH few of his literary contemporaries has Mr. Dickens held more cordial and pleasant relations than with the late Douglas Jerrold. During all the years of their intercourse there sympathy and friendship existed between them which two minds so thoroughly manly and honorable could hardly help feeling for each other. Dickens, though considerably the younger of the two, had won earlier the prizes of his profession. But there was no mean envy and jealousy on the one side, and no mean assumption on the other. The letters that passed between the two men are altogether delightful to read. We shall proceed to give, as far as our space will allow, a few extracts from those of

Dickens to Jerrold, with intercalary elucidations explanatory of the circumstances under which they were written.

In the year 1843, Douglas Jerrold wrote to Mr. Dickens from Herne Bay, where he had taken up his abode in "a little cabin, built up of ivy and woodbine, and almost within sound of the sea."

Mr. Dickens replies:

"Herne Bay. Hum! I suppose it's no worse than any other place in this weather, but it *is* watery, rather, isn't it? In my mind's eye, I have the sea in a perpetual state of small-pox, and the chalk running down hill like town milk. But I know the comfort of getting to work 'in a fresh place,' and proposing pious projects to one's self, and having the more substantial advantage of going to bed early, and getting up ditto, and walking about alone. If there were a fine day, I should like to deprive you of the last-named happiness, and to take a good long stroll."

In the summer of 1844, "Come," wrote Mr. Dickens temptingly, "come and see me in Italy. Let us smoke a pipe among the vines. I have taken a little house surrounded by them, and no man in the world should be more welcome to it than you."

Again from Cremona (November, 1844), Dickens writes:

"You rather entertained the notion once of coming to see me at Genoa. I shall return straight on the ninth of December, limiting my stay in town to one week. Now couldn't you come back with me? The journey that way is very cheap, costing little more than £12, and I am sure the gratification to you would be high. I am lodged in quite a wonderful place, and would put you in a painted room as big as a church, and much more comfortable. There are pens and ink upon the premises; orange-trees, gardens, battledores and shuttlecocks, rousing wood fires for evenings, and a welcome worth having. * * *

"Come! Letter from a gentleman in Italy to Bradbury and Evans in London. Letter from a gentleman in a country gone to sleep, to a gentleman in a country that would go to sleep too, and never wake again, if some people had their way. You can work in Genoa—the house is used to it: it is exactly a week's post. Have that portmanteau looked to, and when we meet say 'I am coming!'"

In 1846, again, Mr. Dickens is off to Switzer-land, and still would tempt Jerrold in his wake. "I wish," he writes, "you would seriously consider the expediency and feasibility of coming to Lausanne in the summer or early autumn. I must be at work myself during a certain part of every day almost, and you could do twice as much there as here. It is a wonderful place to see; and what sort of welcome you would find I will say nothing about, for I have vanity enough to believe that you would be willing to feel yourself as much at home in my household as in any man's."

Arrived at Lausanne, Mr. Dickens writes that he will be ready for his guest in June. "We are established here," he says, "in a perfect doll's house, which could be put bodily into the hall of our Italian palazzo. But it is in the most lovely and delicious situation imaginable, and there is a spare bedroom wherein we could make you as comfortable as need be. Bowers of roses for cigar-smoking, arbors for cool punch-drinking, mountain and Tyrolean countries close at hand, piled-up Alps before the windows, etc., etc., etc." Then follow business-like directions for the journey.

But it could not be. Jerrold was busy with his paper and with his magazine, and felt unable to abandon them even for a few weeks. Well, could he reach Paris for Christmas, persisted Mr. Dickens, and spend that merry time with his friend?

Early in 1847 Jerrold thought he did see his way clear at last to make a short visit to Paris, where Dickens was still established. "We are delighted at your intention of coming," writes the latter, giving the most minute details of the manner in which the journey was to be performed; but even this journey was never accomplished. Once only, after all these promises and invitations—and that for but two or three days—did Douglas Jerrold escape from the cares of London literary life, to meet Mr. Dickens at Ostend, on his return from Italy, and have a few days' stroll about Belgium.

Of Douglas Jerrold's "Story of a Feather," Dickens wrote to the author as follows:

"I am truly proud of your remembrance, and have put the 'Story of a Feather' on a shelf (not an obscure one) where some other feathers are, which it shall help to show mankind which way the wind blows, long after *we* know where the wind comes from. I am quite delighted to find that you have touched the latter part again, and touched it with such a delicate and tender hand. It is a wise and beautiful book. I am sure I may venture to say so to you, for nobody consulted it more regularly and earnestly that I did, as it came out in 'Punch.'"

From Cremona Mr. Dickens wrote in 1844: "It was very hearty and good of you, Jerrold, to make that affectionate mention of the 'Carol' in 'Punch;' and, I assure you, it was not lost upon the distant object of your manly regard, but touched him as you wished and meant it should. I wish we had not lost so much time in improving our personal knowledge of each other. But I have so steadily read you, and so selfishly gratified myself in always expressing the admiration with which your gallant truths inspired me, that I must not call it lost time either."

Writing to Jerrold in 1845, respecting his comedy of "Time works Wonders," Dickens said:

"I am greatly struck by the whole idea of the piece. The elopement in the beginning, and the consequences that flow from it, and their delicate and masterly exposition, are of the freshest, truest, and most vigorous kind; the characters, especially the governess, among the best I know; and the wit and the wisdom of it are never asunder. I could almost find it in my heart to sit down and write you a long letter on the subject of this play, but I won't. I will only thank you for it heartily, and add that I agree with you in thinking it incomparably the best of your dramatic writings."

A year later the friends are still exchanging friendly words. Mr. Dickens writes this time from Geneva:

1846.

MY DEAR JERROLD,—This day week I finished my little Christmas book (writing towards the close the exact words of a passage in your affectionate letter received this morning; to wit, "After all, life has something serious in it)," and ran over here for a week's rest. I can not tell you how much true gratification I have had in your most hearty letter. F. told me that the same spirit breathed through a notice of "Dombey" in your paper; and I have been saying since to K. and G., that there is no such good way of testing the worth of a literary friendship as by comparing its influence on one's mind with any that literary animosity can produce. Mr. W. will throw me into a violent fit of anger for the moment, it is true; but his acts and deeds pass into the death of all bad things next day, and rot out of my memory; whereas a generous sympathy, like yours, is ever present to me, ever fresh and new to me—

always stimulating, cheerful, and delightful. The pain of unjust malice is lost in an hour. The pleasure of a generous friendship is the steadiest joy in the world. What a glorious and comfortable thing that is to think of!

No, I *don't* get the paper* regularly. To the best of my recollection I have not had more than three numbers—certainly not more than four. But I knew how busy you must be, and had no expectation of hearing from you until I wrote from Paris (as I intended doing) and implored you to come and make merry with us there. I am truly pleased to receive your good account of that enterprise. I feel all you say upon the subject of the literary man in his old age, and know the incalculable benefit of such a resource. * * * Anent the "Comic ——" and similar comicalities I feel exactly as you do. Their effect upon me is very disagreeable. Such joking is like the sorrow of an undertaker's mute, reversed, and is applied to serious things with the like propriety and force. * * *

Paris is good both in the spring and in the winter. So come, first at Christmas, and let us have a few jolly holidays together at what Mr. Rowland, of Hatton Garden, calls "that festive season of the year when the human hair is peculiarly liable to come out of curl, unless," etc. I hope to reach there, bag and baggage, by the twentieth of next month. As soon as I am lodged I will write to you. *Do* arrange to run over at Christmas-time, and let us be as English and as merry as we can. It's nothing of a journey, and you shall write "o' mornings," as they say in modern Elizabethan, as much as you like. * * *

The newspapers seem to know as much about Switzerland as about the Esquimaux country. I should like to show you the people as they are here, or in the Canton de Vaud—their wonderful education, splendid schools, comfortable homes, great intelligence, and noble independence of character. It is the fashion among the English to decry them, because they are not servile. I can only say that, if the first quarter of a century of the best general education would rear such a peasantry in Devonshire as exists about here, or about Lausanne (bating their disposition towards drunkenness), it would do what I can hardly hope in my most sanguine moods we may effect in four times that period. The revolution here just now (which has my cordial sympathy) was conducted with the most gallant, true, and Christian spirit—the conquering party moderate in the first transports of triumph, and forgiving. I swear to you that

---

* "Douglas Jerrold's Weekly Newspaper."

some of the appeals to the citizens of both parties, posted by the new government (the people's) on the walls, and sticking there now, almost drew the tears into my eyes as I read them; they are so truly generous, and so exalted in their tone—so far above the miserable strife of politics, and so devoted to the general happiness and welfare. * * *

I have had great success again in magnetism. E., who has been with us for a week or so, holds my magnetic powers in great veneration, and I really think they are, by some conjunction of chances, strong. Let them, or something else, hold you to me by the heart. Ever, my dear Jerrold,

Affectionately your friend,   C. D.

The following curious and interesting letter was addressed by Dickens to Douglas Jerrold on the subject of public hanging, respecting which the latter held conservative opinions.

"Devonshire Terrace, November 17, 1849.

"In a letter I have received from G. this morning he quotes a recent letter from you, in which you deprecate the 'mystery' of private hanging.

"Will you consider what punishment there is, except death, to which 'mystery' does not attach? Will you consider whether all the improvements in prisons and punishments that have been made within the last twenty years have or have not, been all productive of 'mystery?' I can remember very well when the silent system was objected to as mysterious, and opposed to the genius of English society. Yet there is no question that it has been a great benefit. The prison vans are mysterious vehicles; but surely they are better than the old system of marching prisoners through the streets chained to a long chain, like the galley slaves in Don Quixote. Is there no mystery about transportation, and our manner of sending men away to Norfolk Island, or elsewhere? None in abandoning the use of a man's name, and knowing him only by a number? Is not the whole improved and altered system, from the beginning to end, a mystery? I wish I could induce you to feel justified in leaving that word to the platform people, on the strength of your knowledge of what crime was, and of what its punishments were, in the days when there was no mystery connected with these things, and all was as open as Bridewell when Ned Ward went to see the women whipped."

On the last Sunday of May, 1857, Douglas Jerrold was to be one of Mr. W. H. Russell's dinner-party at Greenwich. He was ailing the day before.

Mr. Dickens met him, on the morning of the Greenwich dinner, at the Gallery of Illustration, in Regent Street. They had been advising their friend Mr. Russell in the condensation of his Lectures on the War in the Crimea; and they had engaged with him to go over the last of the series, at the Gallery, at one o'clock that day. "Arriving some minutes before the time," says Mr. Dickens, in a letter to Mr. Blanchard Jerrold, "I found your father sitting alone in the hall.

"'There must be some mistake,' he said. No one else was there; the place was locked up: he had tried all the doors; and he had been waiting a quarter of an hour by himself.

"I sat down by him in a niche on the staircase, and he told me that he had been very unwell for three or four days. A window in his study had been newly painted, and the smell of the paint (he thought it must be that) had filled him with nausea and turned him sick, and he felt weak and giddy, through not having been able to retain any food. He was a little subdued at first, and out of spirits; but we sat there half an hour talking, and when we came out together he was quite himself.

"In the shadow I had not observed him closely, but when we got into the sunshine of the streets I saw that he looked ill. We were both engaged to dine with Mr. Russell at Greenwich, and I thought him so ill then that I advised him not to go, but to let me take him, or send him, home in a cab. He complained, however, of having turned so weak (we had now strolled as far as Leicester Square) that he was fearful he might faint in the cab, unless I could get him some restorative, and unless he could 'keep it down.' I deliberated for a moment whether to turn back to the Athenæum, where I could have got a little brandy for him, or to take him on to Covent Garden for the purpose. Meanwhile he stood leaning against the rails of the inclosure, looking, for the moment, very ill indeed. Finally, we walked on to Covent Garden, and before we had gone fifty yards he was very much better. On our way Mr. Russell joined us. He was then better still, and walked between us unassisted. I got him a hard biscuit, and a little weak cold brandy and water, and begged him by all means to try to eat. He broke up and ate the greater part of the biscuit, and was much refreshed and comforted by the brandy. He said that he felt that the sickness was overcome at last, and that he was quite a new man. It would do him good to have a few quiet hours in the air, and he would go with us to Greenwich. I still tried to dissuade him; but he was by this time bent upon it; his natural color had returned, and he was very hopeful and confident.

"We strolled through the Temple on our way to a boat; and I have a lively recollection of him, stamping about Elm-tree Court (with his hat in one hand, and the other pushing his hair back), laughing in his heartiest manner at a ridiculous remembrance we had in common, which I had presented in some exaggerated light to divert him. We found our boat and went down the river, and looked at the Leviathan which was building, and talked all the way.

"It was a bright day, and as soon as we reached Greenwich we got an open carriage, and went out for a drive about Shooter's Hill. In the carriage Mr. Russell read us his lecture, and we discussed it with great interest. We planned out the ground of Inkermann on the heath, and your father was very earnest indeed. The subject held us so that we were graver than usual; but he broke out at intervals, in the same hilarious way as in the Temple, and he over and over again said to me, with great satisfaction, how happy he was that he had 'quite got over that paint.'

"The dinner-party was a large one, and I did not sit near him at table. But he and I had arranged, before we went in to dinner, that he was to eat only of some simple dish that we agreed upon, and was only to drink sherry and water. We broke up very early, and before I went away with Mr. Leech, who was to take me to London, I went round to Jerrold and put my hand upon his shoulder, asking him how he was. He turned round to show me the glass beside him, with a little wine and water in it.

"'I have kept to the prescription; it has answered as well as this morning's, my dear old boy. I have quite got over the paint, and I am perfectly well.'

"He was really elated by the relief of having recovered, and was as quietly happy as I ever saw him. We exchanged 'God bless you!' and shook hands.

"I went down to Gadshill next morning, where he was to write to me after a little while, appointing his own time for coming to see me there. A week afterwards, another passenger in the railway carriage in which I was on my way to London Bridge, opened his morning paper, and said, 'Douglas Jerrold is dead!'"

"Few of his friends," Mr. Dickens writes, again addressing the son of his old friend, "I think, can have had more favorable opportunities of knowing him in his gentlest and most affectionate aspect than I have had. He was one of the gentlest and most affectionate of men. I remember very well that when I first saw him, in about the year 1835, when I went into his sick-room in Thistle Grove, Brompton, and found him propped up in a great chair, bright-eyed, and quick, and eager in spirit, but very lame in body, he gave me an impression of tenderness. It never became dissociated from him. There was nothing cynical or sour in his heart, as I knew it. In the company of children and young people he was particularly happy, and showed to extraordinary advantage. He never was so gay, so sweet-tempered, so pleasing, and so pleased as then. Among my own children I have observed this many and many a time. When they and I came home from Italy, in 1845, your father went to Brussels to meet us, in company with our friends, Mr. Forster and Mr. Maclise. We all travelled together about Belgium for a little while, and all came home together. He was the delight of the children all the time, and they were his delight. He was in his most brilliant spirits, and I doubt if he were ever more humorous in his life. But the most enduring impression that he left upon us, who are grown up—and we have all often spoken of it since—was, that Jerrold, in his amiable capacity of being easily pleased, in his freshness, in his good-nature, in his cordiality, and in the unrestrained openness of his heart, had quite captivated us.

"Of his generosity I had a proof within these two or three years, which it saddens me to think of now. There had been an estrangement between us—not on any personal subject, and not involving an angry word—and a good many months had passed without my even seeing him in the street, when it fell out that we dined, each with his own separate party, in the STRANGERS' ROOM of a club. Our chairs were almost back to back, and I took mine after he was seated and at dinner. I said not a word (I am sorry to remember), and did not look that way. Before we had sat so long, he openly wheeled his chair round, stretched out both his hands in a most engaging manner, and said aloud, with a bright and loving face that I can see as I write to you, 'For God's sake let us be friends again! A life's not long enough for this.'"

CHARLES DICKENS AS A POET.

THERE are several among our foremost prose writers in the present century, who, possessing high imagination, and a considerable power of rhythmical expression, have occasionally produced verse of a high though not of the first order. Lord Macaulay will not be remembered either by his prize poems or by his " Lays of Ancient Rome," but one who wrote such eloquent prose could hardly fail ignobly when he attempted verse. Thomas Carlyle, in spite of his energetic denunciation of modern poetry as mere dilettantism and trifling, has occasionally courted the muse, and, were the original pieces and translations from the German which lie scattered through his earlier writings collected together, they would form by themselves a volume of no mean value. They have a wild, rugged melody of their own, as have also the occasional verses of Emerson; the latter bear in many respects a remarkable resemblance to those of Blake. The author of " Modern Painters " might also have gained some reputation as a poet, had he chosen to preserve in a more permanent form his scattered contributions to annuals. Indeed, it would seem that no eloquent writer of prose is altogether devoid of the lyric gift if he chooses to exercise it. The only attempt at poetry by Charles Dickens which is at all known to the general public is the song of " The Ivy Green," in the Pickwick Papers. This exquisite little lyric, with its beautiful refrain, so often wedded to music and so familiar to us all, would alone suffice to give him no mean rank among contemporary writers of verse. But in the Comic Opera of the " Village Coquettes,"[*] to which we alluded in our Introduction, there were a dozen songs of equal tenderness and melody, though, as the author has never thought fit to reprint it, they are now forgotten. From these we have selected a few of the best in proof of our assertion.

The first is a song of Harvest-Home, supposed to be sung by a company of reapers:

I.

" Hail to the merry Autumn days, when yellow corn-fields shine,
Far brighter than the costly cup, that holds the monarch's wine!

---

* " The Village Coquettes: a Comic Opera in Two Acts." By CHARLES DICKENS. The music by John Hullah. London: Richard Bentley, 1836.

Hail to the merry harvest-time, the gayest of the year,
The time of rich and bounteous crops, rejoicing and good cheer!

" 'Tis pleasant, on a fine spring morn, to see the buds expand;
'Tis pleasant, in the summer-time, to view the teeming land;
'Tis pleasant, on a winter's night, to crouch around the blaze,
But what are joys like these, my boys, to autumn's merry days!

" Then hail to merry autumn days, when yellow corn-fields shine,
Far brighter than the costly cup that holds the monarch's wine!
And hail to merry harvest-time, the gayest of the year,
The time of rich and bounteous crops, rejoicing and good cheer!"

It must be mentioned that this and the following songs had the advantage of being set to music by John Hullah. Our next selection, " Love is not a feeling to pass away," was a great favorite at the time:

II.

" Love is not a feeling to pass away,
Like the balmy breath of a summer day;
It is not—it can not be—laid aside;
It is not a thing to forget or hide.
It clings to the heart, ah, woe is me!
As the ivy clings to the old oak-tree.

" Love is not a passion of earthly mould,
As a thirst for honor, or fame, or gold:
For when all these wishes have died away,
The deep strong love of a brighter day,
Though nourish'd in secret, consumes the more,
As the slow rust eats to the iron's core."

Our next selection is a Bacchanalian song, supposed to be sung by a country squire:

III.

" That very wise head, old Æsop, said,
The bow should be sometimes loose;
Keep it tight forever, the string you sever;
Let's turn his old moral to use.
The world forget, and let us yet,
The glass our spirits buoying,
Revel to-night, in those moments bright
Which make life worth enjoying.
The cares of the day, old moralists say,
Are quite enough to perplex one;
Then drive to-day's sorrow away till to-morrow,
And then put it off till the next one.

" Some plodding old crones, the heartless drones !
Appeal to my cool reflection,
And ask me whether such nights can ever
Charm sober recollection.

Yes, yes! I cry, I'll grieve and die,
 When those I love forsake me;
But while friends so dear surround me here,
 Let Care, if he can, o'ertake me."

But the gem of all these little songs, in our opinion, is that of "Autumn Leaves," of which the refrain strikes us as being peculiarly happy. The reader, however, shall judge for himself:

IV.

"Autumn leaves, autumn leaves, lie strewn around
 me here;
Autumn leaves, autumn leaves, how sad, how cold,
 how drear!
 How like the hopes of childhood's day,
  Thick clustering on the bough!
 How like those hopes is their decay,
  How faded are they now!
"Autumn leaves, autumn leaves, lie strewn around
 me here;
Autumn leaves, autumn leaves, how sad, how cold,
 how drear!
"Wither'd leaves, wither'd leaves, that fly before the
 gale;
Wither'd leaves, wither'd leaves, ye tell a mournful
 tale,
 Of love once true, and friends once kind,
  And happy moments fled:
 Dispersed by every breath of wind,
  Forgotten, changed, or dead!
"Autumn leaves, autumn leaves, lie strewn around
 me here!
Autumn leaves, autumn leaves, how sad, how cold,
 how drear!"

The next lyric we shall quote was sung by Braham at different concerts, long after the piece from which it is taken had been forgotten, and was almost invariably encored.

"The child and the old man sat alone,
 In the quiet, peaceful shade
Of the old green boughs that had richly grown
 In the deep thick forest glade.
It was a soft and pleasant sound,
 That rustling of the oak;
And the gentle breeze play'd lightly round,
 As thus the fair boy spoke:

"'Dear father, what can honor be,
 Of which I hear men rave?
Field, cell and cloister, land and sea,
 The tempest and the grave:
It lives in all, 'tis sought in each,
 'Tis never heard or seen:
Now tell me, father, I beseech,
 What can this honor mean?'

"'It is a name—a name, my child,
 It lived in other days,
When men were rude, their passions wild,
 Their sport, thick battle frays.
When in armor bright, the warrior bold
 Knelt to his lady's eyes:
Beneath the abbey pavement old,
 That warrior's dust now lies.

"'The iron hearts of that old day
 Have moulder'd in the grave;
And chivalry has pass'd away,
 With knights so true and brave;
The honor which to them was life,
 Throbs in no bosom now;
It only gilds the gambler's strife,
 Or decks the worthless vow.'"

We close our extracts with the following:

"How beautiful at eventide
 To see the twilight shadows pale
Steal o'er the landscape, far and wide,
 O'er stream and meadow, mound and dale!
How soft is Nature's calm repose
 When evening skies their cool dews weep:
The gentlest wind more gently blows,
 As if to soothe her in her sleep!

 The gay morn breaks,
 Mists roll away,
 All Nature awakes
 To glorious day.
 In my breast alone
 Dark shadows remain;
 The peace it has known
 It can never regain."

Mr. Dickens's poetical attempts have not, however, been confined to song-writing. In 1842 he wrote for a friend a very fine Prologue to a new tragedy. Coming to London in his twenty-first year, Mr. Westland Marston resolved to try his success in the world of letters: after writing for several of the second-class magazines, he finished his tragedy of the "Patrician's Daughter," and introduced himself to Mr. Dickens, who became interested in the play. Struck with the novelty of "a coat-and-breeches tragedy," the good-tempered novelist recommended Macready to produce it, and after some little hesitation this distinguished actor took himself the chief character—Mordaunt, and also recited the following prologue by Mr. Dickens:

PROLOGUE TO THE "PATRICIAN'S DAUGHTER."*

BY CHARLES DICKENS.

"No tale of streaming plumes and harness bright
 Dwells on the poet's maiden theme to-night;
No trumpet's clamor and no battle's fire
Breathe in the trembling accents of his lyre.
Enough for him if in his lowly strain
He wake one household echo not in vain;
Enough for him if in his boldest word
The beating heart of man be faintly stirr'd.
That mournful music, that, like chords which sigh
Through charmed gardens, all who hear it die;
That solemn music he does not pursue,
To distant ages out of human view;
Nor listen to its wild and mournful chime,
In the dark caverns on the shore of Time:
But musing with a calm and steady gaze
Before the crackling flame of living days,
He hears it whisper, through the busy roar
Of what shall be, and what has been before.
Awake the present! Shall no scene display
The tragic passion of the passing day?
Is it with man as with some meaner things,
That out of death his solemn purpose springs?
Can this eventful life no moral teach,
Unless ye be for aye beyond its reach;
Obscurely shall he suffer, rot, and fade—
Made noble only by the sexton's spade?
Awake the present! though the steel-clad age
Find life alone within the storied page.

---

* Produced for the first time at the Theatre Royal, Drury Lane, on Saturday, December 10, 1842.

Iron is worn at heart by many still;
The tyrant custom binds the self-like will;
If the sharp rack and chain and screw be gone,
These latter days have tortures of their own.
The guiltless writhe, while guilt is stretch'd in sleep,
And virtue lies, too often, dungeon-deep.
Awake the present! What the past has sown
Is in its harvest garner'd, reap'd, and grown.
How pride engenders pride and wrong breeds wrong,
And truth and falsehood hand in hand along
High places walk in monster-like embrace,
The modern Janus with a double face;
How social usage hath the power to change
Good thought to evil in its highest range,
To cramp the noble soul, and turn to ruth
The kindling impulse of the glowing youth,
Crushing the spirit in its house of clay,—
Learn from the lesson of the present day.
Not light its import, and not poor its mien,
Yourselves the actors, and your home the scene."

We now come to a very curious fact. Mr. R. H. Horne pointed out twenty-five years ago* that a great portion of the scenes describing the death of little Nell in the "Old Curiosity Shop," will be found to be written—whether by design or harmonious accident, of which the author was not even subsequently fully conscious—in blank verse, of irregular metre and rhythms, which Southey, Shelley, and some other poets have occasionally adopted. The following passage, properly divided into lines, will stand thus:

NELLY'S FUNERAL.

"And now the bell—the bell
She had so often heard by night and day,
And listened to with solemn pleasure,
Almost as a living voice—
Rung its remorseless toll for her,
So young, so beautiful, so good.

"Decrepit age, and vigorous life,
And blooming youth and helpless infancy,
Pour'd forth—on crutches, in the pride of strength
And health, in the full blush
Of promise, the mere dawn of life—
To gather round her tomb. Old men were there,
Whose eyes were dim
And senses falling—
Grandames, who might have died ten years ago,
And still been old—the deaf, the blind, the lame,
The palsied,
The living dead in many shapes and forms,
To see the closing of this early grave.
What was the death it would shut in,
To that which still could crawl and creep above it!

"Along the crowded path they bore her now;
Pure as the new-fall'n snow
That cover'd it; whose day on earth
Had been as fleeting.
Under that porch, where she had sat when Heaven
In mercy brought her to that peaceful spot,
She pass'd again, and the old church
Received her in its quiet shade."

Throughout the whole of the above only two unimportant words have been omitted—*in* and *its;* and "grandames" has been substituted for "grandmothers." All that remains is exactly as in the original, not a single word transposed, and the punctuation the same to a comma.

Again, take the brief homily that concludes the funeral:

"Oh! it is hard to take to heart
The lesson that such deaths will teach,
But let no man reject it,
For it is one that all must learn,
And is a mighty, universal Truth.
When Death strikes down the innocent and young,
For every fragile form from which he lets
The parting spirit free,
A hundred virtues rise,
In shapes of mercy, charity, and love,
To walk the world and bless it.
Of every tear
That sorrowing mortals shed on such green graves
Some good is born, some gentler nature comes."

Not a word of the original is changed in the above quotation, which is worthy of the best passages in Wordsworth, and thus, meeting on the common ground of a deeply truthful sentiment, the two most dissimilar men in the literature of the century are brought into the closest approximation.

Something of a similar kind of versification in prose may be discovered in Chapter LXXVII. of "Barnaby Rudge;" and there is an instance of successive verses in the third part of the "Christmas Carol," beginning

"Far in this den of infamous resort."

The following is from the concluding paragraph of "Nicholas Nickleby:"

The grass was green above the dead boy's grave,
Trodden by feet so small and light
That not a daisy droop'd its head
Beneath their pressure.
Through all the spring and summer time
Garlands of fresh flowers, wreathed by infant hands,
Rested upon the stone."

The following stanzas, entitled "A Word in Season," were contributed by Mr. Dickens in the winter of 1843 to an Annual edited by his friend and correspondent, the Countess of Blessington. Since that time he has ceased to write, or, at any rate, to publish any thing in verse.

This poem savors much of the manner of Robert Browning. Full of wit and wisdom, and containing some very remarkable and rememberable lines, it will fitly close this chapter of our volume.

A WORD IN SEASON.

BY CHARLES DICKENS.

They have a superstition in the East,
That ALLAH, written on a piece of paper,
Is better unction than can come of priest
Of rolling incense, and of lighted taper:
Holding, that any scrap which bears that name,
In any characters, its front impress'd on,
Shall help the finder thro' the purging flame,
And give his toasted feet a place to rest on.

* In "A New Spirit of the Age." (Lond., 1844), vol. i. pp. 65–68.

Accordingly, they make a mighty fuss,
  With every wretched tract and fierce oration,
And hoard the leaves—for they are not, like us,
  A highly civilized and thinking nation:
And, always stooping in the miry ways,
  To look for matter of this earthy leaven,
They seldom, in their dust-exploring days,
  Have any leisure to look up to Heaven.

So have I known a country on the earth,
  Where darkness sat upon the living waters,
And brutal ignorance, and toil, and dearth
  Were the hard portion of its sons and daughters:

And yet, where they who should have oped the door
  Of charity and light, for all men's finding,
Squabbled for words upon the altar floor,
  And rent The Book, in struggles for the binding.

The gentlest man among these pious Turks
  God's living image ruthlessly defaces;
Their best High-Churchman, with no faith in works,
  Bowstrings the Virtues in the market-places:
The Christian Pariah, whom both sects curse
  (They curse all other men, and curse each other),
Walks thro' the world, not very much the worse—
  Does all the good he can, and loves his brother.*

CHARLES DICKENS'S READINGS.

ONE glance at the platform is sufficient to convince the audience that Mr. Dickens thoroughly appreciates " stage effect." A large screen of maroon cloth occupies the background; before it stands a light table of peculiar design, on the inner left-hand corner of which there peers forth a miniature desk, large enough to accommodate the reader's book. On the right hand of the table, and somewhat below its level, is a shelf, where repose a carafe of water and a tumbler. This is covered with velvet, somewhat lighter in color than the screen. No drapery conceals the table, whereby it is plain that Mr. Dickens believes in expression of figure as well as of face, and does not throw away every thing but his head and arms, according to the ordinary habit of ordinary speakers. About twelve feet above the platform, and somewhat in advance of the table, is a horizontal row of gas-jets with a tin reflector; and midway in both perpendicular gas-pipes there is one powerful jet with glass chimney. By this admirable arrangement, Mr. Dickens stands against a dark background in a frame of gaslight, which throws out his face and figure to the best advantage.

He comes! A lithe, energetic man, of medium stature, crosses the platform at the brisk gait of five miles an hour, and takes his position behind the table. This is Charles Dickens, whose name has been a household word for thirty years in England. He has a broad, full brow, a fine head—which, for a man of such power and energy, is singularly small at the base of the brain—and a cleanly cut profile. There is a slight resemblance between Mr. Dickens and the Emperor of the French in the latter respect, owing mainly to the nose; but it is unnecessary to add that the faces of the two men are totally different. Mr. Dickens's eyes are light-blue, and his mouth and jaw, without having any claim to beauty, possess a strength that

is not concealed by the veil of iron-gray mustache and generous imperial. His head is but slightly graced with iron-gray hair, and his complexion is florid. There is a twinkle in his eye as he enters, that, like a promissory note, pledges itself to any amount of fun—within sixty minutes.

"THE CHRISTMAS CAROL."

"Ladies and gentlemen, I have the honor to read to you 'A Christmas Carol,' in four staves. Stave one, Marley's Ghost. Marley was dead. There is no doubt whatever about that. The register of his burial was signed by the clergyman, the clerk, the undertaker, and the chief mourner. Scrooge signed it. And Scrooge's name was good upon 'Change, for any thing he chose to put his hand to. Old Marley was as dead as a door-nail."

At the close of this paragraph our first impression is that Mr. Dickens's voice is limited in power, husky, and naturally monotonous. If he succeeds in overcoming these defects, it will be by dramatic genius. We begin to wonder why Mr. Dickens constantly employs the rising inflexion, and never comes to a full stop; but we are so pleasantly introduced to Scrooge, that our spirits revive.

"Foul weather didn't know where to leave him. The heaviest rain and snow, and hail, and sleet could boast of the advantage over him in only one respect—they often 'came down' handsomely, and Scrooge *never did*." Here the magnetic current between reader and listener sets in, and when Scrooge's clerk "put on his white comforter, and tried to warm himself at the candle; in which effort, not being a man of strong imagination, he failed;" the connection

---

* "The Keepsake for 1844: edited by the Countess of Blessington," pp. 73, 74.

is tolerably well established. We see old Scrooge very plainly, growling and snarling at his pleasant nephew; and when that nephew invites that uncle to eat a Christmas dinner with him, and Mr. Dickens goes on to relate that Scrooge said "he would see him—yes, I am sorry to say he did—he went the whole length of the expression, and said he would see him in that extremity first." He makes one dive at our sense of humor, and takes it captive. Mr. Dickens is Scrooge; he is the two portly gentlemen on a mission of charity; he is twice Scrooge when, upon one of the portly gentlemen remarking that many poor people would rather die than go to the work-house, he replies: "If they would rather die, they had better do it, and decrease the surplus population;" and thrice Scrooge, when, turning upon his clerk, he says, "You'll want all day to-morrow, I suppose?" It is the incarnation of a hard-hearted, hard-fisted, hard-voiced miser.

"If quite convenient, sir." A few words, but they denote Bob Cratchit in three feet of comforter exclusive of fringe, in well-darned, thread-bare clothes, with a mild, frightened voice, so thin that you can see through it.

Then there comes the change when Scrooge, upon going home, "saw in the knocker, Marley's face!" Of course Scrooge saw it, because the expression of Mr. Dickens's face makes us see it "with a dismal light about it, like a bad lobster in a dark cellar." There is good acting in this scene, and there is fine acting when the dying flame leaps up as though it cried, "I know him! Marley's ghost!" With what gusto Mr. Dickens reads that description of Marley, and how, "looking through his waistcoat, Scrooge *could see the two buttons on his coat behind.*"

Nothing can be better than the rendering of the Fezziwig party, in Stave Two. You behold Scrooge gradually melting into humanity; Scrooge, as a joyous apprentice; that model of employers, Fezziwig; Mrs. Fezziwig "one vast substantial smile," and all the Fezziwigs. Mr. Dickens's expression as he relates how "in came the housemaid with *her cousin* the baker, and in came the cook *with her brother's particular friend the milkman,*" is delightfully comic; while his complete rendering of that dance where "all were top couples at last, and not a bottom one to help them," is owing to the inimitable action of his hands. They actually perform upon the table, as it were the floor of Fezziwig's room, and every finger were a leg belonging to one of the Fezziwig family. This feat is only surpassed by Mr. Dickens's illustration of Sir Roger de Coverley, as interpreted by Mr. and Mrs. Fezziwig, when "a positive light

appeared to issue from Fezziwig's calves," and he "cut so deftly that he appeared to wink with his legs!" It is a maze of humor. Before the close of the stave, Scrooge's horror at sight of the young girl once loved by him, and put aside for gold, shows that Mr. Dickens's power is not purely comic.

But the best of all, is Stave Three. We distinctly see that "Cratchit" family. There are the potatoes that "knocked loudly at the saucepan-lid to be let out and peeled;" there is Mrs. Cratchit, fluttering and cackling like a motherly hen with a young brood of chickens; and there is every body. The way those two young Cratchits hail Martha, and exclaim—"There's *such* a goose, Martha!" can never be forgotten. By some conjuring trick, Mr. Dickens takes off his own head and puts on a Cratchit's. Later Bob Cratchit and Tiny Tim come in. Assuredly it is Bob's thin voice that pipes out, "Why, where's our Martha?" and it is Mrs. Cratchit who shakes her head and replies, "not coming!" Then Bob relates how Tiny Tim behaved: "as good as gold and better. Somehow he gets thoughtful, sitting by himself so much, and thinks the strangest things you have ever heard. He told me, coming home, that he hoped the people saw him in the church, because he was a cripple, and it might be pleasant to them to remember, upon Christmas-day, who made lame beggars walk, and blind men see." There is a volume of pathos in these words, which are the most delicate and artistic rendering of the whole reading.

Ah, that Christmas dinner! We feel as if we were eating every morsel of it. There are "the two young Cratchits," who "crammed spoons into their mouths, lest they should shriek for goose before their turn;" there is Tiny Tim, who "beat on the table with the handle of his knife, and feebly cried, 'Hoorray,'" in such a still, small voice. And there is that goose! I see it with my naked eye. And O the pudding! "A smell like a washing-day!" That was the cloth. A smell like an eating-house and a pastry-cook's next door to each other, with a laundress's next door to that! That was the pudding." Mr. Dickens's sniffing and smelling of that pudding would make a starving family believe that they had swallowed it, holly and all. It is infectious.

What Mr. Dickens *does* is very frequently infinitely better than any thing he says, or the way he says it; yet the doing is as delicate and intangible as the odor of violets, and can be no better described. Nothing of its kind can be more touchingly beautiful than the manner in which Bob Cratchit—previous to proposing "a merry Christmas to us all, my dears, God bless us"—stoops down, with tears in his eyes, and places Tiny Tim's withered little hand in his, "as if he loved the child, and wished to keep him by his side, and dreaded that he might be taken from him." It is pantomime worthy of the finest actor.

Admirable is Mrs. Cratchit's ungracious drinking to Scrooge's health, and Martha's telling how she had seen a lord, and how he "was much about as tall as Peter."

It is a charming cabinet picture, and so likewise is the glimpse of Christmas at Scrooge's nephew's. The plump sister is "satisfactory, O perfectly satisfactory," and Topper is a magnificent fraud on the understanding — a side-splitting fraud. We see Fred get off the sofa and *stamp* at his own fun, and we hear the plump sister's voice when she guesses the wonderful riddle, "It's your uncle Scro-o-o-o-oge!" Altogether, Mr. Dickens is better than any comedy.

What a change in Stave Four! There sit the gray-haired rascal "Old Joe," with his crooning voice; Mr. Dilber and those robbers of dead men's shrouds; there lies the body of the plundered, unknown man; there sit the Cratchits weeping over Tiny Tim's death, a scene that would be beyond all praise were Bob's cry, "My little, little child!" a shade less dramatic. Here, and only here, Mr. Dickens forgets the nature of Bob's voice, and employs all the power of his own, carried away apparently by the situation. Bob would not thus give way to his feelings. Finally, there is Scrooge, no longer a miser, but a human being, screaming at the "conversational" boy in Sunday clothes, to buy him the prize turkey "that never could have stood upon his legs, that bird. He would have snapped 'em off in a minute, like sticks of sealing-wax." There is Bob Cratchit behind time, trying to overtake nine o'clock, "that fled fifteen minutes before." There is Scrooge poking Bob in the ribs, and vowing he will raise his salary; and there is at last happiness for all, as Tiny Tim exclaims, "God bless us every one!"

It is difficult to see how the "Christmas Carol" can be read and acted better. The only improvement possible is in the ghosts, who are, perhaps, too monotonous; a way ghosts have when they return to earth. Solemnity and monotony are not synonymous terms, yet every theatrical ghost insists that they are, and Mr. Dickens is no exception to the rule. If monotony is excusable in any one, however, it is in him; for, when one actor is obliged to represent *twenty-three different characters*, giving to every one an individual tone, he may be pardoned if his ghosts are not colloquial.

Talk of sermons and churches! There never was a more beautiful sermon than this of "The Christmas Carol." Sacred names do not necessarily mean sacred things.

SIKES AND NANCY.*

"Although among his friends, and such of the outside world as had been admitted to the private performances of the Tavistock House theatricals, Mr. Dickens was known to possess much dramatic power, it was not until within the last few weeks† that he found scope for its exhibition on the platform. Although the characters in his previous readings had each a distinct and defined individuality—and in true artistic spirit the comparatively insignificant characters have as much finish bestowed upon their representation as the heroes and heroines, *e. g.* the fat man on 'Change who replies 'God knows,' to the query as to whom Scrooge had left his money—a bit of perfect Dutch painting— one could not help feeling that the personation was but a half-personation given under restraint; that the reader was 'under-acting,' as it is professionally termed, and one longed to see him give his dramatic genius full vent. That wish has now been realized. When Mr. Dickens called round him some half-hundred of his friends and acquaintances on whose discrimination and knowledge of public audiences he had reliance, and when, after requesting their frank verdict on the experiment, he commenced the new reading, 'Sikes and Nancy,' until, gradually warming with excitement, he flung aside his book, and acted the scene of the murder, shrieked the terrified pleadings of the girl, growled the brutal savagery of the murderer, brought looks, tones, gestures simultaneously into play to illustrate his meaning, there was no one, not even of those who had known him best, or who believed in him most, but was astonished at the power and the versatility of his genius.

"Grandest of all the characters stands out Fagin, the Jew. The voice is husky and with a slight lisp, but there is no nasal intonation; a bent back, but no shoulder shrug; the conventional attributes are omitted, the conventional words are never spoken; and the Jew fence, crafty and cunning even in his bitter vengeance, is there before us, to the life.

"Next comes Nancy. Readers of the old editions of 'Oliver Twist' will doubtless recollect how desperately difficult it was to fight

---

* Extracted (by kind permission) from a criticism by Mr. Edmund Yates.
† Written in 1868.

against the dreadful impression which Mr. George Cruikshank's picture of Nancy left upon the mind, and how it required all the assistance of the author's genius to preserve interest in the stunted, squab, round-faced trull whom the artist had depicted. Accurately delineating every other character in the book, and excelling all his previous and subsequent productions in his etching of ' Fagin in the Condemned Cell,' Mr. Cruikshank not merely did not convey the right idea of Nancy, which would have been bad enough, but conveyed the wrong one, which was worse. No such ill-favored slut would have found a protector in Sikes, who amongst his set and in his profession was a man of mark. We all know Nancy's position ; but just because we know it we are certain she must have had some amount of personal comeliness, which Mr. Cruikshank has entirely denied her. In the reading we get none of the common side of her character, which peeps forth occasionally in the earlier volumes. She is the heroine, doing evil that good may come of it—breaking the trust reposed in her that the man she loves and they amongst whom she has lived may be brought to better lives. With the dread shadow of impending death upon her, she is thrillingly earnest, almost prophetic. Thus, in accordance with a favorite custom of the author, during the interview on the steps at London Bridge, not only does the girl's language rise from the tone of every-day life and become imbued with dramatic imagery and fervor, but that eminently prosaic old person, Mr. Brownlow, becomes affected in the same manner, saying, ' before this river wakes to life,' and indulging in other romantic types and metaphors. This may be scarcely life-like, but it is very effective in the reading, enchaining the attention of the audience and forming a fine contrast to the simple pathos of the dialogue in the murder-scene, every word of which is in the highest degree natural and well-placed. It is here, of course, that the excitement of the audi-

ence is wrought to its highest pitch, and that the acme of the actor's art is reached. The raised hands, the bent-back head, are good ; but shut your eyes, and the illusion is more complete. Then the cries for mercy, the ' Bill ! dear Bill ! for dear God's sake !' uttered in tones in which the agony of fear prevails even over the earnestness of the prayer, the dead, dull voice as hope departs, are intensely real. When the pleading ceases, you open your eyes in relief, in time to see the impersonation of the murderer seizing a heavy club, and striking his victim to the ground.

"Artistically speaking, the story of Sikes and Nancy ends at the point here indicated. Throughout the entire scene of the murder, from the entrance of Sikes into the house until the catastrophe, the silence was intense—the old phrase ' a pin might have been heard to drop' could have been legitimately employed. It was a great study to watch the faces of the people—eager, excited, intent—permitted for once in a life-time to be natural, fogetting to be British, and cynical, and unimpassioned. The great strength of this feeling did not last into the concluding five minutes. The people were earnest and attentive ; but the wild excitement so seldom seen among us died as Nancy died, and the rest was somewhat of an anti-climax.

" No one who appreciates great acting should miss this scene. It will be a treat such as they have not had for a long time, such as, from all appearances, they are not likely to have soon again. To them the earnestness and force, the subtlety, the *nuances*, the delicate lights and shades of the great dramatic art, will be exhibited by one of the first—if not the first—of its living masters ; while those of far less intellectual calibre will understand the vigor of the entire performance, and be specially amused at the facial and vocal dexterity by which the crafty Fagin is instantaneously changed into the chuckle-headed Noah Claypole."

CHARLES DICKENS.

BY G. A. SALA.

"It is as natural to die as to be born; and to a little infant, perhaps, the one is as painful as the other. He that dies in an earnest pursuit is like one that is wounded in hot blood; who, for the time, scarce feels the hurt. And therefore a mind fixed and bent upon somewhat that is good, doth avert the dolours of death. But above all, believe it, the sweetest canticle is *Nunc Dimittis*; when a man hath attained worthy ends and expectations. Death hath this also, that it openeth the gate to good fame, and extinguisheth envy."—BACON: *Essay on Death.*

HE is gone, then!—the gifted writer, the prince of story-tellers, the most genial of essayists, the master of humor and pathos, the compeller of laughter and of tears, the wisest and kindest of moralists. All the world admired his genius; all those who were privileged to know him loved him. On him were bestowed, ere the silver cord was loosened, and the golden bowl was broken, an imperishable treasure of renown and an immeasurable endowment of affection. He appealed not only to the intellect, but to the heart of the entire civilized community. In him even those who have never looked upon his face may deplore the loss not only of a master and a teacher, but of a friend. Into well-nigh every living language which has a grammar and a form of printed expression, his words had been translated; and among nations too rude to read or too ignorant to understand him, his name at least was known—as the names of Shakspeare and Napoleon are known —as that of a Great Man. The most carping of his critics, the most malignant of his detractors—he could not have been great without having both to bark at his heels, and annoy and malign him—will scarcely now dare to deny that his memory is one which posterity will NOT let die. He had been famous, ere he was called away, for nearly five and thirty years: but the day of his death saw the dawn of even mightier fame—fame which years shall be impotent to measure—fame that shall know extinction only when Time forgets who lies at Stratford-on-Avon, and can summon up no memory of the two blind men, one of whom wrote of the War of Troy and the other of the Loss of Eden. Such an inheritance is the portion only of those who create. "The highest praise of original genius," wrote the great scholiast on Milton, "is invention;" and Charles Dickens, in degree, was as original an inventor as he who imagined Achilles' wrath, as he who conjured up Falstaff's salt humors, and who painted Satan in awful blackness. The record of Charles Dickens is

an essential part of the nineteenth century and of the Victorian era; and it would be as difficult to obliterate from the chronicle of our time the remembrance of who he was and what he did, as to ignore Fulton or Stephenson, Brewster or Faraday.

It was said by Johnson of Garrick, that by his death was eclipsed for a season "the gayety of nations." The nations are more populous; they are busier and noisier than they were a hundred years ago; and even as the world rolls, day by day, society must scramble and jostle, traders must strive, lawyers must wrangle, legislators must debate, the great city must whirl in its maelstrom of passion, and ambition, and intrigue, unchecked for one moment even by the consciousness of the loss they have sustained— by the knowledge that Charles Dickens is dead.

On the day that Goldsmith died, Sir Joshua Reynolds threw down his pencil to resume it no more until his friend had been laid in the earth; but such a tribute of sorrow could hardly be spared by the toiling workers of to-day. The roaring looms can not for one instant be arrested; the whirling and clanking of the machine can not for one moment be hushed. Charles Dickens himself died at his post, in full and earnest and active pursuit of his vocation, and at an age when many men less earnest and less active would have withdrawn from public life to enjoy honorable and well-deserved repose. All that his contemporaries can do is to snatch a few hours from their appointed labor to record his good deeds and to bewail his loss. That loss will be felt by the entire community as a national one, and the actual and personal sorrow experienced for the death of Charles Dickens may equal in wide-spread feeling the sorrow which saddened the country at the death of the great Sir Robert Peel.

That illustrious statesman, in old age not extreme, in the fullness of his fame, and in the mature vigor of his faculties, was called away, through a terrible accident, as suddenly as

Charles Dickens by a natural spasm was summoned away on Thursday, the ninth of June; but the shock to the public mind, the impression on the public heart, will be the same. The face, the form, the garb, of Sir Robert were as familiar to the people twenty years ago as those of Dickens were only a few days since. There were few who did not recognize, in his daily rides, the popular Baronet, with his cheerful countenance and light hair, his blue frock-coat and buff waistcoat. There were as few last week who would have been unable to point out the famous novelist, with his thought-lined face, his grizzled beard, his wondrous searching eyes, his bluff presence and swinging gait, as, head aloft, he strode now through crowded streets, looking seemingly neither to the right nor the left, but of a surety looking at and into every thing—now at the myriad aspects of London life, the ever-changing raree-show, the endless round-about, the infinite kaleidoscope of wealth and pauperism, of happiness and misery, of good and evil in this Babylon; now over the pleasant meads and breezy downs which stretched around his modest Kentish demesne hard by the hoary tower of Rochester.

Just as the Kentish farmers and peasants would greet with simple, rural courtesy the neighbor they knew so well, and esteemed so highly for his frank and cordial bearing, so would London folks draw aside as the great writer—who seemed always to be walking a match against Thought—strode on, and, looking after him, say, "There goes Charles Dickens!" The towering stature, the snowy locks, the glistening spectacles, the listless, slouching port, as that of a tired giant, of William Makepeace Thackeray, were familiar enough likewise in London, a few years since, but, comparatively speaking, only to a select few. He belonged to Club-land, and was only to be seen sauntering there or in West-end squares, or on his road to his beloved Kensington, or in the antique hall at Charterhouse on Founders' Day, or on Eton Bridge on the Fourth of June, or sometimes, haply, on the top of a Richmond omnibus, journeying to a brief furlough at Rose Cottage.

Thackeray in Houndsditch, Thackeray in Bethnal Green or at Camden Town, would have appeared anomalous; as well could we picture Carlyle at Cremorne, or Tennyson at Garraway's; but Charles Dickens, when in town, was ubiquitous. He was to be met, by those who knew him, everywhere—and who did not know him? Who had not heard him read, and who had not seen his photographs in the shop-windows? The omnibus conductors knew him, the street-boys knew him; and perhaps the locality where his recognition would have been least frequent—for all that he was a member of the Athenæum Club—was Pall Mall. Elsewhere he would make his appearance in the oddest places, and in the most inclement weather: in Ratcliff Highway, on Haverstock Hill, on Camberwell Green, in Gray's Inn Lane, in the Wandsworth Road, at Hammersmith Broadway, in Norton Folgate, and at Kensal New Town.

A hansom cab whirled you by the Bell and Horns at Brompton, and there was Charles Dickens striding, as with seven-leagued boots, seemingly in the direction of North-end, Fulham. The Metropolitan Railway disgorged you at Lisson Grove, and you met Charles Dickens plodding sturdily towards the Yorkshire Stingo. He was to be met rapidly skirting the grim brick wall of the prison in Coldbath Fields, or trudging along the Seven Sisters' Road at Holloway, or bearing, under a steady press of sail, through Highgate Archway, or pursuing the even tenor of his way up the Vauxhall Bridge Road. He seemed to prefer for mere purposes of exercise the lengthy thoroughfares of our exterior boulevards, to narrow and intricate streets. They offered, perhaps, a better opportunity for fair and honest walking, and for the performance of that self-appointed task of pedestrianism which for so many years he had undertaken daily, and which well-nigh undeviatingly, and wherever he was—in London, at home at Gadshill, in France, in Italy, or in America—he performed to the last rood and furlong of a mentally-measured route. It was one of Mr. Dickens's maxims that a given amount of mental exertion should be counteracted by a commensurate amount of bodily fatigue; and for a length of years his physical labors were measured exactly by the duration of his intellectual work.

It is idle at this time to inquire whether he took too much exercise, and whether, in some cases, Nature will not resent unvarying regularity in the observance of her laws, or refuse to respond by the gift of health and long life to the most rigidly-pursued system of hygiene. If Charles Dickens erred in this respect, he erred with Cornaro, with Franklin, and with Prescott, all of whom lived by line and rule; measuring the sands of their time by the grain, weighing out their sustenance by the ounce and the gill, adjusting even the weight of the garments they wore in summer or in winter to the minutest flections of the balance. Charles Dickens was a man who never exceeded in aught save pedestrianism; whose nature, strongly impulsive as it was, seemed to have been brought under an inexorable discipline.

Those who had followed him from the morning of his career to its dazzling noontide, and so to its golden evening—those who, knowing him of old, watched the man as well as the master with that reverent love which Raphael's scholars, which Luther's disciples, and which the personal attendants of the First Napoleon bore for their chief—might now, in very mournful retrospect, call to mind the different phases of personal aspect of him who was at once the leader and the friend, the king and the colleague.

The photographic portraits of Charles Dickens form a legion; and the more recent ones give a life-like resemblance of him as he seemed to the present generation—a bronzed, weather-worn, hardy man, with somewhat of a seaman's air about him. His carriage was remarkably upright, his mien almost aggressive in its confidence. He was one of the few men whose individuality was not effaced by the mournful conventionality of evening dress. Many a prince, many a peer, would, but for their stars and ribbons, be absorbed at public dinners or evening parties by the terrible dead level of the black coat and white cravat; but under such circumstances the face and figure of Charles Dickens were always unmistakably conspicuous. The same prominence of individuality was strongly manifest in Mr. Leslie's well-known picture of Mr. Dickens as the Copper Captain, in "Every Man in his Humor," in the recent Exhibition of Deceased Masters at the Royal Academy. The dramatic *travestissement* was complete; the picturesque "make up" was perfect; the simulated captain was the genuine bearded, whiskered swashbuckler and braggadocio of Ben Jonson; and yet beneath all these there shone forth, strongly as the sun darting from behind a summer cloud, the searching eyes, the determined visage, the irresistible smile of Charles Dickens.

His appearance in walking-dress in the streets, during his later years, was decidedly "odd," and almost eccentric, being marked by strongly-pronounced colors, and a fashioning of the garments which had somewhat of a sporting and somewhat of a theatrical guise.

To those who did not know that he was Charles Dickens, he might have been some prosperous sea-captain home from a long voyage, some Western senator on a tour in Europe, some country gentleman of Devon or of Yorkshire who now and then bred a colt or two, and won a cup, but never betted. But those who could look far back remembered when Charles Dickens was in countenance, like Milton in his youth, "eminently beautiful," and when in attire he was, next to Count D'Orsay, the choicest and most tastefully dressed dandy in London. For the similitude of the elderly Dickens we must rely upon the wonderfully faithful photographic portraits lately published; for the Dickens of middle age, we must refer to the noble portrait by Mr. Frith, or to the grand, but somewhat dusky, picture by Ary Scheffer, or to the engraving from the delicate miniature by Margaret Gillies, prefixed to Mr. Horne's "New Spirit of the Age;" but for the Dickens of thirty years since, for the "unknown young man" who, as his greatest critic and admirer, Mr Thackeray, said, "calmly and modestly came and took his place at the head of English literature," we must turn to the portrait by his early friend, Daniel Maclise, an engraving of which forms the frontispiece, we think, to the first completed edition of "Nicholas Nickleby."

There is also a very characteristic sketch of the youthful Dickens in an etching by George Cruikshank, illustrating one of the "Sketches by Boz," and in which both the author and the artist are depicted with wands in their hands, as stewards at a public dinner at the Freemasons' Tavern; but for grace, and refinement, and intellectual force we must go to Maclise's canvas, and ponder over that exquisite delineation of the young man with the long silky hair, the fascinating smile, and the marvellous clear and inquiring eyes which, even from the copperplate, seem to follow the beholder everywhere, as the eyes of Guido's Beatrice do in that gallery at Rome.

This was the Charles Dickens who, in high satin stock and double breast-pin, in glossy frock-coat and velvet collar, in cut velvet waistcoat and glistening chain, was, in the early days of Queen Victoria's reign, one of the best-looking and best-dressed young fellows about town; or who, a few years later, in a blue frock, white vest, and white trowsers, looked even nattier and comelier.

This was the brilliantly successful young author who, without effort, as it seemed, had risen from the lowest to the topmost rung of the ladder of literature; who the day before yesterday, as it were, lawyer's clerk, reporter at a police-court, short-hand writer in the House of Commons gallery, scribbler of fugitive articles in an evening paper, found himself suddenly followed, admired, courted, lionized, almost idolized, by almost all that was wealthy, and dignified, and beautiful in society; who, emerging from a model middle-class home and middle-class surroundings, found himself all at once the peer and the associate of Bulwer and Milnes, of Lockhart and Jeffrey, of Moore and Campbell, of Talfourd, and Proctor, and who, ere he had long enjoyed his first wreath of laurels, had the high honor to be virulently abused by the Right Honorable John Wilson Croker.

About four-and-thirty years have elapsed since the publication of "Pickwick." Lifted into immediate and prodigious celebrity, Charles Dickens, until the day of his death, never knew what it was for that celebrity to have decreased one jot.

In 1836, England and all America knew him, rejoiced in him, and were proud of him; all England and all America, and all the civilized world beside, know and are proud of him in 1870; although, alas! their rejoicing is turned to sorrow, and the greenest bays of all their chaplets, which they would have wreathed round the brows of the author of the "Mystery of Edwin Drood," must now be laid upon a grave.

There is something eminently touching and consoling in this thoroughness and completeness of the good writer's life—in this insoluble continuity of success, in this long day of renown, whose brightness knew no overclouding, no storms, no dank chilliness of gradual fading and decay. And as, in the tropics, there is no twilight; and while the sky is all ablaze with the crimson and gold of the setting sun a great black pall suddenly falls and extinguishes all in Night, so, while the genius of Charles Dickens was at its brightest, and the splendor of his name most luminous, comes Death, and drops a cloak over all the light and splendor, and shuts it up; and there is night—and we can only hope that it will be a night of stars.

> "Le pauvre en sa cabane où le chaume le couvre
>   Est sujet à ses lois ;
> Et la garde qui veille aux barrières du Louvre
>   N'en défend pas nos rois."

In such magnificent lines has Malesherbes echoed the eloquent warning of the heathen poet.

But it boots not to dilate on the brevity or the uncertainty of life, to strain rhetoric into high-flown reflections on this transitory existence, or to indulge in vain lamentations on the suddenness of the event, for which it is impossible to know whether the deceased was prepared or unprepared. Who shall tell, and who shall say as much more or as much less, or aught that is certain of any human creature? Our shrifts may be as short as the lightning's flash, or we may tell our beads for fourscore years, and yet die unready. It is sufficient to know that God took him in His own good time, and that he had been permitted to fill a place in the history of his age, to enjoy a career, and to accomplish a life-work, the completeness of which kings and conquerors might envy. He scarcely ever failed in any thing he undertook. It would be rash to say that he was born to succeed in any thing he might have attempted; but it is certain that he had so brought his powers under mastery, that he had so disciplined his capacity, that he had so trained and developed the direction of his genius, as to be able to insure and to command a certain amount of success in every one of his endeavors. His triumphs were neither fortuitous nor accidental. They were premeditated, consummated, and deserved.

His introduction to Messrs. Chapman and Hall—his earliest, his latest, and his most appreciative publishers—had, perhaps, some appearance of "luck" about it; and it might be argued that if poor Seymour had not proposed to execute a series of humorous etchings for Messrs. Chapman and Hall, and if those gentlemen had not been compelled to cast about for a clever young man to "write to the engravings," Charles Dickens might have continued, for many years longer, to vegetate in his chambers in Furnival's Inn.

We all know with what painful, toilsome slowness Thackeray ascended the staircase of renown; in how many ante-chambers he was forced to wait; at how many doors he was fain to knock unavailingly; how he toiled in obscurity in magazines, and reviews, and newspapers, and weekly serials, until at length, but tardily, success, celebrity, and glory came. And yet Thackeray was, in his sphere of letters, as distinctly original and as distinctly unapproachable as Dickens. Both men have had followers and imitators by the score—doleful creatures, who have copied the faults of their models, even as monkeys mimic the meanest motions of men, but who have been wholly impotent to imitate

their beauties. There were few social satirists of note to compete with Thackeray when he began "Vanity Fair." There were few humorists of note extant to compete with Dickens when he began "Pickwick." The last sprang, at once, in early youth, into transcendent fame; the first —who was a practised member of Fraser's staff before Dickens had been heard of—had come to be nigh forty years old before "Vanity Fair," bandied about, rejected from publisher to publisher, was at length accepted. The reason for the long-deferred recognition in the one case, and the immediate and tremendous acclaim in the other, was, probably, that Thackeray only appealed to a cultivated and a somewhat cynical section of the world, and that Dickens appealed to all humanity. "Vanity Fair" was but an alterative for some of the morbid humors of society. "Pickwick" was a literary panacea.

The Spanish king who from his palace window saw on the banks of the Mançañares a student rolling in ecstasies of laughter, with a book in his hand, remarked to his courtiers, "That scholar must either be mad or reading 'Don Quixote.'" And Philip III. had very probably, just before, been reading Cervantes's masterpiece, himself. It was every one's portion. Only a limited number of scholars and worldlings could understand the mordant satire, the delicate equivoque, the scathing irony of Thackeray's prose epic, or could understand the glittering comedy of Becky Sharpe and the Marquis of Steyne, or of Major Pendennis and Captain Costigan. Thackeray essayed to construct an English Quixote in Colonel Newcome, but he succeeded only in producing a beautiful work of art, on a personage whose most natural acts were less true to nature than the wildest Quixotisms of the Ingenious Hidalgo. On the other hand, every one—the prince, the peasant, the judge, the charity-boy, the learned professor, and the servant-maid—could understand, and could enjoy, "Pickwick." It was the universal recreation and solace.

When the luckless Irish rebel, John Mitchel, after his condemnation to transportation in Dublin, was conveyed in a war steamer to the convict dépôt at Spike Island, the officer commanding the ship mercifully lent the prisoner in his lonely cabin some novels of Charles Dickens to read. Mitchel, in his "Jail Journal," has recorded the consolation their perusal afforded him. And precisely the same alleviation of suffering, or weariness, or low spirits might have been felt by a Princess of the Blood turning over the pages of "Pickwick" or "Nickleby" at the very moment that the wretched Irish convict was likewise deep in Dickens, and endeavoring to divert his thoughts from the imminent hulks.

The only "luck" experienced by Charles Dickens at the outset of his career was, that he discovered a great national want which had not yet been supplied. The age would no longer tolerate the grossness of Smollett and Sterne, and could not comprehend the philosophy, while it still applauded the wit, of Fielding. The "comic" literature of the decade preceding the advent of Dickens was simply deplorable in its dull idiocy. When it happened to be somewhat funny, it was usually ribald. Charles Lamb had written, and written exquisitely; but the circulation of his essays, from the medium adopted for their publication, was restricted; and even at the present day the people at large fail to appreciate the arrowy wit and delicate fancy of Elia.

But to whom are Sam Weller, Mr. Alfred Jingle, Mr. Winkle, Mr. Snodgrass, Mr. Tupman, Mr. Jingle, and the immortal Fat Boy, mysteries? Who has ever found Bob Cratchit, Scrooge, Tiny Tim, or even Marley's Ghost recondite? Is any scholastic experience necessary to understand Mrs. Gamp? Need we be cynical to enjoy Mr. Pecksniff? It was through the universality of his drama and the thorough humanity of his personages that Charles Dickens at once attained world-wide fame. He was "lucky" to find liberal publishers in the Strand for the "Pickwick Papers;" but had he never written that enchanting piece of drollery he would have been as "lucky" with Mr. Macrone in St. James's Square with his "Sketches by Boz," as "lucky" with Mr. Bentley in New Burlington Street with "Oliver Twist."

His genius was bound to "pierce." It was the Hour for him—the hour when the schoolmaster began to be abroad; when a young generation was rising, determined to be kept no longer in ignorance; when the presence of a young and blameless Queen on the throne made thoughtful men reflect with horror on the scurrility and the ribaldry of by-gone literature—and for that Hour Charles Dickens was the Man. Had he approved himself nothing but a comic writer, his celebrity, vast as it would have been for a time, might very soon have waned. Samuel Foote was called "The English Aristophanes;" yet what sane publisher would undertake, at the present day, to reissue Foote's works? Rabelais was the merriest droll imaginable; his writings are a mine of roaring fun; yet who, save laborious scholars, read Rabelais through? Was there ever a funnier fellow than Theodore Hook? Yet where is his fun now? Scarron, Tom Brown, D'Urfey, George Colman have all been laughed at—and forgotten; and even the reputation of the arch-wag, Tom Hood, would have been ephemeral but for his noble services to humanity as a serious poet—as the writer of the "Song of the Shirt" and the "Bridge of Sighs." When Charles Dickens was about midway in his career, it was a favorite device with those who decried him to exaggerate beyond measure the merits of "Pickwick," to the disparagement of his later and more serious works, and to declare that he would never again write any thing half so good as his first, his most facetious, but certainly his least artistically-constructed novel. But these backbiters were speedily silenced when it was found that the great master of farce was likewise a great master of sentiment; that Dickens could be, on oc-

casion, not only irresistibly comic, not only slyly humorous, not only inimitably quaint, but that he could be infinitely tender, graceful, and pathetic—that he could be dramatic, tragical, and terrible. The hand which drew Mr. Pickwick "in the Pound" gave us, almost simultaneously, Fagin in the condemned cell. From the same teeming brain have come the death of Little Nell, and the marriage of Mrs. M'Stinger; the description of Mr. John Smawker's "Swarry," and the picture of the Gordon Riots; the terrific combat of Mr. Crummles and his sons, and the storm in "David Copperfield;" the christening of little Paul Dombey, and the murder of Mr. Tulkinghorne. I conscientiously believe that, had Charles Dickens never written "Pickwick" at all, his tenure of the public mind and on the public love would have been as great and as promising of permanence as it is now.

He was a great traveller. We are not alluding to his two journeys to the United States, to his long residence in Italy, to his frequent excursions to France, or even to his prolonged explorations—now on business, now on pleasure —of his own country. Where he had travelled longest, where he had looked deepest and learned most, was in inner London. He is no Regent Street lounger: he scarcely ever mentions Pall Mall; he rarely alludes to Piccadilly; he is not much at home in fashionable squares; he is not to be found in the Ladies' Mile; he is out of his element at Brompton, or in the Regent's Park, or in Great Gaunt Street, or at Greenwich, or Richmond, or in any of the localities so well beloved by Thackeray. But he knew all about the back streets behind Holborn, the courts and alleys of the Borough, the shabby sidling streets of the remoter suburbs, the crooked little alleys of the City, the dank and oozy wharfs of the water-side. He was at home in all lodging-houses, station-houses, cottages, hovels, Cheap Jacks' caravans, work-houses, prisons, school-rooms, chandlers' shops, back attics, barbers' shops, areas, back-yards, dark entries, public-houses, rag-shops, police-courts, and markets in poor neighborhoods. And, curiously, from these localities, unseemly and unsavory as they might be, he brought pictures of life and manners, and produced characters of men and women and children, that have been the wonder and delight and edification of millions, not only of his own countrymen, but of strangers at the uttermost ends of the earth. He was the good genius who turned every thing into gold. Upon offal and garbage, upon crime and misery, upon poverty and pestilence, upon the dullest, densest, ugliest things the bright light of his amazing fancy shone, and of the social reptiles he held up to view only the precious jewels in their heads remained. He was a great traveller—as earnest and as eloquent a pilgrim, indeed, as that wanderer whom John Bunyan has shown us travelling from this world to the next. And he, too, like Christian, has got to his journey's end—to the cold, dark river with the shining city beyond.

9

His travels in town were obviously offshoots and extensions of those long daily walks which he undertook for purposes neither of intellectual study nor of relaxation, but in the stern endeavor to preserve his health. But when his walking work was done—work scarcely less arduous than the crank or treadmill toil of a convict, one can imagine him beginning to loiter a little; to toy with his road; to look into shops; to linger at street corners; to watch street comedies, street pastimes, street brawls, as Hogarth watched them; to branch off to the right or the left; to explore unknown regions, losing himself purposely, and trusting to blind chance to find the straight road again. It must have been in these desultory wanderings that he lighted on the out-of-the-way places which with such matchless fidelity and graphic force he has described; that he came upon "Tom all Alone's" and Bleeding-Heart Yard; upon the court in "Bleak House," where the "Follower" died, and where the inquest was held upon the law writer; upon the den where Fagin lived; and the garret where Kaggs died; upon the abode of the R. Wilfer family, and the residence of the Golden Dustman; upon the quiet nook where Bob Cratchit held his Christmas dinner, and where Tiny Tim did *not* die; upon the half-college half-almshouse where the moody chemist who had "hewn himself steps out of the rock of knowledge whereby to rise to fame and fortune" was confronted by his own spectre; upon Mrs. Chickenstalker's chandler's shop, and upon those immortal door-steps, close to the church tower which held The Chimes, where the political economist devoured the tripe of Trotty Veck. The pictures he drew were clearly not imaginary, for no sooner were they drawn than all the world recognized their amazing vividness and veracity, and only wondered that such scenes had not occurred to them before: and herein his greatness as an artist was conspicuous; for it is one of the distinctive privileges of genius to utter thoughts and to portray objects which at once appear to us obvious and familiar, but of which no definite idea or impression had hitherto been presented to our minds. Few of us have passed through life without meeting with some gross fat man, full of vice, and profligacy and impudence—vainglorious, dishonest, and a coward, but who was tolerated for the drollery of his manners and the facetiousness of his conversation. But in the hands of genius this sufficiently common personage becomes suddenly typical, representative, and unique. He becomes Sir John Falstaff. Who has not known some oily, specious humbug, the pilferer of other men's laurels, the weasel sucking other men's brains, the shabby, shuffling schemer, weaving his dirty webs under pretense of candor and simplicity? We know these cogging knaves, and pass them by unregardingly; but genius takes up our smooth scoundrel, and brands him to all time as Pecksniff. The sayings and doings of the rascally architect, like those of the Fat Knight, have become proverbial. There is nothing so common as a proverb; but it is only genius that can first give tangible form and expression to proverbial wisdom. Every body knew Mrs. Gamp years before Dickens was born; but nobody had thought about painting her. Many had done business with Ralph Nickleby, but none had thought of describing him. Mr. Squeers had figured in a dozen lawsuits for cruelty and neglect ten years before "Nicholas Nickleby" was written; yet Dotheboys Hall was hailed as a country I newly brought within human cognizance as California or Queensland.

These travels in London were alternated by travels in the country—journeys as patient, as earnest, and as fruitful in result. To these rural pilgrimages we owe numbers of exquisite descriptions of scenery and village life; we owe the fair in "Our Mutual Friend;" the forge in the marsh where Pip in "Great Expectations" lived; the ark on the sands which harbored the Peggoties; the cosy nook where Mrs. Jarley encamped with her wax-work show; the churchyard where the Punch and Judy showmen met the boy and girl on stilts; the ill-omened glade where Tigg was murdered by Jonas Chuzzlewit. I do not know whether Charles Dickens was in the habit of taking manuscript notes of the places or the people that came under his observation, as Honoré de Balzac did, at whose death, according to M. Armand Baschet, there were brought to light piles of memoranda, or *petits papiers "plein des chambres, plein des maisons."* I am the rather inclined to think that Mr. Dickens did *not* take such notes, but that he had a wonderfully receptive and tenacious ocular memory:—"collodion in the eye," as has been said of Gustave Doré, who rarely makes preliminary sketches of the scenes which he afterwards reproduces with such wonderfully picturesque vigor. There is some curious internal evidence of the theory I hold to be found in the circumstance that in one of Charles Dickens's later novels, "Little Dorrit," there is described, with the minuteness of an Ostade or a Teniers, a place which had been utterly demolished at least fifteen years before the novel was written. This was the Marshalsea prison in Southwark. When he recounted in "Pickwick" the adventures of Mr. Smangle and Mr. Mivins in the Fleet, or the humors of the cobbler who had been ruined by having a legacy left him, and who slept under a table because it reminded him of a four-post bedstead; when he expatiated on the sorrows of the Chancery prisoner, and the miseries of the unhappy wretches on the "Poor Side," the infamous place of legal torture in Farringdon Street was in full activity; yet the description of the Marshalsea, which was pulled down long before he sat down to compose "Little Dorrit," and the very fact of whose existence had well-nigh passed from the ordinary memory of man, is to the full as elaborate and (as those who know the hideous old den can vouch) as faithful as any of those priceless pictures of Fleet Prison life which have moved so many thousands to uproarious laughter and to scalding tears; for who can forget the inimitable fun of Mr. Pickwick's first night in the Marshal's room, or the entertainment by Sam Weller of the Rev. Mr. Stiggins in the Snuggery, or the infinite pathos of Jingle in his decadence, and the Chancery Prisoner on his death-bed?

Thus gifted with two of the most essential adjuncts of the traveller's outfit—eyes swift to see, sense to perceive, and tenacious to treasure up—Charles Dickens must undoubtedly have possessed another faculty inestimable to travellers. He must have been a wonderful listener. He has "reported," so to speak, the utterances of the meanest of mankind with the same nervous and textual truth with which, long years before, he reported the speeches of statesmen for the "Morning Chronicle" and the "Mirror of Parliament." All of his contemporaries in the gallery whom I have ever known—and I have known many—have concurred in stating that he was the quickest, the readiest, the aptest, and the most faithful stenographer of this time. He had completely mastered the difficult and ungrateful art of short-hand: a mistress whom you may woo indeed to conquest, but upon whom the door must be locked, and who must be bound in links of iron, lest she run away from you five minutes after she has given you her heart. The late Angus Reach, himself an accomplished Parliamentary reporter as well as a distinguished man of letters, used to say that, next to the difficulty of learning the signs and characters in short-hand came that of understanding their purport after they had been written. Charles Dickens, however, retained his proficiency to the last.

At one of the dinners of the Newspaper Press Fund, at which he presided, and in the course of a speech, in which he recalled, with delightful pleasantry, his experiences on the "intellectual treadmill" of reporting, he mentioned that the old capacity had never left him, and that often, while listening to other speeches, he found himself tracing on the table-cloth, half mechanically, half in pastime, notes of the phrases he was listening to, just as though he were taking his "turn" in the Commons' gallery. And, twenty years after he left that gallery he retained enough of his ancient craft to teach the art of short-hand very thoroughly and completely to a young brother-in-law, who was entering on the career of journalism.

Now it is manifest that a deaf or a dull-eared man can not be a good reporter, were he to use "long-hand" even, instead of short-hand—as some of the best reporters have done; or were he to report from memory, quickening his reminiscences by drinking two pots of porter after a debate—as Woodfall did. In his time, Charles Dickens must have listened to and taken down the words of the speeches of nearly every public man of the last generation. He reported Brougham's great speech at Edinburgh, after his resignation of the Chancellorship. He may have reported Lord Stanley's famous oration on the Irish Church. He must have reported habitually the speeches of Peel and Grey, of Denman, of Lyndhurst, of Ellenborough, of Hume, and Melbourne, and Grote.

There can be little doubt that this early training in listening and transcribing was of infinite service to him in enabling him to develop the utterances of his inborn genius in a clear, concise, and perspicuous style. He had listened to masters in every style of rhetoric: he had followed Henry Brougham the Demosthenes, Shiel the Cicero, O'Connell the Mirabeau, of their age; and albeit in dialogue and in description the eccentricity of his humor and the quaintness of his conceits sometimes marred the purity of his fabric, and betrayed him into exaggeration and into mannerism, he was, in genuine essay, in grave and deliberate statement, and in his culminating passages of invective or of eulogium, a well-nigh unrivalled master of racy, pungent, idiomatic English. In nobility of diction, strength of expression, harmonious balance of phrases, and unerring correctness of construction, very many of Charles Dickens's short essays equal the grandest of Dryden's prose prefaces, and surpass the most splendid dialectical flights of Macaulay. He was rarely involved and never florid. I do not know whether he ever wrote a leading article in a newspaper, or whether he could have written one had he attempted the task. I am inclined to think that he felt too strongly, and that his earnestness was of a nature too natural and individualized to be subjected to the constraints of the conventional "we," or fo bring himself down to the level of the leader-writer, who, in his articles, at least, should have neither personality, likings, dislikings, anger, placability, enthusiasm, heart, nor soul—nothing but brains, in fine, and the art of hiding himself from public ken. Whenever it can be ascertained, from internal evidence, who writes the "leader," that leader must be faulty.

It is remarkable that, while the magnificent examples of oratory to which he had been a listener, had evidently sunk deep into his mind, and had had as evidently a powerful influence in bracing and clarifying that which I may term his didactic style, it would seem that he suffered while in the House from so abundant a surfeit of parliamentary verbiage of the lower kind, and that he had been so frequent and so unwilling a listener of the heavy verbosity of the Noble Lord and the dull platitudes of the Right Honorable Gentlemen, that he was ever afterwards careful to eliminate, so far as ever he could, the sayings and doings of the small fry of the literary world from his narratives. For greatness, in whatever rank of life it might be found, he had a congenial reverence. For great men he had as congenial an affection. If among his most intimate friends I mention at random the names of Earl Russell, Lord Lytton, Lord Houghton, and Sir Alexander Cockburn—friends as dearly cherished by him as were ever his own colleagues and companions, Thackeray, Douglas Jerrold, Leech, Mark Lemon, Albert Smith, Stanfield, Frith, Leslie, Maclise, Collins, Macready, and Fechter—it would seem plain that he was as equally devoid of an intolerant radical hatred of persons born to or elevated to high social station, as of the pitiable foible of toadying noblemen, simply because they belonged to the nobility. Still the small fry he had watched from afar off in his gallery days had clearly left a very disagreeable taste in his mouth; and neither "rank" nor "gentility" shine to any great advantage in his writings. A young lord is introduced for a moment in "Pickwick" (at the Bath Assembly Rooms), and he is an idiot; Lord Frederick Verisopht in "Nickleby" is a good-natured fool; Sir Mulberry Hawk is a sharper and a blackguard; Sir Leicester Dedlock in "Bleak House," on the delineation of whose character he bestowed great pains, and whom he endeavored to make a chivalrous, high-minded, though obstinate and prejudiced Tory gentleman, is a mere stilted bore; and Cousin Feenix in "Dombey and Son" is, although a well-meaning creature enough, a fatuous dotard. The Tite Barnacle family in "Little Dorrit" are, from the prosperous placemen of the tribe to the genteel pensioners at Hampton Court, a mean, shabby, and contemptible crew; and in "Barnaby Rudge," he has bestowed on Sir John Chester —one of the most elaborate of his creations—all the vices of Chesterfield, without any of his virtues; and has drawn the unhappy Lord George Gordon even madder than he was. The unfavorable light in which the patrician classes are, as a rule, depicted in his works, was, I remember, good naturedly resented by Lord Houghton, in his speech at the Liverpool banquet in 1869; and in the course of his speech, the accomplished nobleman I have mentioned, while expressing a wish that the name of Dickens itself might one day be inscribed on the roll of peers, twitted him with the discourteous treatment the peerage had hitherto received at his hands in a literary sense, and hinted that were he a member of the House of Lords, he might learn to know the aristocracy better. Mr. Dickens did not lose his temper, but he retorted somewhat sharply, asking, "What amazing devil" could have possessed Lord Houghton, when he accused him of disparaging the patrician order?

That he did so disparage dignified rank by implication, seeing that the majority of his titled personages are either rogues or simpletons, while he has left out the talented or the virtuous nobles altogether, seems undeniable; and I repeat that I ascribe the fact not to democratic prejudice, but to his horror of those minor magnificoes to whose folly or whose dullness he had been compelled to lend his ears in youth. He reverted, as for change and relief, to the very opposite pole of society, and "reported," as faithfully as he had reported any Noble Lord, who was "free to confess," or any Honorable Gentleman who "came down to this House"—

to say nothing at all worth listening to—the parlance of barbers and beadles; of costermongers and rag-shop keepers; of hostlers and hospital nurses; of grooms and porters; of mudlarks and Jacks-in-the-water; of the derelicts of the gutter; the thin remains of decayed humanity in the work-house; the draff of felony and vagabondage, and the scum of the detective police A preposterous Frenchman, by the name of Edmond Scherer, commenting only a few days since in a Paris newspaper, "Le Temps," on the literary merits of Charles Dickens, asserts that he had "a propensity to depict hideous and atrocious things," and to drag his readers "through revolting scenes where children are martyrized, through jails where convicts are rotting away, surrounded by maniacs and mendicants." Setting aside the fact that convict prisons are not usually found in combination with lunatic asylums and work-houses, no English reader need be told, that while many of the scenes and the characters depicted by Charles Dickens were painful, and even repulsive, those scenes were drawn with a distinct and deliberate purpose—that of exposing and denouncing flagrant social evils;—and that in many cases the end he had in view, that of obtaining the redress of the evil he denounced, was either directly or remotely obtained. His novels acted upon journalism; journalism reacted upon public opinion; public opinion became at last a pressure; and that pressure was ultimately adequate to change or to abrogate old laws or to enact new ones. There can not be the slightest doubt that Yorkshire schools were knocked on the head by the portraiture of Dotheboys Hall, where, to use Mr. Scherer's words, little children were really and truly "martyrized;" and it is equally incontrovertible that the movements to which we owe Refuges and Reformatories, the Industrial Schools Act, and the reforms in the Court of Chancery and the Ecclesiastical Courts, and the Abolition of Imprisonment for Debt, received a direct and a powerful impetus from his writings. Let it be remembered that in this respect he did not (as is the case with most writers "with a purpose") follow public opinion. He led it. He depicted the horrors of a debtor's prison, and the cruelty and delay of the Court of Chancery, in "Pickwick," before Lord Eldon, so to speak, was cold in his grave, and four years before Lord Brougham obtained the abolition of arrest on mesne process; and he returned to the charge long years afterwards in his doleful tableau of the Marshalsea, and in his withering satire on the suit of Jarndyce versus Jarndyce. Continually to do battle with these social wrongs necessitated the production on the stage of his works of those who from those wrongs had suffered most grievously; and these sufferers generally belonged to the wretchedest and worst-favored classes in the community. Fagin, Bill Sikes, Nancy, Squeers, Smike, are all repulsive characters; but their appearance in public was inevitable.

It would be difficult to imagine a more loathsome character than the ignorant, gin-drinking, abusive, venal harridan, Mrs. Gamp; yet who shall say that the exposure of the malpractices of hospital nurses five-and-twenty years ago had not some part, and an important one, in bringing about the beneficent reforms which we owe directly to Florence Nightingale, and which have substituted patient, loving, tenderly sedulous "sisters" in our hospital wards and sick-rooms for the careless, thieving, drunken beldames of the last generation? Thus, bringing such creatures into the light, he was constrained to listen to them, to observe, and to "report" them. He could have had no special preference for the delineation of revolting scenes or ugly people. He revelled, on the contrary, in describing beautiful scenery, or quiet households, or the happy sports of innocent children. That there was a strong melodramatic side to his intellect I shall hereafter show; but at present I have to deal only with his pictures of "low life." He had enjoyed as many opportunities of observing polite and fashionable society as he had of observing that which is no society at all, but a social chaos. Every kind of society was open to him. He was free to mingle, whenever it pleased him, with all that was illustrious, and exalted, and good. He would have been as welcome at Windsor Castle as he was at the Garrick Club, or in his favorite box at the Albion Tavern. He had not been born in poverty, but in a respectable middle-class family. He had never known—save, perhaps, in early youth, the occasional "hard-uppishness" of a young man striving to attain a position—actual poverty. He had never been a "Bohemian." He had no terrible experiences to tell, as Johnson and Goldsmith, as Crabbe and Gifford had, of days passed in slavish toil, in dirt, and destitution, and opprobrium—of nights spent upon the bulks of shops, or under the lee of glass-house kilns; or in pacing the stony-hearted streets, bedless and breadless. He had never, like Goldsmith, "lived in Axe Lane among the beggars," or eaten his meals, in a ragged horseman's coat, behind a screen, being thought unfit to join Mr. Cave's well-dressed contributors at table. From youth to age he lived in honor, and affluence, and splendor; as prosperous and honored an English gentleman as Shakspeare was at New Place; but without having known what it was, as Shakspeare knew it, to fly from the ire of a county justice, or to dance attendance in the player's tiring-room, or to hold horses (if the legend be true) at the play-house door. Thus he never "mingled" with paupers, and thieves, and wantons. He merely listened to and "reported" them. Shakspeare, perchance, had slept on the same bench with Christopher Sly; had, waking, thirsted like him for a cup of small ale, and had been denied by a churlish hostess. But Dickens had only passed by where the drunken tinker wallowed, and had marked his staggering gait and tipsy leer, and listened to his bald chat.

It is reasonable to infer from sundry chapters in "Pickwick" and "Oliver Twist," and from the intimate knowledge of police-court procedure and of the purlieus of Westminster Hall, the Inns of Court, and the Judges' Chambers displayed therein, that, prior to his admission to the gallery, Charles Dickens had served a brief apprenticeship as a reporter in a police-court and as an "out-door" clerk in some attorney's office. He seems as well acquainted with the ways of jailers, justices' clerks, Bow Street runners, pickpockets, and "night charges," as with those of process-servers, law-writers, tipstaves, and sham bail—of turnkeys in debtors' prisons, and of janitors to spunging-houses. With all these people he may have come in contact (without personally knowing them), as in his parliamentary career he came in contact with Peers and Knights of the Shire; with the Sergeant-at-Arms and the Gentleman Usher of the Black Rod; with Nicholas the plump butler, and Jane the frolicsome handmaiden at "Bellamy's." And, looking at his police-court scenes and his debtors' prison episodes, one glance at them is sufficient to show how immeasurably superior were his capacity and his perception to those of writers who at the same time were watching the self-same things and endeavoring to describe them. Compare the examination of the Artful Dodger, or the arraignment of little Oliver before the brutal bully, Mr. Fang (a faithful portrait of a truculent personage who then disgraced the magisterial bench), with the best of the "Mornings at Bow Street"—papers which enjoyed in their day considerable popularity, thanks to the exquisitely-beautiful designs by George Cruikshank. The "Mornings at Bow Street" articles are merely the production of a smart penny-a-liner; the police-court papers of Dickens are the early yet bright emanations of a pure and original genius.

The history of an artist's life should be, in the main, only the history of his works. As that people which has no history is said to be the happiest, so will the career of that man of genius concerning whose private life the least can be said prove to have been most strongly marked by felicity. The adventurous authors, the painters whose biographies are picturesque, have, as a rule, been wretched. Mr. Forster did well to call his admirable monograph of the author of the "Vicar of Wakefield" the "Life and Adventures of Oliver Goldsmith." Those "adventures" were, we know, to live in a lane among beggars, to be threatened with a jail by the bookseller, whose hack he was, for illegally pawning a suit of clothes; to wander on foot through France and Germany, dependent on the talents of an itinerant minstrel for subsistence; and to die at last, famous, and two thousand pounds in debt. There are very few "adventures" to record in the life of Charles Dickens. He never slew a man in a brawl, as Savage and as Baretti did; he never languished in a Bastille, as Voltaire, or in a dungeon of Sant' Angelo, as Benvenuto Cellini did; he was never the pet of a Czarina, as Diderot, or a slave among the Moors, as Cervantes was. His life was as exclusively and entirely devoted to the pursuit of letters as was that of Dryden; but he was never, like the illustrious writer of "Alexander's Feast," cudgelled by a courtier's bravoes: nor was his funeral "conducted" by a drunken lord and his boon companions. It was a calm, peaceful, and (I should say) happy life. I have neither the means, the power, nor the inclination to attempt an elaborate biography of the man whose death I am merely lamenting, and of whose character and place in letters I am striving to trace a faint sketch; but to give some definite purport to these remarks I may set down in something like coherent order the principal dates and the governing events in his public career.

Charles Dickens was born at Portsmouth in 1812, and was the son of Mr. John Dickens, a gentleman who was in the Government service (the Navy Pay Office), but who retired at the peace, and came to London, where he obtained an engagement as a reporter on a daily paper. The connection of the elder Mr. Dickens with the press continued until his death, which took place but a very few years ago, when he was still on the staff of the journal (the "Daily News") of which his illustrious son had been the first editor. Of Charles Dickens's three younger brothers, it may suffice to mention that one, Frederick, held for many years an appointment in the War Office; that another, Alfred, was a pupil of Brunel, and as an engineer held a post under Government in connection with the Board of Health and the Local Government Act; that the third, Augustus, went to the United States, and was engaged in the office of a railway company at Chicago, and that all of them are dead. Charles received a portion of his education—a strictly middle-class one—in or near Rochester; and it is very pleasant to have heard, recently, that he entertained sincere esteem for his old schoolmaster, Mr. Giles, and was instrumental, in later life, in presenting him with a testimonial. Otherwise he exhibits in his works a very thorough aversion to middle-class schools and middle-class schoolmasters. Squeers is a monster of cruelty, rapacity, and meanness. Crinkle, in "David Copperfield," is a ferocious and dastardly tyrant; Bradley, the National schoolmaster in "Our Mutual Friend," begins as a misanthrope, and ends as a virtual murderer; and even Doctor Blimber in "Dombey," although he does not torture his boys, crams them to death. If the account of "our old school" in one of the early numbers of "Household Words," and manifestly from Charles Dickens's pen, was drawn from personal experience, that school could scarcely have been the one at Rochester. There is a good schoolmaster in the "Sketches by Boz," a better one in the "Old Curiosity Shop," a charming one (although he dotes) in "Copperfield:" not Crinkle, but the good old Dominie at Canterbury. To schoolmistresses Charles Dickens was kinder; for gov-

ernesses and their sorrows he always evinced intense sympathy; but for the genus pedagogue he seemed to have an instinctive abhorrence; differing in this respect very widely from Thackeray, who bears no more malice to the real Dr. Raine than he does to the imaginary Dr. Birch; and who is never tired of dwelling on the learning, the conviviality, and the fundamental kindness of heart of his Orbilius, all *plagosus* as he may have been in early days to little boys who stumbled in their Greek verbs.

When quite a lad, Charles Dickens entered, as has been often repeated, a lawyer's office, and thence passed to the "Morning Chronicle," then a newspaper whose power and influence were second only to the *prestige* of the "Times," but which died a very miserable death some years ago, under the baleful patronage of the French Government. Charles Dickens's editor was Mr. or "Dr." Black, a hard-headed, clear-minded, warm-hearted Scotchman, and who wielded with remarkable vigor the sceptre once held by that noted journalist, Mr. Perry. I remember some years ago to have met one of Mr. Perry's sons (another is Sir Erskine Perry, a retired Indian judge), who was (and still is, I hope) her Majesty's Consul-General at Venice; and he mentioned to me the curious coincidence that the house so long occupied by Charles Dickens in Tavistock Square had formerly been the residence of his father, Mr. Perry, of the "Morning Chronicle," who there held those well-remembered evening parties at which Moore, Campbell, Hazlitt, Jerdan, Leigh Hunt, e tutti quanti, were frequent visitors. The apartments of Tavistock House were destined, under a more illustrious tenancy, to harbor a still more distinguished train of guests. The proprietor of the "Morning Chronicle" in young Charles Dickens's time was, I think, Sir John Easthope, a well-known stockbroker; and it was in the "Evening Chronicle," if I mistake not—an offshoot of the morning edition, and belonging to the same proprietors—that the pictures of London life and manners which were afterwards collected under the title of "Sketches by Boz," were first printed. They were republished originally by John Macrone, a young Manxman, who had been in partnership with Mr. Cochrane in Waterloo Place, but subsequently set up for himself as a publisher in St. James's Square. He was unsuccessful, ultimately, in business; and died early, leaving a widow and a young family. It was to help these bereaved creatures that Charles Dickens (by that time become eminent), in conjunction with many other well-known men of letters, brought out two handsome volumes of Tales and Sketches under the title of the "Pic Nic Papers." Dickens was the editor. The enterprise was obviously undertaken in generous emulation of a similar joint-stock work published by a society of French authors for the benefit of the widow of Ladvocat, the bookseller, and called "Le Livre des Cent et un;" but the "Pic Nic Papers," albeit illustrated by the pencils of

Cruikshank and Hablot Browne, failed to attain the success which had been achieved by their French exemplar. Under all reserve I may, with regard to the "Sketches by Boz," recall the statement which was current at the time of their first appearance; that the price paid to Charles Dickens for the copyright was seventy-five pounds, and that Mr. Macrone, falling soon afterwards into difficulties, disposed of the copyright to another publisher for eleven hundred pounds.* The newspapers of the day also recorded that "a young and beautiful countess" (supposed to be Lady Blessington) had had a personal altercation, and even a physical struggle, with Mr. Macarone in her zeal to secure one of the first impressions of the "Sketches by Boz;" but those were the halcyon days of newspaper puffs; and the newspaper *canard* was, perhaps, stronger on the wing than it is now, when our journals have become so very keen of perception and so very critical of each other's shortcomings—or long comings—that one section of the press seems systematically occupied in plucking out the "enormous gooseberry" from its neighbor's eye, quite unconscious of the "shower of frogs" in its own organ of vision.

The origin of the grotesque signature "Boz" was explained by Mr. Dickens in a preface to one of the late editions of his works, in which he mentioned that one of his younger brothers had been nicknamed in the family circle "Moses," after the celebrated speculator in spectacles in the "Vicar of Wakefield." "Moses," pronounced through the nose, became "Boses;" and this, again, by elision, became "Boz." Very soon after the Sketches appeared, this pseudonym of "Boz" became a household word, not only in a modest English home but throughout a great empire. The publication of the Sketches was the stepping-stone to that of the "Posthumous Papers of the Pickwick Club." The story of the author being sought out by Messrs. Chapman and Hall to furnish text for Mr. Seymour's illustrations of sporting adventures I have already touched upon. It has been told five hundred times, and will not bear repetition here. Equally familiar is the circumstance that Mr. Thackeray, who had been studying high art in the Louvre—and drew, perhaps, rather worse than he had done before beginning that course of study—was very anxious to try his hand at illustrating "Pickwick," and waited on Mr. Dickens for the purpose of tendering his pictorial services, which were thankfully declined. It is, however, not quite so generally known that Thackeray, about this time, did actually furnish a series of etchings to illustrate Douglas Jerrold's "Men of Character." Those etchings were prodigies of badness.

It was an odd game of literary and artistic cross-purposes altogether: reminding one of Goya's weird masquerade scene, "*Nadie se conoce.*" Charles Dickens, in 1836-'7, was "Boz;" Thackeray was "Yellowplush," or "Major Gahagan," or "Michael Angelo Titmarsh," or "Ikey Solomons, Junior." He was to become the "Fat Contributor," "Lancelot Wagstaffe," "Fitz-Boodle," and "Mr. Snob," before he was to be known to all the world as "William Makepeace." A sobriquet was speedily found for the artist selected to succeed Mr. Seymour (with the brief interval of Mr. Buss) in the illustration of "Pickwick." This was a young man named Hablot Browne, who, if my memory of a certain print I once saw in a shop-window in Wardour Street does not play me false, had, prior to his engagement by Messrs. Chapman and Hall, won a medal from the Society of Arts for a large etching of John Gilpin scattering the pigs and poultry in his never-to-be-forgotten ride. Mr. Browne was forthwith, for publishing purposes, rechristened "Phiz;" and he retained his *sobriquet* (which had more meaning in it than that assumed by Charles Dickens) for many years after "Boz" had become obsolete. Mr. Hablot Browne's first illustrations to "Pickwick" were exceedingly humorous, but exceedingly ill-drawn. The amazing success of his author seems, however, to have spurred the artist to sedulous study, and to have conduced in a remarkable degree towards the development of his faculties. A surprising improvement was visible in the frontispieces to the completed volumes of "Pickwick." Corresponding progress was manifest in "Nicholas Nickleby," and in the illustrations (drawn on wood) to the "Old Curiosity Shop" and "Barnaby Rudge." The landscape illustrations to these novels were drawn by the late George Cattermole.

The drawing in the first-named work of the drowned corpse of Quilp lying in the ooze and sedge of the river bank, and in the second, of Hugh tied to the trooper's horse after the suppression of the riots of '80, are really noble performances. "Phiz" reached his *acme*, perhaps, as an illustrator in "Martin Chuzzlewit." His Tom Pinch, his Jonas Chuzzlewit, and especially his Pecksniff, are masterly creations of comic art. In "Copperfield" there is a slight falling off, although there have been few finer etchings from his needle than the picture of little Davy giving his "tremendous order" for a glass of ale in the public-house. In "Bleak House" and in "Little Dorrit," Mr. Hablot Browne unhappily adopted a style of engraving (a level ruled tint being laid over the free-handed etching, and touched up here and there with high lights) which although soft and pleasing to the eye, and productive occasionally of Rembrandt-like effect, undoubtedly militated against the graphic vigor of his designs; this style was not pursued in the illustrations to the "Tale of Two Cities," an essentially melodramatic work, where the Rembrandt-like effects would

* On a fly-leaf in the original edition of the "Sketches" appeared the advertisement of a forthcoming work to be written by Mr. Harrison Ainsworth, illustrated by George Cruikshank, and published by Mr. Macrone under the title of "The Lions of London," but this work never appeared, and like the "Life of Talleyrand," by W. M Thackeray, promised nearly thirty years ago by Messrs. Chapman and Hall, must be added to the list of luckless literary embryos.

have been valued; and when "Our Mutual Friend" was commenced, Mr. Dickens, for some reason or another, chose to change his artistic interpreter, and the illustrations were drawn on wood by Mr. Marcus Stone, a young painter of very signal merit and of still greater promise, whose picture of "The first Suspicions of Catherine of Aragon," is one of the most prominent in the Academy Exhibition of the current year, and who is the son of the late Mr. Frank Stone, R.A., one of Mr. Dickens's dearest friends. For the "Mystery of Edwin Drood," Mr. Dickens chose yet another illustrator—a Mr. Fildes—although the task had in the first instance been apportioned to his son-in-law, Mr. Charles Collins, the brother of the author of the "Woman in White" and the "Dead Secret."

Any notice of the scene-painters to that human comedy of which Charles Dickens was the exponent would be incomplete were I to omit the name of George Cruikshank. To that gifted artist—that pure and good English worthy—was confided the task' of illustrating the "Sketches by Boz;" and the publisher, nervous as to the first literary venture of a young and unknown man, was probably moved by politic reasons in securing the co-operation of an artist who knew London and London life better than the majority of Sunday-school children know their Catechism, and who in 1836 had already been for twenty years in the enjoyment of well-earned celebrity. It was something for the young reporter of the "Morning Chronicle" to have for coadjutor an artist who had caricatured "Boney" ere ever Waterloo was fought; who had been a thorn in the side of the Prince Regent; who had illustrated Hone's "Slap at Slop," and "The Political House that Jack built;" whose pictures to "Life in London" had made Pierce Egan notorious, and who had been dubbed "Glorious George" in one of the earliest numbers of "Blackwood." George Cruikshank's etchings in the "Sketches" were admirable. One—that of "The Streets: Morning"—a view of some slum near Seven Dials, deserted in the bright dawn save by a saloop-woman, a sweep, and a policeman leaning against a post, is incomparably fine. George Cruikshank took a yet higher flight in the illustrations to "Oliver Twist." Who does not recollect the tragic force of "Sikes attempting to destroy his dog"—with that wondrous view of distant London in the background? Who has not felt a shuddering horror creep over him at the sight of "Fagin in the condemned cell?" George Cruikshank likewise illustrated for Charles Dickens a pamphlet—now exceedingly scarce—called "Sunday in London," and two volumes of the "Memoirs of Grimaldi" (the famous clown), edited by Dickens for Mr. Bentley. I have seen stated recently that Mr. Dickens only lent his name to the title-page of this publication, and that no line of his original writing appears therein. From this I dissent. The stories of Little Joey giving away the

guinea; of the man who had but three fingers to one of his hands, and, in particular, the appalling account of the death of Grimaldi's wayward son, are unmistakably from the hand of the Master.

The name of "Dickens" was first appended to the completed volumes of "Pickwick;" and in the year 1837 the first installment of "Oliver Twist" appeared in "Bentley's Miscellany"—a publication of which the young author became editor. To the "Miscellany" he likewise contributed some short miscellaneous papers, among which I especially remember an exquisite piece of drollery on the transactions of "the Mudfog Association for the Advancement of Science." This racy pasquinade served undoubtedly as a model to Mr. Gilbert A'Beckett, when, some years afterwards, he wrote in the "Times" his memorable leading articles in ridicule of the meetings of the British Association. "David Copperfield" was, it has always been assumed, Mr. Dickens's favorite work; and—rather absurdly, I think—it is supposed to possess strongly autobiographical features; although it is patent that its author never had a stepfather who ill-treated him; never ran away from home, to be brought up by an eccentric aunt; never groaned under the sway of a brutal flogging schoolmaster like Crinkle; was never employed to wash bottles in a wine-merchant's cellar; and was never articled to a proctor in Doctors Commons.

It is questionable even if a genius so catholic as his would have shown any preference to one of his works over another; but, if he did so prefer a book of his own, I should imagine that one to have been "Oliver Twist." Quite recently, in very forcible and eloquent language, he vindicated the intent and the scheme of that work—seemingly uneasily conscious that his characters might be classed, by unthinking persons, with the bandits and wantons over whom, in an indefensibly mischievous romance, called "Jack Sheppard," Mr. Harrison Ainsworth has thrown a halo of tawdry picturesqueness—of sham gold lace, second-hand brocaded petticoats, thread-bare velvet masks, and "property" pistols that won't go off. "Once upon a time," wrote Charles Dickens, in his latest preface to "Oliver Twist," "it was held to be a coarse and shocking circumstance that some of the characters in these pages are chosen from the most criminal and degraded of London's population. As I saw no reasons, when I wrote this book, why the dregs of life (so long as their speech did not offend the ear) should not serve the purpose of a moral as well as the froth and cream, I made bold to believe that this same once upon a time would not prove to be all time, or even a long time. I saw many strong reasons for pursuing my course. I had read of thieves by scores; seductive fellows (amiable for the most part), faultless in dress, plump in pocket, choice in horseflesh, bold in bearing, fortunate in gallantry, great at a song, a bottle, a pack of cards or dice-box, and fit companions for the bravest.

But I had never met (except in Hogarth) with the miserable reality. It appeared to me that to draw a knot of such associates in crime as really did exist; to paint them in all their deformity, in all their wretchedness, in all the squalid misery of their lives; to show them as they really were, forever skulking uneasily through the dirtiest paths of life, with the great black ghastly gallows closing up their prospect, turn them where they might, it appeared to me that to do this would be to attempt a something which was needed, and which would be a service to society. And I did it as I best could." Surely no stronger or more convincing vindication than this was needed for a work which, for the strength of its construction, the verisimilitude of its scenes, and the impressiveness of the moral it points, can find in modern letters only one compeer — the "Splendeurs et Miseres des Courtisanes" of Balzac.

More recently still, half with the preoccupying wish to vindicate "Oliver," half, perhaps, in unconscious gratification of that melodramatic *penchant* in his mind (and which was developed occasionally to a morbid degree), he determined to introduce the harrowing description of the murder of Nancy by Sikes into his public readings. The determination was not arrived at without anxious and mature deliberation, and a private "test" reading was given before a select company of critics convened for the purpose. The select company of critics were unanimously of opinion that the murder scene should be given publicly. They would, I take it, have been unanimous in favorable opinion had the lecturer recited "My name is Norval," or stood upon his head. The murder scene, then, was given to the world at large: it was acted rather than read—and acted magnificently by Mr. Dickens; but I questioned at the time, and I question still, the taste and the usefulness of the display. The audience whom Mr. Dickens addressed was composed of educated and cultivated persons, who would have looked upon a real murder with as much horror as they would have displayed aversion from the spectacle of the hanging of the murderer; and no healthy feelings could possibly be awakened by the simulation, in marvellous fluency of language and facundity of gesture, of a revolting and sanguinary scene.

"Oliver Twist" was followed by "Nicholas Nickleby," and by this time the author had become renowned. He was married, too, to Miss Catherine Hogarth, the daughter of Mr. George Hogarth, a distinguished musical critic and writer on the history and literature of music. On the sudden deaths of two of his connections by marriage there may be read in Kensal Green Cemetery a strikingly eloquent epitaph, manifestly written by Charles Dickens. But fame and fortune now began to pour down upon him; he was fêted, courted, petted, lionized, and—I need scarcely say it—abused. A year or two afterwards, in the preface (I think) to "Master Humphrey's Clock" (the father of

what may be called "Novels with machinery," and in which Mr. Pickwick and Sam Weller were, by an error in judgment, resuscitated), he pleasantly alludes to some kind friends who had circulated the report that he had gone raving mad, adding that the intelligence had been the cause of great mirth round his hearth at Christmas. I perfectly remember, when he moved from his modest residence in Doughty Street to a much grander but still not very palatial house in Devonshire Terrace, an old gentleman calling one day upon my mother, and telling her, with a grave countenance, that Dickens had pawned his plate, and had been waited upon for the last fortnight by bailiffs in livery. As, about this time, my eyes were just beginning to open to the pomps and vanities of the world, and I conceived a powdered footman to be about the most gorgeous spectacle of which it was possible to have any conception, I own that it did not appear to me very dreadful that "Boz" should be waited upon by bailiffs; while I certainly felt a swelling pride in the thought that the author of whom I had already heard so much should have people in livery to stand behind his chair at all.

It was Mr. Croker, as before hinted, to whom was ascribed the neat saying that Charles Dickens "had gone up like a rocket, and would come down like the stick." I do not quarrel with Croker—contemptible as he was in a hundred ways, and branded as he has been with undying obloquy by Disraeli in "Coningsby" and by Thackeray in "Vanity Fair"— or with the venerable but somewhat purblind sages of Albemarle Street whom Cobbett was wont to call "the old Shufflebreeches of the 'Quarterly Review'"—for their inability to comprehend at first the sudden, the well-nigh sidereal rise of Charles Dickens, or their readiness to assume that a flight so rapid and so lofty could not be sustained, and must speedily terminate in exhaustion and collapse. There had been precedents, indeed, for literary triumphs as brilliant and as spontaneous achieved by genius as precocious.

Byron and Shelley were both mere lads when they found themselves the cynosures of the world of literature; but neither Byron nor Shelley attained middle age. Pope indeed enjoyed a life moderately prolonged, and the productions of his later years are as fresh and as sparkling and brilliant as those of his nonage; but Pope, and Byron, and Shelley to boot, were all ripe and cultivated scholars after Albemarle Street's own heart. The two former had been students in our great universities; the last had been most carefully trained in classical knowledge by private tutors; and all three were young men of leisure who had never known what it was to earn their bread by the sweat of their brow. But here was a young man barely five-and-twenty years of age, whose livelihood, as every body knew, had until very recently depended on his weekly salary as a newspaper reporter; who was avowedly of no public school and of no university; who had received, at the most, only what is known as a "commercial" education; who had never imitated Horace, never translated Greek epigrams, and who knew nothing about the Protagorean Dilemma or the Square of the Hypotenuse. Mr. George Canning had written some delicious drolleries—the "Loves of the Triangles" and the "Needy Knife-Grinder," for example; but then Mr. George Canning had had a brilliant career at Eton and Oxford, and had been introduced to the great world by the most distinguished wits and statesmen of the day. Richard Brinsley Sheridan was a sot, a spendthrift, and an adventurer, but at least he was the son of a classical scholar who had written a Pronouncing Dictionary and delivered lectures on elocution; and he himself had been at Harrow, and had eaten his terms at the Middle Temple. Gifford, indeed, had been a cobbler, a cabin-boy, and next door to a beggar, but his precocity had been early perceived, fostered, and controlled, and his genius had been trained into classical channels. Lord Grosvenor had patronized him, and he had gone the grand tour with his lordship's son. But here was a young man without Latin, without Greek, without logic, without mathematics, as destitute of a patron as he was of a degree, who suddenly uprose and took the literary world by storm. The venerable sages of Albemarle Street regarded the prodigy not unmingled with horror. No such subversion of the established order of things had taken place since the evil days at the end of the preceding century when Mack and Wurmser and Beaulieu and other highly respectable Austrian commanders of the antediluvian period watched, half perplexed and wholly terrified, the impertinent career of conquest of the boy-general, Napoleon Bonaparte. And at least those bewildered ancients might have derived a meagre consolation from the assertion that the Republican general had received a "regular education" at an established college, had graduated at the Ecole Militaire, and taken high honors in mathematics. Still the uprising of Napoleon was as sudden and startling as that of Dickens. It was in contravention of established rules. It was revolutionary; and of course, to complicate the embarrassment of Albemarle Street, it speedily turned out that the young conqueror was a Radical of the most pronounced description, who scoffed at Grampound, who had no reverence for Gatton, and refused to drop one tear for old Sarum; who spoke lightly of the Bench of Bishops—is there not a song in "Pickwick" describing an onslaught made by the depraved Turpin on a Right Reverend Prelate as he was proceeding in his carriage over Hounslow Heath?—and who bantered the Lord High Chancellor. And such a Radical did Charles Dickens continue until the end of his days. I can remember but one instance in which he opposed, even by implication, in his works a Liberal measure: that measure was the New Poor Law, and against that cruel and unjust code, as

it existed in the days when "Oliver Twist" was written, he certainly waged uncompromising war.

By 1840, "Pickwick," "Nicholas Nickleby," "Oliver Twist," had become such patent and accomplished facts, and the trilogy of humor, pathos, and dramatic interest had become so universally recognized, that the deprecators of revolutionary measures were somewhat puzzled where next to strike the innovator on the hip. A writer in that then good old Tory magazine, "Fraser's"—the journal in which Thomas Moore was, in mere waggery, merely accused of having stolen from the Greek, and disguised in English dress epigrams and anacreontics which never existed—adopted the ingenious hypothesis that the humor of Charles Dickens consisted solely in, and was entirely dependent on, the quaint extravagance of his diction. This Sage took the trouble to translate into German a whole page from "Nickleby" descriptive of the visit of Mr. Lillyvick, the tax-collector, to the Kenwigs family, and then to re-translate it into English. Of course the re-translation was very dull and very verbose; and the critic pointed triumphantly to its dullness and verbosity as proofs that the much-vaunted Dickens was merely a *joueur de gobelets* —a word-trickster, and a phrase-jingler. It is Voltaire, is it not, who remarks that there is one class in humanity who never forgive, never forget—who are implacable and inexorable? The blockheads are that class, and in the eyes of a literary blockhead there is no offense so intolerable or so unpardonable, next to possessing any literary style at all, as that of writing in a new style. Nobody ever written before as Charles Dickens wrote; and he was excommunicated by the blockheads accordingly. They had scarcely forgiven him for having a style of his own on the day before his death; although now, fifty thousand strong, they are whining and snivelling over his grave.

It chanced that about 1840, Mr. Dickens, with a momentary lack of prudence, chose to alter the form of his serials—to abandon the green covers which, though they were but four years old, had become familiar throughout the length and breadth of the land—and to issue, in weekly instead of monthly parts, a publication of which the plan did not seem to have been, in the outset, very definitely arranged, called "Master Humphrey's Clock." There were some very charming stories in the earlier numbers of the "Clock"—a marvellously melodramatic one, especially, about a murder—but the public resented desultoriness or brevity from the writer to whom they were never tired of listening. They thirsted for the long continuous tale, the crowded scene, the characters developing in magic accretion, the action gloriously progressing. Master "Humphrey's Clock" did not weary, but it failed to satisfy the sharp appetite of the reading community. The blockheads were in ecstasies. To them the fact was plain and palpable. Dickens had "written himself out," and was no more capable of constructing another lengthy novel than he was of draining Chat Moss, or piercing the Box Tunnel with his single arm. The rocket had scattered its last brilliant sparks, and the stick was coming down heavily.

"Censure," says Swift. "is a tax which a man pays to the world for being eminent." There are a great many more imposts which an eminent literary man is called upon to disburse to his kind friends the public. One tax-gatherer's name is Envy; his brother assumes all Hatred, Malice and all Uncharitableness. A rogue thunders at the door, and cries: "I am Lying Slander; pay me." Another tugs at the bell fiercely, and yells: "I am Domestic Espionage; pay me." A third rascal—who has come from a great distance—peeps through the keyhole and whispers: "I am the London Correspondent; I am the Foreign Eavesdropper; you'll pay me, I guess." And the eminent man must pay willy-nilly, else the tax-gatherers will distrain on his goods, and seize the clothes from his back and the hat from his head; a crowd of libellers and scandal-mongers, plagiarists, and pirates looking on approvingly. With regard to piracy, the Red Rovers of the land, not only in America, but in this country, became aware of Charles Dickens early, and strove to despoil him with an ardor worthy of Blackbeard and Captain Kyd in their best days. When the popularity of the "Pickwick Papers" was at its height, it occurred to a wretched bookseller in Bloomsbury, but who should have lived in Holywell Street, that although the publication of the work was protected by the then existing (although very imperfect) copyright laws, a good stroke of business might be done by mutilating, forging, and parodying Charles Dickens, and accordingly the "Penny Pickwick" appeared in weekly numbers, written by some gutter-blood hack, and illustrated in the first style of Seven Dials art. Forced by an injunction to remove the title of "Pickwick" from the rag he had put forth, the publisher continued his forgery under some name which I am glad to forget, and in which the exquisitely humorous creations of Dickens were vilely distorted and mangled. This disgraceful fabrication had an enormous sale; and fraudulent as was the enterprise, and base as were the motives of the publisher, they could not fail to testify to the wonderful and universal popularity of Charles Dickens. A pleasanter and more graceful recognition of his hold on the public mind was the appearance, in Mr. Ackermann's shop window in Regent Street, of a number of beautiful little statuettes modelled in wax, and colored to the life, representing Mr. Pickwick with his hands beneath his coat-tails, electrifying the club with his eloquence; Sam Weller cleaning the shoes of the spinster with whom Mr. Jingle eloped; the Fat Boy asleep on the door mat; Mr. Weller, senior, delivering his caveat against widows, and so forth. A higher compliment was to be paid to the young au-

thor. In England one of the most shining tributes rendered to the celebrity of the hour is to name a dahlia, a Derby favorite, or a set of quadrilles after him. At Havana, when a distinguished stranger visits the tobacco factory of Señor Cabana or Partagas, the custom is to offer him an "obsequio," by striking a new brand of cigars in his honor. To this we owe the excellent cigars known as the "Serrano" and the "Henry Clay;" and were the great leaders of the Conservative and the Liberal party to visit Havana, Señores Anselmo del Valle and Partagas would very soon be consigning "Gladstones" or "Juventus Mundis," "Disraelis" or "Lothairs" to the European market. The London tobacco manufacturers elected to pay Charles Dickens the Cuban compliment. A neat little cigar, costing only a penny, was devised, and was christened the "Pickwick;" and it still retains its popularity. Such an ingenious stretch of courtesy has not been equalled save by the patriotic coach-builder who constructed the first private four-wheeled cab and dubbed it a Brougham.

A modified form of piracy to which the author was subjected was in the publication in the cheap (and nasty) periodicals of that day, and in the Sunday newspapers, of inordinately long extracts from his works, whole chapters being often coolly appropriated; but these semi-buccaneering raids did the writer no harm; since they only whetted the public appetite for more and more Dickens, and excited those who had only read him piecemeal to lay out their shillings on the green covers, and read him consecutively. I hesitate to brand as piratical the numerous dramatic adaptations of his novels, which very soon took possession of the stage of nearly every theatre in London and the provinces; because, although I hold, myself, that every part and parcel of an author's brains belong to him, and can only be alienated by his legally assigning his copyright, and that he should be entitled either to warrant or to prohibit the transference of his plot, his characters, and his dialogue to the boards of a play-house, I know that such a doctrine is not universally held, and, at the time to which I refer, was held by very few persons indeed. An English novelist was considered by the hack playwright to be as perfectly fair game as the French dramatist; and the industrial who stole "Passé Minuit" from the French and christened it "Two in the Morning," would naturally feel no hesitation in compressing a three-volume English novel into a two-act drama without the permission of the author. An amusing version of "Pickwick" was produced at the Strand Theatre, the part of Sam Weller being supported with real humor and appreciativeness by the late Mr. W. J. Hammond, and that of Mr. Pickwick himself by Mr. Reynoldson, a voluminous translator of French farces. At the Adelphi Theatre very able and striking adaptations of "Oliver Twist" and "Nicholas Nickleby" were produced, and with immense success. I have seen both pieces played in one night, and the scenery and costumes were modelled in scrupulous conformity with George Cruikshanks's designs. Of the powerful nature of the "cast" some notion may be formed when I mention that in "Oliver Twist" the part of Oliver was performed by the admirable Mrs. Keeley (she played Smike, I think, in Nickleby); that of Fagin by Mr. Frederick Yates; Bill Sikes by the terrible O. Smith; Mr Grimwig by Mr. Wilkinson (a most humorous comedian); and the Artful Dodger by Mr. Wright. With the exception of Mrs. Keeley, all these actors and actresses are dead. The Adelphi adaptations had, I believe, the sanction and approbation of Charles Dickens; but he resented with some bitterness the continuous appearance at innumerable theatres of brutally blurred and disfigured caricatures of the productions on which he had bestowed long labor and infinite pains. With his customary eloquence, when moved to wrath, he alludes to the adaptation grievance in one of the concluding portions of "Nicholas Nickleby," which, be it observed, had been dramatized, without his consent, long before the novel had been concluded. A literary gentleman is introduced at Mr. Crummles's farewell supper, who has dramatized books unnumbered, and thinks that he has done the authors thereof great honor by robbing them. This literary gentleman considers Shakspeare to have been an "adapter," who "adapted very well—considering; but," the literary gentleman continues, "human intellect, sir, has progressed since his time, is progressing, will progress." To this Nicholas Nickleby, or rather Charles Dickens, retorts, "Shot beyond him, I mean, in quite another respect, for whereas he brought within the magic circle of his genius traditions peculiarly adapted for his purpose, and turned familiar things into constellations which should enlighten the world for ages, you drag within the magic circle of your dullness subjects not at all adapted to the purposes of the stage, and debase as he exalted. For instance, you take the uncompleted books of living authors fresh from their hands, wet from the press, cut, hack, and carve them to the powers and capacities of your actors and the capabilities of your theatres, finish unfinished works, hastily and crudely vamp up ideas not yet worked out by their original projector, but which have, doubtless, cost him many thoughtful days and sleepless nights: by a comparison of incidents and dialogue, down to the very last word he may have written a fortnight before, do your utmost to anticipate his plot—all this without his permission and against his will; and then, to crown the whole proceeding, publish in some mean pamphlet an unmeaning farrago of garbled extracts from his work, to which you put your name as author, with the honorable distinction annexed, of having perpetrated a hundred other outrages of the same description. Now show me the difference between such pilfering as this and picking a man's pocket in the street; unless, indeed, it be that the Legislature has a regard for pocket handker-

chiefs, and leaves men's brains (except when they are knocked out by violence) to take care of themselves." To this somewhat vigorous reproof the literary gentleman replied, shrugging his shoulders, "That man must live." "That," resumes Nicholas, "would be an equally fair plea in both cases; but if you put it upon that ground, I have nothing more to say than if I were a writer of books, and you a thirsty dramatist, I would rather pay your tavern score for six months, large as it might be, than have a niche in the Temple of Fame with you for the humblest corner of my pedestal through six hundred generations."

A "thirsty dramatist" of the epoch, considering himself directly alluded to, and feeling personally aggrieved by this onslaught, penned a reply to Mr. Dickens's strictures, which reply was published in some Sunday print or "mean pamphlet," and was much applauded in the tap-rooms of theatrical taverns about Broad Court and Vinegar Yard. But the "thirsty dramatist" did not, in the end, take more by his motion than that Yorkshire schoolmaster who suspected that his own portrait had been drawn in that of Mr. Squeers, because his neighbors concurred in saying that "it was so like him," and threatened an action for libel, which, however, he had sense enough not to bring. The adaptation to the stage of Charles Dickens's works continued for some years. Mrs Keeley was called upon to play Barnaby Rudge, and again to sustain—the which she did with infinite humor and spirit—the onerous buckskins and top-boots of Young Bailey in "Martin Chuzzlewit." In his time, also, Mr. Samuel Emery created a marked impression by his very powerful impersonation of Quilp in "The Old Curiosity Shop." By degrees the fact dawned upon the public, and even on the dramatist's mind, that it was grossly unfair to the author to "adapt" his works to the stage before they were finished as books. By slower degrees it came to be acknowledged that the juster and the gracefuller part would be to ask his permission ere his works were dramatized at all. Thus, at the Lyceum, under the management of Madame Celeste, "A Tale of Two Cities" was brought out under the direct authorization, and, to some extent, under the supervision of Charles Dickens; and in a more recent instance he has directly authorized the very ingenious version of "Copperfield," under the title of "Little Em'ly," by Mr. Andrew Halliday, at the Olympic Theatre.

I revert to the literary career of Charles Dickens. Shortly after the completion of "Barnaby Rudge," he undertook, accompanied by his wife, a journey to the United States, and for many months his progress through the Northern and the less remote Western States was one continuous triumph. He appears to have had an instinctive horror of penetrating into the (then) Slave States; but he went to Washington, and to the President's levee; and he crossed the Potomac and visited Richmond, the capital of

Virginia, where, as I was told in America. when he entered the Senate House, the legislators were in session, but with one accord they all rose to welcome Charles Dickens. A grander compliment has rarely been paid to a private man. He returned to England after having contracted a close intimacy with Washington Irving, who had just been appointed United States Ambassador to the Court of Spain. Of course, Charles Dickens recounted his American experiences in a book, to which was given the title "American Notes for General Circulation." Some strictures bearing upon social usages in the States awakened a stoim of indignation in New York. The people of New England, and the Bostonians in particular, were not nearly so enraged, for Dickens had said very little in their social disfavor, and, besides, he had won their esteem and admiration by his uncompromising denunciations of slavery. He was abused to a considerable extent in the American newspapers; and in this country a reply to his book was put forth, under the name of "Change for American Notes," and which proposed to turn the tables on the English author by describing the experiences of an American in England. It was not, however, the production of an American, but of a gentleman of Yorkshire, named Henry Wood, who subsequently became sub-editor of "Douglas Jerrold's Weekly Newspaper."

In 1844 Mr. Dickens, slightly embittered perhaps by the Billingsgate so freely lavished upon him by transatlantic journalists, returned to the American charge in "Martin Chuzzlewit;" and while the American Adventures of Martin and his friend Mark Tapley have little to do with the conduct of the real drama, of which the immortal Pecksniff—the English Tartuffe as the Italian "Diritto" lately called him—is the real hero, the American episodes of "Chuzzlewit" will always be read with interest, as a very lively, an exceedingly humorous, but a very one-sided satire on the manners and customs of the American people. In the "American Notes," while dwelling on the foibles he has rendered some justice to the good qualities of the nation who gave him so magnificent and so generous a reception. In "Chuzzlewit," with the single exception of the gentleman who lends Martin enough money to come home again. his American dramatis personæ are made up of rowdies, loafers, stump orators, "cusses," and "scally-wags." The Americans, however, who are the most irritable and the most placable nation on the face of the earth, very freely forgave him almost so soon as the ink in his terrible pen was dry, and when he went for a second time to the United States, in 1867, gave him a reception as generous and more magnificent than the first.

After the completion of "Chuzzlewit" he went to Italy with his wife and family, fixing upon his residence at Genoa, and making, thence, excursions to nearly every part of the Italian Peninsula and the south of France. On his return to England in 1845 he became the first editor of the "Daily News," in which appeared his "Pictures from Italy," and some very powerful letters on social subjects, notably one on Capital Punishment, in which he advocated the establishment of the system of private executions. Twenty-four years afterwards his suggestions were adopted by Parliament. The editorial chair in Whitefriars, however, soon became irksome to him, and after a brief occupancy he resigned it. Let me pause for an instant here to notice the charming series of Christmas Carols—of which he may be said to have been the inventor—which flowed from his pen between the years 1843 and 1848. These were the inimitable "Christmas Carol," "The Chimes," "The Cricket on the Hearth," "The Battle of Life," and "The Haunted Man, or the Ghost's Bargain." These delightful treatises were full of sparkling illustrations by Daniel Maclise, Edwin Landseer, Clarkson Stanfield, and John Leech. "Dombey and Son" was published in 1847–'8, "David Copperfield" in 1849–'50; "Bleak House" in 1853, "Little Dorrit" in 1856. "Hard Times," "A Tale of Two Cities," "Great Expectations," and the "Uncommercial Traveller," together with the Christmas "numbers" comprising "The Seven Poor Travellers," "The Haunted House," "The Wreck of the Golden Mary," "Mrs. Lirriper's Lodgings," "Tom Tiddler's Ground," "Somebody's Luggage," and "No Thoroughfare," appeared originally in the pages of "Household Words," a weekly journal conducted by him and founded in 1850, and which in 1859, after his quarrel with Messrs. Bradbury and Evans and his purchase of their interest in "Household Words," was incorporated in a new journal, precisely similar, however, in character and scheme to the old one, and called "All the Year Round." This periodical he has bequeathed to his eldest son Charles, who has publicly announced that he intends to continue its publication on the "old lines" so firmly laid down by his father. Of the "Christmas numbers" he was always the deviser, and to them he generally contributed one or two original stories, the remainder being written by the brilliant staff of authors he had gathered about him in "Household Words" and "All the Year Round." Among these contributors the most conspicuous were R. H. Horne (the author of "Orion"), Charles Knight, Henry Morley, W. Moy Thomas, John Hollingshead, Percy Fitzgerald, W. H. Wills (his assistant in the editorship), Wilkie and Charles Collins, William Jerrold, Sidney Blanchard, Mrs. Gaskell, Mrs. Linton, W. Allingham, Andrew Halliday, Walter Thornbury, Robert Brough, Edmund Yates, Miss Amelia Edwards, J. C. Parkinson, with others of minor note. His penultimate serial, "Our Mutual Friend," commenced in May, 1864. The novel which he was not destined to finish, but of which about one half is said to have been completed before his death, was begun in March of the present year.

It is probable that, gauging his literary productions only as so much printed matter, there have been authors who, in a career of letters of equal length to his, have produced more "copy." Rousseau wrote more; Dryden wrote more; Diderot wrote more; William Godwin wrote more; G. P. R. James wrote more; Lord Lytton has written more; Anthony Trollope has written more; Charles Lever has written as much. As an author, Charles Dickens has been famous for about four-and-thirty years, and, certainly, he has not written four-and-thirty novels. Beyond his works of fiction, his only literary productions have been the "Sketches by Boz," the "American Notes," the "Pictures from Italy," a few essays in the "Daily News," the "Household Words" and "All the Year Round" papers. Stay, there was also the "Child's History of England," and one or two dramatic pieces; and the libretto to the opera of the "Village Coquettes," the music of which was composed by his friend Mr. John Hullah, and which was produced at the St. James's Theatre under the management of Mr. John Braham.

Charles Lamb used humorously to say that his own genuine "works" were entombed in the bulky day-books and ledgers of the India House. Similarly the great bulk of Charles Dickens's "copy" may be lying perdu in the short-hand notes he took and transcribed when he was a reporter in the gallery of the House of Commons. But mere manifest production weighs very little in the scale by which a man's work should be tested. The idlest men have often been the most prolific producers. There was no end to George Morland's pictures. Raffaelle is said to have lacked industry; yet Raffaelle, who died before he was forty, has left far more on record, in the way of quantity, than Michael Angelo, who lived to be nearly ninety, and worked like a day-laborer to the last of his life. In the "Horned Moses" there is a whole gallery of sculpture. In "David Copperfield" may there not be said to be an entire library of fiction? Surely art is not to be measured by line and rule, and ticked off at per inch. If this were the case, the brick wall of Whitechapel Work-house would bear away the bell from the Banqueting-house at Whitehall, and Mr. Sandys's "Medea" would have to yield the palm to Banvard's Panorama of the Mississippi. Apart from his literary labors, which, in their result, have been tremendous, Charles Dickens worked continuously, earnestly, sedulously, unflinchingly, from the first dawn of his adolescence to the golden autumn of his age. Never had there been a busier man, in the best sense of the term; never one who was so fully aware that the power of genius and all the fertility of imagination can not compensate for the lack of application and for the want of punctuality.

His liking for the stage—for theatrical representations, theatrical scenes, and theatrical people, attained nearly the proportions of a passion. He is said to have contemplated at one time entering (in conjunction with some friends similarly minded) upon the management of a London theatre, and was never so happy as when he was engaged in private theatricals. He organized and sustained prominent parts in numerous amateur performances, now for the benefit of the funds of the Guild of Literature and Art, now in substantial memory of the talents and the worth of Douglas Jerrold. He had a private theatre of his own at Tavistock House, and some of the principal scenes painted by Clarkson Stanfield for Mr. Wilkie Collins's dramas of "The Light-House" and "The Frozen Deep" were subsequently transferred to Gadshill, where, framed and glazed in the hall, they had, for all the rapidity of their execution, the appearance of cabinet paintings. He had been in early life a close friend of William Charles Macready, and in later years he was affectionately intimate with the versatile French actor, Mr. Fechter. A beautiful little summer-house, on the model of a Swiss châlet, in the grounds of Gadshill, and in which, in warm weather, he often wrote his "copy," was a gift from Mr. Fechter. His love for the stage was very manifest in his wonderful readings—readings from his own works with which he delighted countless audiences in England and the United States; gaining by these performances many thousands of pounds, but losing, I am afraid, many years of the life which he might have reasonably hoped to attain. His delivery was measured, sonorous, and emphatic; he could make his audience laugh, or weep, or shudder, as he chose; the effect he produced was thrillingly impressive; but his manner was undeniably "stagey," and not unfrequently, on the platform, he overacted his part. While engaged in these readings his life must have been that of a convict in golden fetters. Still, for all the prodigious amount of work he went through—body work, brain work, hand work, foot work—for in pedestrianism he rivalled Deerfoot and Captain Patten Saunders—he looked a hale, bright, valid man. His recent speech at Birmingham convinced the world that his withers were still unwrung. Yet a little before that, as we all know, he was forced to break off for a while in his course of readings—readings which were resumed early in the next year. The man was manifestly tired out, tired to death's door—tired of having to keep with rigid punctuality appointments at five hundred miles' distance from each other; tired of discounting the future, and knowing with grim certainty what he was going to do, or at least was expected to do, in the middle of next month; tired of express trains and hotel dinners, and saying the same things night after night, and seeing the same sea of upturned, eager faces; tired of gas and waiters, and money-takers, and rounds of applause, and neat criticisms in provincial newspapers. He wanted rest. His doctors told him that he must take it, and he took it. I fear that he took it too late, and that in addition to the exhaustion to his frame consequent on his incessant journeys, his nervous system had been seriously affected in the shock of the horrible railway accident at Staplehurst. He was in one of the carriages at that frightful catastrophe, and but narrowly escaped the fate which overtook so many of his fellow-travellers. Depend upon it that the tax-gatherers rubbed their hands gleefully when they heard that Charles Dickens had been forced to pause for a while.

There is one collector whom I have not yet named—the man who calls for that tax called "Hypocritical Commiseration." It is a commutation of the old Spite, Malice, and Impatience at Continuous Success duties. "Ah! poor fellow," sighed the commiserators; "broken down —quite broken down—sinking by the head. The pitcher goes often to the well, but gets broken at last. He will never be himself again. A clear case of physical collapse, the sure forerunner of mental decay. 'Sick body, sick brain,' you know. We always thought he would overdo it at last." And so, from decade to decade, does one generation of affable vipers succeed another; and we dare say there were good souls in Shakspeare's time, who confidentially imparted to another their conviction that Mr. S. was really working the mine of his brain too freely, that he was writing himself out, and that this kind of thing could not last long, you know.

The time and the manner of his death and of his burial are matters too recent to need detailed account here; but as memoranda they will be found elsewhere set down.

Of his private life it behooves me not at this time to speak. I have dealt with him mainly as a public man, and as the foremost writer of the Victorian era. His Life, in an extended, substantial, and authorized form, will, ere long, I doubt it not, be written: and I hope that the writer of such a Life may be either his constant and noble-minded friend John Forster, or his near connection and co-laborer in letters, Wilkie Collins. Both are admirable writers, both experienced men of the world; and both had opportunities of studying and of judging the personal character of Charles Dickens—opportunities possessed by none other of his contemporaries. Biographers there will be also in plenty who, at no distant date, may retail his minutest words and deeds; who will make public his private correspondence with his friends, and who will do justice to the integrity of his character, to the cordiality of his manner, to the charms of his conversation, to the generosity of his hospitality, to the inflexible integrity which he ever showed in his dealings with his fellow-men, to his private charities — which were innumerable, untiring, and unostentatious — to his public spirit and lofty sense of right, to his unflagging industry, his wonderful strength of will and tenacity of purpose, his undeviating punctuality, his forbearance under provocation, his placable nature after wrong. It has been my task only to touch upon the leading points in his literary career, and to re-

call the outward aspect of the man who but a few days since was so warm a friend, so kind a host, so true a master, so ready a writer, so eloquent a speaker, so merry a companion—and who now lies cold and dumb. He is gone. There is no longer a Charles Dickens — our Charles Dickens, at least; and to the veterans —to the jaded coursers in the race of life whose old feet seem to do nought but stumble at graves, this last yawning tomb can but suggest the grim question—"Who is to go next, and next?"

Scrupulously as I have endeavored to avoid prying into secrets which do not concern me, and which can not concern any of us now, I am aware that it would be an act of cowardly dishonesty to suppress the fact that twelve years since a great shadow fell across his hearth. He chose — whether well or ill advised I am not called upon to pronounce—to make the fact of his domestic troubles public; although into the circumstances thereof he did not enter. But he published in his own journal, in "The Times" newspaper, and in other channels of common information, a vehement vindication of himself from some attacks, or some scandalous imputations so wildly improbable in their nature, and so obscure that their very existence was ignored by ninety-nine out of every hundred men and women, who began to wonder at the passionateness of his defense. The refusal on the part of the proprietors of "Punch"— Messrs. Bradbury and Evans—and of the editor of that essentially high-minded journal, the late Mr. Mark Lemon—to give publicity to this document, led to a rupture between Charles Dickens, his esteemed publishers, and his intimate personal friend. I am glad, however, to say that he was reconciled to Mark Lemon ere the former died. Nothing more need or can be said concerning the domestic troubles and the appearance of that luckless vindication. Those who have a right to speak have not spoken; and the world has no right to inquire into the mystery—if any mystery there be—nor will have, any time these fifty years.

I have frequently asked myself, in the course of this retrospect, whether, dazzled by the brilliance of his genius, or rendered a fanatic by the length of years during which his written and spoken words had been Household Words to me, I have over-estimated his powers, have exaggerated his qualities, have ranked him too high in the hierarchy of great men. I have ventured to predict for him such a perpetuity of renown as has been the guerdon of the great writers of antiquity; as has been the portion of those who wrote "Hamlet" and "Paradise Lost." I can only plead that, if I have erred, the error must be attributed to ignorance—but to an ignorance which may be palliated by its sincerity. I may be a dullard or a zealot, but I believe in his greatness and in the universality of his name—on this side the decay and the oblivion which must sooner or later overtake all human things. And my fanaticism, if fanaticism it be, may lose some of its apparent insanity if I mention that when he first came before the world as an author I was an illiterate child, gifted with a strongly retentive memory, but blind; that the chief solace in my blindness was to hear my sister read the "Sketches by Boz;" that when I recovered my sight it was out of "Pickwick," and by the same loving teacher, that I was taught to read; and that finally I knew him from 1836 upward, and, in literature, served him faithfully for nineteen years. My *cultus* of him, therefore, may be that of Garrick's "dresser," of Rubens's color-grinder. Critics who are cooler and calmer than I am, and who are thus enabled to judge him with greater impartiality, may make light of the praises I have given, may deny the rank I claim for him. In their eyes, perhaps, he is not destined to climb to the topmost grade of the staircase of glory; he is not fated to occupy the supreme step—to stand where, little less than Light, the Only Shakspeare is, his hands fast locked in those of Milton and Dante, and Homer in the Sun shining on all their heads. But I maintain that his renown will be progressive, and that he will March. He will march in the great company—with rare Ben Jonson, with glorious John Dryden, with kind Molière and patient Cervantes, with noble Walter Scott, with gentle William Thackeray—all great humorists, all great masters of pathos, all good and honest men. He will march until not only this pin's-head England, not only the great American Republic, not only the vast empire which is to be in Australia, but the extremest limits of a new civilized China, the farthest borders of a re-civilized Hindostan shall be full of the sound of the footsteps of his fame.

My task ends here. I have striven to accomplish it without servility and without impertinence. Only the other day the sorrowing crowds were pressing round his tomb in Poet's Corner, and so throwing garlands into his grave as to make it a well of flowers. Men plucked the sprigs from their button-holes; women took the posies from their bosoms to place them on his coffin-plate. I wait for the crowd to disperse, and, as quietly as I may, I place one green chaplet on the brink of the tomb of one I knew so long, I reverenced so deeply, I loved so dearly.

DEAN STANLEY ON CHARLES DICKENS.

ON Sunday, June 19, the Rev. Dr. Stanley, Dean of Westminster, preached a sermon in Westminster Abbey on the death of the latest addition to the line of English worthies who are buried within the walls of that edifice. As on the recent occasion, when the funeral service was read over the remains of Mr. Peabody, there was an immense congregation, consisting very largely of the working-classes. The service took place in the chancel and choir. A few seats were kept within the altar-rails for a small number of privileged persons, one of whom was Mr. Alfred Tennyson, the poet laureate. While the vast congregation awaited in silence the commencement of the service, the music of Spohr's beautiful anthem, "Blessed are the dead that die in the Lord," was softly played on the organ.

The Dean took as his text the verses in the 15th and 16th chapters of St. Luke, which embody the parable of the rich man and Lazarus —"He spoke this parable. There was a certain rich man which was clothed in purple and fine linen, and fared sumptuously every day. And there was a certain beggar named Lazarus, which was laid at his gate, full of sores, and desiring to be fed with the crumbs which fell from the rich man's table: moreover the dogs came and licked his sores." There are some passages of Scripture, he said, which when read in the Sunday services almost demand a special notice, from their extraordinary power and impressiveness. Such is the parable of the rich man and Lazarus, read in the gospel of this day. There are some incidents of human life which almost demand a special notice, from the depth and breadth of the feelings which they awaken in the heart. Such was the ceremony which on Tuesday last consigned to his grave within these walls the lamented and gifted being who had for years delighted the generation to which he belonged; and if the Scripture of the day and the incident of the week direct our minds to the same thoughts, and mutually illustrate each other, the attraction becomes irresistible, and the lesson which each brings is doubly strengthened. Let me attempt to draw out these lessons this afternoon.

I will speak first of the form of instruction which we are called upon to notice in to-day's gospel. Not only is it, like most of our Lord's instruction—parable, but, as it were, it is a parable of the parables. It is the last of a group which occurs in the 15th and 16th chapters of St. Luke, where the story is taken in each case, not as in the other gospels, from inanimate and irrational creatures, but from the actions and characters of men. First comes the story of the good shepherd, with all its depth of tenderness; then the story of the indefatigable searcher, with all its depth of earnestness; then the story of the prodigal son, with all its depth of pathos; then the story of the unjust steward, with all its depth of satire; and last of all comes this story of the rich and poor man, drawn from the varied stir of human enjoyment and suffering in the streets and alleys of Jerusalem. It is a tale of real life—so real that we can hardly believe it is not history. It is nevertheless a tale of pure fiction. Dives and Lazarus are as much imaginary beings as Hamlet or Shylock, and the scene in Abraham's bosom and the rich man in Hades is drawn from popular Jewish conceptions current at the time.

This parable, then, is the most direct example which the Bible contains of the use and value and sacredness of fictitious narrative. There are, doubtless, many other instances in the Old and New Testaments; but the highest sanction to this mode of instruction is that, as in this parable, given by our Lord himself, it was his favorite mode of teaching. He stamped it with his peculiar mark. Without parable, without fable, without an invented story of this kind, he rarely opened his lips. He, the Example of examples, the Teacher of teachers, spoke many things in parables. Through this parable form, His gravest instructions have had double life given to them. If we were to ask for the most perfect exposition of the most perfect thing respecting God and man which the world contains, it would be found not in discourse, nor in a creed, nor in a hymn, nor even in a prayer; but in a parable story such as those which I have cited. I have dwelt upon these characteristics of the Gospel teaching, because it is well to see how the Bible sanctions a mode of instruction which has been in a special sense God's gift to our own age. In various ages this, no doubt, has assumed various forms—the divine flame of poetry, the far-reaching gaze of science, and the searching analysis of philosophy, the glorious page of history, the burning eloquence of speaker or picture, the grave addresses of moralists and divines—these have we had in ages that are past. Their memorials are all around us here. These, too, have we had in our measure, some more, and some less, in the age in which we live; but it is, perhaps, not too much to say that in no age of the world, and in no country of the world, has there been developed upon so large a scale, and with such striking effects, as in our own, that gift of speaking in parables, and addressing mankind through romance, novel, tale, and fable. For proof of this there comes, first, that greatest of all the masters of fiction, the glory of Scotland, whose romances have refreshed and exalted our childhood, as they still refresh and exalt our advancing years; and I would to God they might still continue to refresh and exalt the children of many in the years that are to be. He rests not here. He rests beside his native Tweed. Long may he yet charm and purify us; long may yonder monument of the Scottish youth whom he has immortalized in one of his noblest works keep him in our memory, as, one by one, the lesser and later lights follow in his track.

It is because one of these bright lights has just passed from us—one in whom this generation seemed to see the most vivid exemplification of the Heaven-sent power of fiction—that I would thus speak to-day for a few moments of its most general aspects. There was a truth—let me confess it—in the old Puritan feeling against an exaggerated enjoyment of romances, as tending to loosen the fibre of the moral character. That was, as it seems to me, a wholesome restraint I remember in my childhood, which kept me from revelling in fiction until the day's work was over, and which thereby impressed upon us that the reading of pleasant fiction was the holiday of life, and not its serious business. It is this which, if it constitutes also the danger of fictitious narratives, constitutes also their power. They approach us at times when we are indisposed to attend to any thing else. They fill up those odd moments of life which exert so wide an influence over the whole tenor of our characters. Poetry may enkindle a loftier flame, the drama may rivet the attention more firmly, science may open a wider horizon, philosophy may touch a deeper spring, but no works are so penetrating, none reach so many homes and attract so many readers, as the romance of modern times. Those who read nothing else read eagerly the exciting tale. Those whom sermons never reach, whom history fails to arrest, are reached and are arrested by fictitious persons, and by the stirring plots of the successful novels. It is this great power which makes a wicked novel more detestable almost than any other form of wicked words or deeds. It is this which gives to the foolish and worthless novel a demoralizing force beyond its own contemptible demerits. It is this which makes a good novel, pure in style, elevating in thought, and true in sentiment, one of the best blessings to the Christian home and Christian state. How vast the responsibility of those who wield this mighty engine—mighty it may be, and has been, for corruption, for debasement, for defilement; mighty it certainly has been in our own novels for edification and purification, for giving wholesome thoughts, high aspirations, and soul-stirring recollections ! Ye who read those wonderful works of genius, acknowledging them as God's special gifts to us, only remember that the true romance of life is life itself.

This leads me to the further question of the special form which this gift assumed in him whose loss the country now deplores with a grief so deep and genuine as to be itself a matter for serious reflection. What was there in him which called forth this wide-spread sympathy? What is there in this sympathy and in that which created it worthy of our religious thoughts this day? I profess not here to sit in judgment on the character and on the career of this gifted man. That must be left for posterity to fix in its proper niche among the worthies of English literature. Neither is this the place to speak at great length of those lighter and more genial qualities such as rendered his death, like that of one who rests beside him, almost an eclipse of the gayety of nations. Let others tell us of the brilliant and delicate satire, of the kindly art, of the keen and ubiquitous sense of the ludicrous and grotesque. There is a time to laugh and a time to weep. Laughter is itself a good, yet there are moments when we dare not indulge in it. It may even seem hereafter, as it may sometimes have seemed to some of our own age, that the nerves of the rising generation were, for a time at least, unduly relaxed by that inexhaustible outburst of the humorous temper and never-slumbering observation. The flood of drollery and merriment, it may be, brought out the comic and trivial side of life in too startling relief; but even thus, and even in this sacred place, it is good to remember that in the writings of him who has gone we have had the most convincing proof that it is possible to move old and young to inextinguishable laughter without the use of a single expression which could defile the purest or shock the most sensitive. Remember, if there be any who think you can not be witty without being wicked; who think that, in order to amuse the world, and to awaken the interest of hearers or readers, you must descend to filthy jests, and unclean suggestions, and debasing scenes; that so thought not, and so wrote not—to speak only of the departed — Walter Scott, Jane Austen, Elizabeth Gaskell, and William Thackeray; so thought not, and so wrote not, the genial, loving humorist whom we now mourn. However deep his imagination led him to descend into the dregs of society, he still breathed an untainted atmosphere around him; he was still able to show by his own example that, even in dealing with the darkest scenes and most degraded characters, genius could be clean and mirth innocent.

There is another point yet more peculiar and special on which we may safely dwell even in the very House of God, even by the freshly-laid grave. In that long series of stirring tales, now forever closed, there was, amidst all this comic and satiric vein, a profoundly serious, nay, may we not say a profoundly Christian and Evangelical truth, of which we all need to be reminded, and of which he was in his own way a special teacher. It is the very same lesson which is represented to us in the parable of this day: "There was a certain rich man clothed in purple and fine linen, who fared sumptuously every day; and there was a certain beggar named Lazarus who was laid at his gate full of sores, and desiring to be fed from the crumbs which fell from the rich man's table. Moreover the dogs came and licked his sores." This is a picture whose every detail is impressive. It awakens thoughts which live forever. It is true that an Oriental atmosphere hangs round it—the Syrian purple, the fine linen of Egypt, the open banqueting-hall, the beggar in the gateway, the dogs prowling about the city. But the spirit of the parable applies to the West as well as to the East. The contrast—the irregularity of deserts—meets us in the streets of London; and the moral which it was intended we

should draw from the parable is the same spirit which, in some shape or form, is urged upon us with a force unexampled and unrivalled throughout the writings of our lost instructor. Close beside the magnificence and luxury of this great metropolis are those very neighbors whom the parable describes. It has often been observed that the rich man has no name in Scripture; but the poor man has a name given to him in the Book of God. And he has a name given to him, he has many names given to him, in the tales in which the departed one has described the homes and the manners of our poorer brethren. Lazarus—meaning the help of God—a noble name which tells us that God helps those who help themselves, is the very prototype of these outcasts, those forlorn and struggling human beings whose characters were painted by him in such living colors that we shrink from speaking of them here even as we shrink from speaking of living persons. It is of this outlying mass of unseen human suffering we need so constantly to be reminded. It is this contrast between things as they are in the sight of God and as they seem in the sight of men, that so easily escapes our notice in the midst of our busiest civilization. The lesson taught by the parable in that age is still more needed now, and it is to meet this need that our dull and sluggish efforts want all the assistance which can be given by vivid imagination, by genial sympathy, by the dramatic power of making things which are not seen even as they which are seen.

Such were the gifts wielded with wondrous power by him who has just passed away. It is said to have been the distinguishing glory of a famous Spanish saint that she was the advocate of the absent. That is precisely the advocacy of this Divine parable, of the Gospels, and the advocacy of these modern human parables. The advocacy of the neglected and weaker side of life, which, not seeing, we are likely to forget. It is because this susceptibility to things absent is so rare and so difficult to attain, that we ought doubly to value those who have the eyes to see, and the ear to hear, and the tongue to speak, and the pen to describe those who are not at hand to demand their own rights, to set forth their own wrongs, and portray their own sufferings. Such was he who lies yonder; by him that veil was rent asunder which parts the various classes of society. Through his genius the rich man, faring sumptuously every day, was made to see and to feel the presence of the Lazarus at his gate. The suffering inmates of the work-house, the neglected children in the dens and caves of our great cities, the starved and ill-used boys in remote schools, far from the observation of man, felt that a new era of sunshine was pouring on their dark systems, that a new interest was awakened in their forlorn and desolate state. And this was because an unknown friend had pleaded their cause with a voice which ran through the palaces of the great as well as through the cottages of the poor—it was because, as by a magician's wand, those gaunt figures were made to speak for themselves to those who hardly before dreamt of their existence. Nor was it mere compassion which was thus evoked. As the same parable which delineates the miseries of the outcast Lazarus tells us how, underneath that degradation, was nursed a spirit fit for converse with the noble-minded and gentle-hearted in the bosom of the Father of the Faithful; so the same master-hand which drew the sorrows of the English poor drew also the picture of the unselfish kindness, courageous patience, and tender thoughtfulness, that lie concealed behind many a coarse exterior, in many a rough heart, and in many a degraded home. When the little work-house boy wins his way clear and undefiled through the wickedness around him, when the little orphan girl brings thoughts of heaven into the hearts of all around her, and is as a very gift of God to the old man whose desolate life she cheers, there is a lesson taught which touches every heart, and which no human being can feel without being made the better for it. It makes that grave seem to those who crowd around it as though it were the very grave of those little innocents whom he created for our companionship, instruction, delight, and solace. He labored to tell us all in new, very new words, the old, old story that there is even in the humblest and worst of mankind a soul of goodness and nobleness, a soul worth redeeming, worth reclaiming, worth regenerating; he labored to tell the rich and the educated how this better state was to be found and respected even in the most neglected Lazarus; he labored to tell the poor no less to respect those better placed than themselves. And if by any such means he who is gone has brought rich and poor together, and has made Englishmen feel more as one family, he assuredly will not have lived in vain, nor will his bones have been laid without cause in this resting-place of the great ones of the English nation.

There is one more thought which this occasion suggests in the parable of the rich man and Lazarus besides the pungent and pithy lessons of social life which it impresses upon us. It refers to the awful solemnity of the other world. " If they hear not Moses and the prophets, neither will they be persuaded though one rose from the dead." So also on Tuesday there was impressed upon us the solemnity, before which the most lively sallies of wit and the most brilliant splendor of genius went faint and pale—the solemnity of each man's individual responsibility in each man's life and death. When on Tuesday last we stood beside that open grave, in the still deep silence of the summer morning, in the midst of the vast and solitary space, broken only by that small band of fourteen mourners, it was impossible not to feel there was something more sacred, more lofty, than any earthly glory, however bright, or than any historic mausoleum, however august, and that was the return of the individual human soul into the hands of its Maker. Many, many are the feet which have trodden and will tread the consecrated ground around that grave; many, many are the hearts, that both in the Old and in the New World, are drawn towards it, as towards the resting-place of a dear personal friend; many are the flowers that have been strewn, and many the tears shed by the grateful affection of the poor and those that have none to help them. May I speak with these many a few sacred words which may come with a new and deeper meaning, because they come from the lips of our friend—because they are the most solemn utterances of lips now forever closed in the grave. They are extracted from the will of Charles Dickens, dated May 12th, 1869, and they will be heard by many here for the first time. After the most emphatic injunctions respecting the inexpensive, unostentatious, and strictly private manner of his funeral—injunctions which were carried out to the very letter—he thus continues: "I direct that my name be inscribed in plain English letters on my tomb. I conjure my friends on no account to make me the subject of any monument, memorial, or testimonial whatever. I rest my claims to the remembrance of my country upon my published works, and to the remembrance of my friends upon their experience of me in addition thereto. I commit my soul to the mercy of God through our Lord and Saviour Jesus Christ, and I exhort my dear children humbly to try and guide themselves by the teaching of the New Testament, in its broad spirit, and to put no faith in any man's narrow construction of its letter, here or there." In that simple and sufficient faith he lived and died; in that simple and sufficient faith he bids you live and die. If any of you have learned from his works to feel the strong value of generosity, purity, kindness, and unselfishness, and have learned to show these in your hearts and lives, then remember these are the best monuments, memorials, or testimonials to the friend whom you have loved, and who loved with a rare and unselfish love his friends, his country, and his fellow-man. These are monuments which he would not refuse, and which the humblest and poorest and youngest here have it in their power to raise to his memory.

THE END.

whelan

Printed in the United States
834700003B

9 780898 756333